Edinburgh For Under Fives

a handbook for parents

by local members of the National Childbirth Trust

Published by the National Childbirth Trust
Edinburgh Branch Booklet Group

Cover : Ann R Paterson
Cartoons: Davie Smith
Map : Forbes Mutch

Printed by D. & J. Croal Ltd., Haddington

ACKNOWLEDGEMENTS

We would like to thank everyone who has helped in compiling this book. Financial support came from the Miss Beveridge Trust, The City of Edinburgh District Council and the National Childbirth Trust. We would also like to thank everyone who filled in a questionnaire, or supplied us with information. Thanks to all those who gave freely of their time, advice or assistance including Ursula Alexander, Liz Allen, Maggie Anderson, Raoul Barbier, Brenda Bellis, Sue Bird, Tim Birley, Neil Blake, Sandi Bomphray, Sue Brace and the others in the informal 'working parents' group; Jane Bradley, Ken Capewell, Brian Chrystal, Janet Clark, Dave de Feu, Anne Dennis, Donald Dickie, Alistair Dobbin, Mr Dunn EDC, The Edinburgh Advertiser, The Evening News, Sheena Fisher, Gill Fisken, Jane Kelly, Willie Kerr, Iain Lumsden, Ted Matthews, Sue McDermott for acting as Treasurer, Jim McDougal, Janey McDowell, Elaine McFarlane, Kathy McGlew, Lesley McIver, Neil McLeish, Barbara McLeod (snr), Ian Miller, Morna Munro, NCT group leaders, Judy Nussbaum, Gillian Paterson-Brown, Tricia Phoenix, Carol Preston, Jane Robson, St Brides Community Centre, Bob Sargent, all at Smith's Place, Alison Spiers, Barbara Stirling, Kate Streatfield, Maggie Thomson, Gill Waugh, Ken Whitson, Margaret Wragg, and Bronwen Wright. Financial support was also received from Lothian Regional Council.

SUPPORTED BY

CITY OF EDINBURGH
DISTRICT COUNCIL

IMPROVING SERVICES
CREATING JOBS

INTRODUCTION

Even if you have lived in Edinburgh all your life, Edinburgh with babies and small children in tow is quite a different place. Gone is the freedom of the anonymous adult. You become public property; frowned on when your child is having a tantrum, admired when she is asleep in her buggy, and you become public nuisance no. 1 — continually having to ask for toilets, help with doors and stairs, getting on and off buses and to apologise for accidents and spills, grubby fingers and snotty noses. Hardly surprising if parents retreat indoors.

However Edinburgh has a lot going on for small children if you know where to look. This book aims to point you in the right direction, saving you time and frustration. It will provide you with information to help you and your children enjoy Edinburgh with confidence. It can show you, for example, where to have lunch with a toddler and a breastfeeding baby, where to find animals in the city, swimming pools with playpens, parks with swings, where to change a nappy in town. It can also help you plan a birthday party, choose a playgroup and find help in a crisis. It is a book by parents for parents, either living here or visiting.

We hope, also, it will bring awareness to those who have the power to change things. A few small changes could make life a little bit easier for a lot of people.

This book has been compiled by 9 mothers and their children (11 increasing to 16 by the time it is released). We have done most of the research ourselves, accompanied by our children, but also consulted professionals and many other parents. We look forward to your comments. Please send details of any changes, inaccuracies or omissions to Edinburgh For Under Fives P.O. Box 726, Edinburgh EH4 1NX.

We are:—

Margaret Barbier
Kate Birley
Sheila Capewell

Sheila Dobbin
Jackie le Brocq
Barbara MacLeod

Jane McLeish
Alice Miller
Liz Sargent

Contents

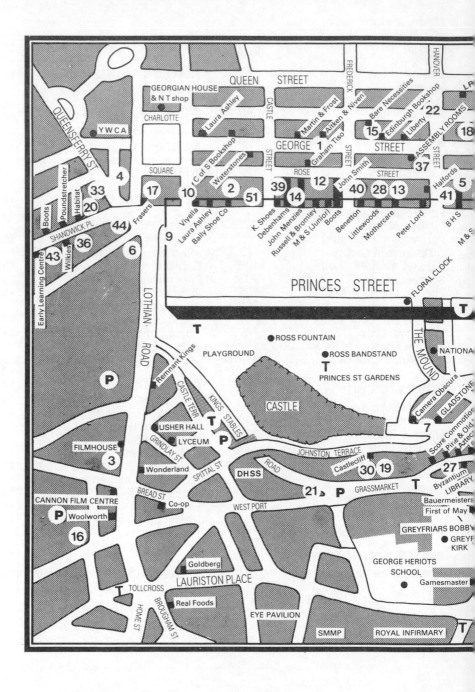

Update

Acknowledgements — We acknowledge with thanks the generous donation from the J. K. Young Endowment Fund

Page 5 **Mothercare** — now has lift in back right of store; Mothers' Room in basement; public toilets on 1st floor (ask staff for key). Dispose of soiled nappies in the Mothers' Room — toilets are frequently blocked due to people trying to flush them away.

Page 7 **The Village** — closed.

Page 23 **Wonderland** , Rose St. — closed.

Page 24 **Bauermeister Bookshop** will allow the use of staff toilet.

Page 24 **Edinburgh Bookshop** — new hours: Mon-Sat 9 am-10 pm, Sun 11-5.

Page 25 **As Good As New** — hours are Tues-Sat 10.30-4; Wed 10.30-2.30.

Page 27 **Little Marco's,** 228 2141. Now open Mon-Fri 10-4. Takes children aged 3-10. Cost: £5 per child for 3 hours. Box of refreshments is included in price.

Page 31 **Kids Stuff**: 10 Hensman Hill, Clifton, *Bristol* BS8 4PE.

Page 32 **Millikids** — no longer trading.

Page 36 **Stork Exchange** — closed.

Page 42 **Edinburgh Bookshop Coffee Room** — new hours are Mon-Sat 9.30-9.30; Sun 11.30-4.30.

Page 45 **North British** — closed.

Page 49 **Waterfront Wine Bar** — children are no longer welcome.

Page 54 **Harp Hotel Restaurant** — telephone number should read 334 4750.

Page 64 **Craigmillar Park Church Mother and Toddler** is in Newington.

Page 64 **Mayfield Mother and Toddler Group** meets 9.30-11.30. Contact: Karen Grant 447 4535.

Page 65 **Southside Community Centre** is in Old Church, Nicolson Street.

Page 68 **Montessori Nursery School**. The Good Shepherd School, The Good Shepherd Church Hall, Murrayfield. Contact Diana Boyd 0835 22225.

Page 68 **Dublin Street Playgroup** — now St Mary's Playgroup, St Mary's Primary School, 3 York Lane/9.15-11.45/Contact Helen Smith 556 9690.

Page 68 **Little Marco's Nursery** — no longer in existence.

Page 69 **Stewart House Nursery**, Craigmillar Park, is in Newington.

Page 70 **Fairmile Church Nursery** — run by Lothian Regional Council; open during school terms.

Page 71 **Mentone Nursery** — now closed.

Page 82 **Queen Margaret College** do not train nursery nurses.

Page 84 **Portobello Library** — children's section is on the ground floor.

Page 86 **Pentland Community Centre Toy Library** — organiser is Mrs Mary Davies 445 5144.

Page 88 **Manor Ballet School** — Director is Mrs Noel Platfoot 220 1466.

Page 90 **Little Marco's** — supervision is no longer free if parents using Marco's.

Page 93 **Dunfermline College of Physical Education** is now Moray House College of Education, Cramond Campus, tel. 312 6001.

Page 93 **Swimming** — New charges. Commonwealth Pool: Adults 75p, children 55p. At Dalry, Glenogle, Infirmary St, Portobello, Leith and Warrender charges are: Adults 45p, children 30p.

Page 113 **Gallery of Modern Art** — new hours Mon-Sat 10-5; Sun 2-5.

Page 114 **Scottish National Portrait Gallery** has a lift.

Page 118 **Gorgie City Farm** — toilets for public and disabled.

Page 119 **Rosebank Open Farm** — new hours. Easter till Sep. Mon-Sat 1-8, Sun 11-8. Other times by appointment. (Last admission 7 pm.)

Page 122 **ABC** is now Cannon Film Centre.

Page 155 **Family Planning Centre** is now called Dean Terrace Centre, and offers also well woman services.

Page 165 **Emergencies** — the Western General Hospital, Crewe Road, also has a Casualty Department which takes children.

T-SHIRTS AND SWEATSHIRTS

These attractive shirts with the distinctive 'EDINBURGH FOR UNDER FIVES' logo (pictured below) are available in a wide variety of sizes (16"-46" chest), colours and styles. You can choose short-sleeved or long-sleeved T-shirts made from 100% cotton, or our comfortable sweatshirts made from 50% cotton, 50% polyester. For extra warmth in winter our sweatshirts can be ordered with a double thickness of fabric front and back. For the fashionable "baggy" look order a size bigger than you normally require. Finally for pregnant women we also offer a specially tailored sweatshirt. All shirts are made in Edinburgh.

Every order will help to fund the next edition of 'EDINBURGH FOR UNDER FIVES'.

COLOURS

Choose from white, red, pale blue, pale pink, beige, buttercup yellow, pale grey all with a **dark blue** logo.

Navy, royal blue, black all with a **white** logo

DELIVERY

Please allow 28 days. You will be notified if there is any delay.

MONEY BACK GUARANTEE

If you are not completely satisfied, please return the item to us in 'as new' condition within seven days. We shall refund your money in full.

PRICES

T-shirts

Chest size		£
	16"-24"	3.75
	26"-32"	4.25
	34"-42"	4.90
	44"-46"	5.40

For **long-sleeved** T-shirts add 50p per shirt.

Sweatshirts

Chest size		£
	16"-24"	5.80
	26"-32"	7.15
	34"-42"	8.45
	44"-46" and Pregnant-style	9.10

For **double thickness** front and back add £2.50 per sweatshirt.

These prices include postage and packing.

HOW TO ORDER

Please send payment and order to Edinburgh for Under Fives, PO Box 726, Edinburgh EH4 1NX.

When ordering please give the following information:

- Size
- Colour
- Style
- No. required
- Your name, address and tel. no.
- Any special instructions (extra long sleeves, etc.)

Please remember to enclose payment with order. Cheques and postal orders should be made payable to Edinburgh for Under Fives.

'EDINBURGH FOR UNDER FIVES' is a project of the National Childbirth Trust in Edinburgh, whose office is at Stockbridge Health Centre, India Place, Edinburgh EH3 6EH. Please telephone Margaret Barbier 332 6092 with any enquiries concerning the shirts.

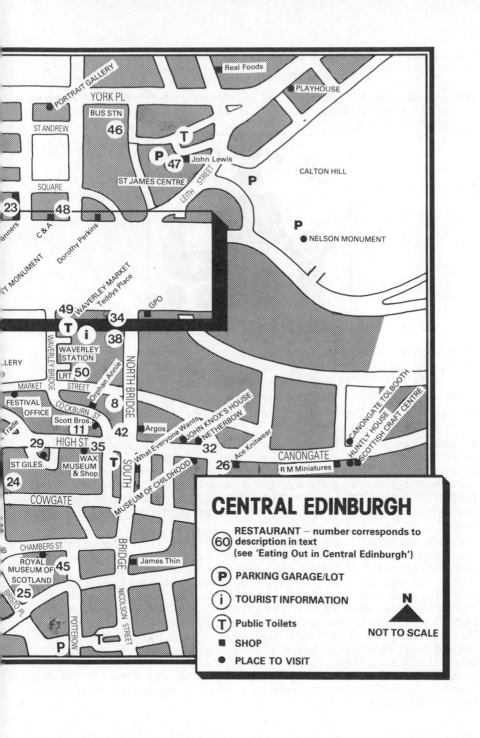

Real Foods

PLAYHOUSE

PORTRAIT GALLERY

YORK PL

BUS STN
46

ST ANDREW

T

SQUARE

P
47 John Lewis

ST JAMES CENTRE

CALTON HILL

23 48

C & A

Dorothy Perkins

P

P
NELSON MONUMENT

T MONUMENT

WAVERLEY MARKET
Teddys Place

GPO

49

T i

38

34

WAVERLEY
STATION

LERY

MARKET

WAVERLEY BRIDGE

LRT 50

STREET

COCKBURN ST

FESTIVAL
OFFICE

Scott Bros.

11

29 HIGH ST 35

Orphan Annie

8

NORTH BRIDGE

42

Argos

What Everyone Wants

JOHN KNOX'S HOUSE

NETHERBOW

32

Ace Knitwear

CANONGATE TOLBOOTH

SCOTTISH CRAFT CENTRE

HUNTLY HOUSE

CANONGATE

26 R M Miniatures

ST GILES

24

WAX
MUSEUM
& Shop

T

SOUTH

MUSEUM OF CHILDHOOD

COWGATE

CHAMBERS ST

ROYAL
MUSEUM OF
SCOTLAND

45

BRIDGE

James Thin

25

BRISTO PL

POTTEROW

NICOLSON STREET

P

T

CENTRAL EDINBURGH

60 RESTAURANT – number corresponds to
description in text
(see 'Eating Out in Central Edinburgh')

P PARKING GARAGE/LOT

i TOURIST INFORMATION

T Public Toilets

■ SHOP

● PLACE TO VISIT

N

NOT TO SCALE

WE WELCOME SMALL CHILDREN

NATIONAL CAMPAIGN

Aims: To improve and promote good facilities for parents with small children. To encourage public places, shops, restaurants, etc., to offer a warm welcome to parents with small children.

This yellow and orange sticker is being awarded nationally. You will see it in the margins of this book and in places where you and your children will be treated in a friendly and considerate manner.

When awarding this symbol the features we have taken into account are:

Access. This should be good and staff should always be willing to help with steps or look after pushchairs.

Facilities. Nappy changing and breastfeeding in separate rooms if possible (who else has to eat lunch in the toilet?). Provision of a play area. In restaurants, high chairs, children's menus or portions, and entertainment (eg crayons and paper) all make eating out more bearable. Whether shops and public places allow the use of a toilet — newly trained toddlers and pregnant Mums often them need quickly! Finally there should be no unprotected hazards.

We have not found it practical to set a rigid standard. We cannot expect a small shop to have the same access or facilities as, perhaps a department store, supermarket or library. The overriding factor has been the general attitude towards parents and young children and the willingness of staff to help. To most parents these will probably seem modest requirements. Nevertheless we have only been able to identify 24 places in Edinburgh which match up to these criteria and have consistently made our families welcome. Please patronise them, and encourage other places to follow their example! The symbol is copyright and even after the sticker is awarded it remains the property of the campaign. Please let us know of your experiences, so we can monitor the service of our 24 recipients. If you discover anywhere else that merits a sticker, by all means write to us at Edinburgh for Under Fives, P.O. Box 726, Edinburgh EH4 1NX.

Shopping

Many families find their shopping habits change when they have children, and not just because they have to buy things for the children. Suddenly the 'I'll just pop into two or three shops in Princes Street in my lunch hour' becomes a major expedition with a nightmare of steps, escalators, hungry screams and urgent toilet requirements. We hope this section will give you clues on how to cope with potential problems. We also suggest that where you find there are difficulties with access or no toilets or changing facilities, you ask and keep on asking for help and advice to make more people aware of the needs of shoppers with children.

We have not included precise opening hours of all the shops but generally Thursday is late night shopping in the city centre; on Tuesday mornings some central shops open late at 9.30 after staff training; Tuesday or Wednesday is half-day closing in the suburbs; and Sunday and evening opening are more frequent before Christmas and during the Festival. Where we have listed shops with several branches the description generally refers to the main branch and you may find that other, smaller branches, do not have the same choice or availability of goods.

We have used 'baby' to describe clothes for under 2s and 'children's' for over 2s.

Shops which we think are notable for their helpful attitude to under 5s are indicated by the 'We Welcome Small Children' symbol.

Refer to the map to plan an efficient shopping expedition. Unless the name of the suburb is given in the address, shops are located in the central area of the city and are indicated on this map.

DEPARTMENT STORES, LARGE SHOPS, AND CHAIN STORES

Aitken & Niven
77 George St
225 1461
Mon-Sat 9-5

Old-fashioned, expensive, shop with unbuggyable steps throughout and no lift. **Ground:** Good quality, expensive maternity clothes, fitted maternity bras, baby and children's clothes, children's shoes (Startrite), Christening and First Communion dresses, a limited amount of equipment. **Toilets, 1st:** very cramped. **2nd:** Restaurant, see 'Eating Out in Central Edinburgh (1)'.

Boots the Chemist
101 Princes St
225 8331
Mon-Wed, Sat 9-5.30; Thurs 9-7; Fri 9-6

1

Also at 48 Shandwick Pl, St James Centre and suburban locations (see phone book).

See below 'Chemists with extended hours' for out-of-hours dispensing service.

Ground: Nursery equipment, baby clothes, baby shoes, foods, nappies, disposable nappy roll (including home delivery service of own brand nappies at no extra charge) all in 'BabyBoots' back left of ground floor. Seasonal catalogue available. Also dispensing chemist, back right; non-fluoride toothpaste in 'Dental Care'. **1st:** Toys (wider range at Christmas), small selection of books, tapes, videos, greetings cards, paper. In the photographic department there are special letter cards with space for a photo in 'baby' and 'child' designs. Lift on left of ground floor. Escalators up. Staff toilets available. Other branches not so well stocked with nursery equipment or toys.

British Home Stores plc
64 Princes St
226 2621
Mon-Wed 9-5.30; Thurs 9-8; Fri 9-6; Sat 8-6
(Also at Savacentre, Cameron Toll Shopping Centre)

1st: Baby and children's clothes. Small staff lift available if member of staff free to accompany you. Escalators up and down. Patio Restaurant: See 'Eating Out in Central Edinburgh (5).

C & A
33 Princes St
556 4411
Mon-Wed 9-5.30; Thurs 9-8; Fri, Sat 9-6. Suns in summer and at Christmas

2nd: Good selection of reasonably priced baby, children's and maternity clothes. Escalators up and down and large lift with operator, though often a long wait as this lift is also used for stock movement. No toilets.

The Co-op (Scotmid Co-operative Society Ltd)
28-58 Bread St
229 2424
Mon, Tues, Fri, Sat 9-5.30; Thurs 9-7; Wed Closed
(Also at 52 Nicolson St and Chesser Ave)

This store has obviously seen better days. Good access. 3 old fashioned gated and self-operated lifts. Shoe department next to main store. **1st:** Poor selection of baby and children's wear, as well as own brand toiletries and disposable nappies. Toys also on 1st, mostly 'big names'. Wonderful, and precarious, bicycle display. 6 steps up from 1st floor along narrow passage, a warehouse like display of a small amount of nursery equipment including cots and buggies. **Toilets: 1st,** next to toys. Spacious and with wide shelf for changing if desperate, but did not seem clean, and with many locks missing from doors.

Debenhams plc
109-112 Princes St
225 1320
Mon, Tues 9.30-5.30; Wed, Fri, Sat 9-6; Thurs 9-8

Department store with large lift, and escalators, front left, which serve main store; and glass lifts in the back (Rose St) section. These operate from the Menswear Dept. **1st:** Small baby and children's dept, good access from Rose St entrance. Maternity clothes. **Toilets, 4th:** Opposite main lift. Disabled/maternity toilet with chair for feeding, and small changing shelf. **Restaurant, 4th:** See 'Eating Out in Central Edinburgh (14)'.

Frasers Department Store
West End, Princes St
225 2472
Mon-Sat 9-5; Thurs 9-7

Recently modernised department store with lift. Escalators up and down. **2nd:** Maternity bras and occasionally maternity clothes. **4th:** Baby and children's clothes. **Toilets, 5th:** Access almost impossible with buggy, no room to change a nappy or to breastfeed, but they will provide you with a chair if you ask. **Restaurant, 5th:** See 'Eating Out in Central Edinburgh (17)'.

Goldberg, A & Sons plc
High Riggs, Tollcross
(behind NCP Car Park, Lauriston Pl)
229 3391
Mon 9-5; Tues, Wed, Fri 9-5.15; Thurs 9-7.30; Sat 9-5.30; Sun 12-5

Department store with many steps at entrance and easier access from the rear on Lauriston St where there are only 5 steps. Two manned lifts. Escalators up only. **1st:** Baby and children's clothes and shoes (Startrite fitting service), nursery equipment and a large toy department. **Toilets, 1st:** No changing or feeding facilities, but plenty of space. **2nd:** Patio Coffee Bar.

Jenners
48 Princes St/Sth St Davids St/Rose St
225 2442
Mon-Sat 9-5.30; Tues 9.30-5.30

Imposing up-market department store with large galleried light well.

Access problems, badly signed with many different levels and mezzanine floor. The many lifts are small and tend to be crowded. Ask advice on how to get about — it may involve going up and across before going down. In general the central of the entrances on Rose St (where there is a good lift at the Travel Agency) or the Sth St Davids St entrance will be easier with pushchairs than Princes St entrances, unless you are going to the basement toy department (the lift to toys is behind the perfume department on the ground floor). **Basement:** Perserverence is rewarded by discovering an excellent and enormous toy department with everything from cheap party toys to expensive dolls, rocking horses and train sets. Galt toys have an outlet here and provide toys to play with. **Lower ground:** Baby knitting wools, birth sampler kits and good selection of ribbons and buttons. **Ground:** Central collection point, near menswear. **Midway** (above ground and below 1st): large lingerie department with bra fitting. **1st:** Small baby, baby and children's clothes, tartan outfits from 6 months (boys and girls), beautiful Shetland shawls, nappy stackers, quilts. Good play area. **Toilets, 1st:** Conveniently situated next to children's wear. Difficult access (six stairs around two corners), small cubicles (5p charge) no changing facilities, though seats available in cloakroom could be used at a pinch but it's usually very busy. **3rd** (Furniture): Free toilets. Take the Rose St lift, turn right, through swing doors, toilets on left. Not as smart as 1st floor but large tiled floor area for nappy changing Usually quiet. **Restaurants:** See 'Eating Out in Central Edinburgh (23)'.

3

John Lewis plc
St James Centre
556 9121
Mon Closed; Tues, Wed, Fri 9-5.30;
Thurs 9-7; Sat 9-6; Open for 3 Mons
prior to Christmas

Department store with 3 large lifts, escalators (up and down) and easy access between departments. Access from St James Centre Car Park is severely hampered by the lack of a lift and steep stairs. Regular home delivery of big items (including disposable nappy delivery to John Lewis account holders — useful for flat dwellers especially). Central collection point in China Department on ground floor, saves carrying large items around the shop or writing more than one cheque (John Lewis Account Cards are the only credit card accepted by the store). Price promise guarantee. **Basement:** Toy Dept with small selection of books and large and small toys (although the department almost doubles in size in the run up to Christmas). No toys to play with. Children's wallpapers. **Ground:** Toiletries Dept with disposable nappies; soft toy making requisites, samplers, wools and patterns, fabrics and paper patterns; Haberdashery Dept with PVC and cotton children's aprons, small coathangers, nightdress cases, toy boxes, ribbons, buttons, motifs and 'made to order' name tapes; Hosiery Dept Socks and tights from approx age 2. Gloves, a large selection from babies' sheepskin mitts to novelty 'puppet' gloves nearly all ready strung; China Dept Selection of children's china, but displayed from floor height upwards so keep toddlers on a tight rein and beware of little hands stretching out from pushchairs. **1st:** Maternity clothes, bra fittings, baby and children's equipment. Pushchair repairs with the option of hiring one of theirs interim. Premature baby, baby and children's clothes, baby shoes. These departments are extremely congested, certainly difficult with a pram or pushchair and no toys are provided for children to play with. It is very easy to lose a toddler in the racks of clothes but having said that there is a very good selection. There are sometimes 'seconds' nappies from good brand names at sale time — worth looking out for as it is often difficult to tell what is wrong with them. Children's shoes, (Clarks and Startrite) width fittings, usually busy but there is a ticket machine so at least you can look around as you wait. **2nd:** Some nursery rugs, duvet covers, place mats and curtain fabrics in relevant departments. **Toilets, 2nd:** Separate area with three chairs for feeding and a changing shelf with a 3" rim to prevent rolling off. **Restaurant, 2nd:** See 'Eating Out in Central Edinburgh (47)'.

Littlewoods Organisation plc
90/91 Princes St
225 1683
Mon-Wed 9-5; Thurs 9-7; Fri, Sat 9-5.30

Stair and escalator problems in store — the stock lift is available if a member of staff is free (they are usually very obliging!). **1st:** Cheap baby and children's clothes, but not much for young babies. **Toilets:** Right hand back of ground floor are small, busy, difficult to find and not suitable for feeding or changing. **Restaurant, Basement:** See 'Eating Out in Central Edinburgh (28)'.

Marks & Spencer plc
104 Princes St (Children's Wear)
225 2301

Mon, Tues 9.30-5.30; Wed, Fri, Sat 9-6; Thurs 9-8
(Main store 53 Princes St)

Good quality reasonably priced and generously sized baby and children's clothes. Disposable nappies (and terry's in ½ dozen packets). New range of nursery equipment including pushchairs and highchairs all on ground floor. Despite being a new children's store there are no toilets or feeding facilities.

Martin & Frost
83-85 George St
225 2933

Expensive furniture shop with kiddy corner on Saturdays 10-4, with baby minder, videos, sweets and coffees.

John Menzies plc
107 Princes St
226 6214
Mon-Sat 9-6; Thurs 9-7
and smaller branches throughout the city (see phone book)

Magazines, books, toys, records, cassettes and stationery. Used to have good maternity toilets but these were deemed unnecessary when renovation occurred. 2 lifts back left. No toilets.

Mothercare UK Ltd
84a Princes St
226 6503
Mon, Wed, Fri 9-5.30; Tues 9.30-5.30; Thurs 9-8; Sat 9-6

A shop which claims to sell everything for the expectant mother, her baby and children under 10. It may make a useful one-stop shop in the last weeks of pregnancy. There are a couple of armchairs to rest on in the Maternity Clothes section. Shop is on ground and 1st floors with stairs and up only escalator, and stairs to upper mezzanine level. The lack of a lift is much complained about: if staff are available, they will help carry babies, pushchairs etc up and down, or the stocklift may be used on request. You will emerge on mezzanine level. Pushchairs may be left with staff on ground floor who will secure them in a stock cupboard if you wish. **Ground:** Baby clothes, nappies, maternity clothes, bra fitting. Adult toiletries. **1st:** Children's clothes, some shoes (no fitting service), toys including some to play with. **Mezzanine:** Equipment — pushchairs, playpens, highchairs, cots, baby toiletries etc. Excellent changing and baby feeding room located at the very back left corner. Fathers should ask staff before they may be allowed to use this room. Well equipped with sink, changing mats, bins, 4 chairs and bottle warming kit, as well as free first-size nappies, wipes, lotions etc. No toilets but pregnant women and toddlers may use the staff toilet after waiting for a member of staff to accompany them. There is a central collection point, and orders may be taken in advance. Also a home delivery service for own brand disposable nappies. Catalogue available. See 'Shopping from Home, Miscellaneous'.

Woolworth F W & Co Ltd
142 Lothian Rd
229 4644
Mon-Wed, Sat 9-5.30; Thurs, Fri 9-6
(also at 36 Raeburn Pl, Stockbridge 332 2623; St John's Rd, Corstorphine 334 6644; and 170 Constitution St (New Kirkgate Centre), Leith 554 3872

Small sections of baby toiletries, nappies, cheap children's clothes (Ladybird stockists), 'big name' toys, books, cassettes and videos. No toilets.

SHOPPING CENTRES AND MARKETS

Assembly Rooms
54 George St
225 3614

Craft Fairs and Antique and Collectors' Fairs are held approximately once a month, advertised in windows and in press. 'Scotfairs' are the largest antique fairs with a variety of stalls, usually including a few baby and children's items. Craft fairs: Shetland jumpers, wooden toys, patchwork and smocking etc, especially before Christmas. All fairs tend to get very crowded particularly at lunch time, which renders buggy pushing and unrestrained small children a liability.

Large cloakroom on 1st floor where it is possible to feed and change babies. (Also **toilets** right at back of lowest floor).

Usually a **snack bar** on 1st floor. No lifts. Admission charges 30p-£1, adults. Children free-20p. (Fairs are also occasionally held at Adam House, Chambers St).

Byzantium
Victoria St
226 1678
Mon-Sat 10-5.30

An old church dramatically converted to shopping centre for Crafts and Antiques and Specialist Shops. Unusual gifts, abundance of knitwear, some toys. Stairs but no lift or escalator. **Toilets**, 1st. Cafe Kinnell, 2nd. Snacks and coffee, lunches available.

Cameron Toll Shopping Centre
6 Lady Rd
Opening hours of individual shops vary
Boots: Mon-Wed, Sat 9-5.30; Thurs, Fri 9-8; Sun 12-4.30

Savacentre (Sainsburys and British Home Stores) Mon-Thurs 8.30-8; Fri 8.30-9; Sat 8-8; Sun 10-5
Safeway: Mon-Sat 8-8; Sun 10-5

A variety of shops including Savacentre (baby and children's clothes, some toys), Safeway, Boots, K Shoes, Peter Lord (Clarks children's shoes), Dorothy Perkins (including maternity clothes), Mackay's (baby and children's clothes), Forbuoys (newsagents and toys), Seconds and Firsts (limited range of children's clothes), bookshop with small children's section at back, while-you-wait shoe repairs, jeweller with Christening goods — all on ground floor.

Self-opening doors, seats to rest on, plenty of trolleys with baby seats and some with cradles which you can use throughout the Centre, although some shops do not let you in with these unwieldy monsters! Public phones.

Toilets, ground and 1st. Currently very small, difficult with small children and pushchair but new facilities, including a feeding and changing room on 1st floor, are being installed. In the meantime use the disabled toilet (also 1st). There is a lift under the stairs to the left of Savacentre. Difficult to find a parking space at weekends but cheap petrol on the way out.

Restaurant, The Terrace, see 'Eating Out in East Edinburgh'.

Ingliston Market
off A8 at Ingliston on Airport road
333 3801 (Spook Erection)
Sun 10-4

Open-air market of huge proportions with plenty of free parking space and good traffic martialling. Variety of stalls including baby and children's clothing, denim jeans and cheap toys. Be wary, especially with toys, but there are bargains to be had.

Toilets and changing and feeding room for babies, well signed. Clean and comfortable. Lost children's centre at First Aid Post. Tannoy system covers market. Enormous models (King Kong).

Snacks. Stalls selling everything from ice-cream to curry. Some with tables and chairs.

Newkirkgate Shopping Centre
off Great Junction St, Leith
Opening hours of individual shops vary

Includes Presto Supermarket, Woolworth (large, with children's clothes), Mackays (baby and children's clothes), various shoe shops (none with fitting service), Boots, Wool Wearhouse (good selection of baby yarns and patterns), health food store. **Toilets** on 2nd floor of Leith Community Centre. Lift or stairs from shopping area. Very dirty and recommended for emergencies only. No nappy changing surface. **Salad bar/cafe.** Prams and buggies allowed inside.

St James Centre
Princes St/Leith St

Numerous shops including John Lewis (see above 'Department Stores etc'), John Menzies, Adams (see below 'Baby and Children's Clothes'), Bayne and Duckett (see below 'Children's Shoes'), Dorothy Perkins and Chelsea Girl (see below 'Maternity Wear'), Presto Supermarket, Richards, Happit (some children's clothes) — all on one floor. Pedestrian access from the corner of Leith St and Princes St and St Andrews Square Bus Station. Vehicular entrance to multi-storey car park from Leith St and Elder St

(a small street off York Pl). There is no lift in the car park which makes returning to your car with infant(s), pushchair and shopping particularly irksome. The shopping mall is well patrolled by security guards and is clean and litter free. Seats to rest on and public phones. **Toilets** nearby in Bus Station and John Lewis, or Elder St **Restaurant**. For John Lewis Restaurant and Crawfords Country Kitchen, see 'Eating Out in Central Edinburgh (47)'.

The Village
St John's Rd North, Corstorphine

A mini shopping centre, on 2 floors joined by steps, and up steps at the front entrance. There seems to be a fairly rapid turnover in the occupancy of the units. On the ground floor you may find baby clothes, mugs and toys, as well as meat and vegetables. 1st: Mostly antiques, but also a **cafe** (self service), and coin operated children's rides. **Toilets:** 1st, small.

Waverley Market Shopping Centre
Corner of Princes St/Waverley Bridge
Opening hours for individual shops vary. Centre is open on Sun although some shops may not be.

If you regard a trip here as entertainment rather than a shopping expedition it can be fun — glass lift, pools, spectacular fountains, plants, occasionally a piano player. Sometimes there are roundabouts or inflatables on the Princes St level. There are often seasonal displays eg Easter Chicks or Santa, or automatan models in empty units. Other impromptu entertainments sometimes occur. Up-market shops and boutiques, and 'barrows' on 2 floors below street level.

Tourist Information is on the roof (Princes St level).

Only a few shops sell goods for children. Tanya's Toys, Crafts 'n' Puzzles, see below 'Toy Shops etc'. Stockbridge Bookshop and James Thin both stock some children's books. One of the barrows sells unusual wool jumpers with animal motifs and nursery rhymes, in small sizes; another has a large selection of badges and mobiles. However, if you do want to shop here and can't face the prospect of keeping your toddler from taking a dip in the unprotected pools (to collect coins or to catch fish) or negotiating escalators, try 'Teddy's Place' see below 'Creches while Shopping'.

Access. The easiest entrance from Princes St is next to the Waverley Steps where there is a ramp which leads to the small, very busy lift. The Waverley Bridge entrance also has a ramp.

Toilets: There are 2 sets of toilets within the market complex. The smaller of the two is behind Waverley Food Court, has a few cubicles — very small floor space and access would be difficult with a pushchair. The main toilets can be reached by a long steep flight of steps from Waverley Bridge (open 24 hours) at the side of the market entrance, or through a set of heavy double doors marked 'Exit', to the left of Cafe Noir on the lower sales floor. An attendant can show you to the Nappy Change room. There are quite a few cubicles but despite this there are often very long queues.

Restaurants: The Caravelle, Cafe Noir, and Waverley Food Court, see 'Eating Out in Central Edinburgh (49)'.

Wester Hailes Shopping Centre
Wester Hailes Rd
Some shops close Wed pm.

Individual shops and Forum Centre consisting of a complex of 50 shop units, with good parking facilities and travelator access between floors. Includes Presto Supermarket, Drummonds Chemist (buggies, books, clothing, and toys and competitively priced baby foods), Forbuoys (toys), MacKays (baby and children's clothes), Bayne and Duckett (Clarks shoes). Forum has baby and children's clothes, shoes, baby wools, toys. A decorative pool, fountain, cage of budgies, children's pay 'n' ride machines on lower floor. Father Christmas, chicks at Easter, and other events throughout year particularly during the Wester Hailes Festival.

Toilets outside the building — no feeding or changing area although there are seats available on the ground floor of the Centre.
Cafe in Forum Centre (toilet available on request and with deposit for key).

MATERNITY WEAR

There are no specialist maternity shops in Edinburgh but the ones below either have a maternity department or clothes which may be suitable. If you can't find what you want, outsize shops may be worth a look too. If you still have no luck see below 'Make Your Own' and 'Shopping from Home'.

Aitken and Niven

See above 'Department Stores etc'.

Laura Ashley
126 Princes St
225 1218

Often have styles suitable for maternity wear, although no specific maternity section.

C & A
See above 'Department Stores etc'.

Chelsea Girl
St James Centre
556 6374

Cheap fashionable maternity clothes you won't feel forced to wear second time around.

The Chiffonier
98 Morningside Rd, Morningside
447 6715
Mon-Sat 10-6.30

Fitters of maternity and nursing bras and other specialist bras. Wide range of sizes, expensive; pleasant and helpful staff.

Cockburn St
Denim mecca. If you can tolerate loud music, and regarding your potential purchase in the mirror only to see the reflection of the youthful male assistant contemplating your larger-than-usual rear, there are several shops on this steep hill (start from the top on the High St if you can) which often have a selection of fashionable baggy dungarees and jumpsuits which make comfortable maternity wear.

Debenhams
See above 'Department Stores etc'.

Dorothy Perkins
Princes St (east end). Also at St James Centre, and Cameron Toll Shopping Centre 664 7279

A selection of reasonably priced maternity wear. Casual dungarees and jumpsuits to smart dresses.

Frasers
See above 'Department Stores etc'.

Madam H. Lazarska
2 East Preston St, Newington
667 4948

A real corsetière! Specializes in made-to-measure bras in non-standard sizes.

John Lewis
See above 'Department Stores etc'.

Mothercare
See above 'Department Stores etc'.

National Childbirth Trust
Contact Office 225 9191
Mon-Fri 9.30-11.30

Trained volunteers hold specialist fitting sessions for Mava bras, some of which have back lacing (ideal if you lose a lot of weight whilst feeding) and a hooked front opening. Others have zipped openings. High percentage of cotton. Wide range of sizes. A catalogue is available showing swimsuits, nightwear and leisurewear, all designed for maximum comfort during and after pregnancy. Also secondhand maternity wear. Phone office for details of all services.

Stewarts
95 Newington Rd, Newington

Fit maternity and nursing bras. Will allow breast feeding in shop.

Stork Exchange
Secondhand maternity wear, see below 'Secondhand Goods'.

Wilkie's
49-61 Shandwick Pl
229 5333

Bra fitting. Lift in shop. Toilets near the cafe are large enough for a pushchair but down small set of stairs.

BABY AND CHILDREN'S CLOTHES

Most department stores, supermarkets and chemists stock baby and children's clothes, underwear and socks. Not all are listed here; we've mentioned only those with a good range, exciting stock, competitive prices or something special to offer. Apart from the problems of finding the right style, fabric and colour at the right price, there are two bugbears when shopping for children's clothes: the lack of any standard sizing system and seasonal availability.

The large department stores and major brand names all have different sizing systems. Most are based on an out-of-date British Standard, with manufacturers adding their own allowances for growth, comfort etc. The age range given to various sizes is only a guide and you are best to take along your child's measurements and a tape measure for accurate results. Most shops will refund if an item is unsuitable but you <u>must</u> keep receipts. Many of the smaller shops mentioned in this section will make-to-measure, at little or no extra charge for children with, for example, long arms or legs.

One of the first signs of spring is the sudden disappearance (often while snow lies thick on the ground) of warm hats, gloves etc, and the sudden emergence (usually just after the January sales) of T-shirts, shorts etc. If your child does lose gloves in the 'chain store summer' you are probably best to try either boutique-y shops or secondhand and charity shops.

<u>Small baby clothes</u> (from about 3 lb) are available from the Corstorphine and Raeburn Pram Centres (see below 'Nursery Equipment etc') and Jenners and John Lewis (see above 'Department Stores etc').

Ace Knitwear
250 Canongate
557 0104

Includes attractive machine-knitted children's sweaters in Shetland wool.

Adams Children's Wear
16 St James Centre
556 0692

Good value baby and children's clothes. Selection of casuals that co-ordinate well together. MacLaren pushchairs and a small amount of other equipment. Easy access.

Laura Ashley
126 Princes St
225 1218

As well as the traditional 'little girl' smocks and dresses, there are boys' clothes — shorts, shirts, jerseys etc. Small selection of knitwear.

Baggins
18 Deanhaugh St, Stockbridge
332 2290
Tues-Sat 10-4

Good quality children's clothes, in natural fibres, made by shop (will make-to-measure). Ordered goods can take up to 3 weeks. Toys to play with whilst you choose. Access difficult — down a steep flight of steps to a basement. Baggins parties for groups, see 'Shopping from Home, Party Plan'.

Bare Necessities
60 Thistle St
226 4540

Expensive, mostly French and Italian baby and children's clothes (0-16 yrs). Access up a few very steep steps. Blackboard and chalk and toys to play with. Sofa for weary in middle of shop. Staff toilet for changing etc.

Benetton
94 Princes St
225 3140
Mon-Sat 9.30-6; Thurs 9.30-7

This is the only Edinburgh branch which keeps children's wear. Casual, fairly expensive Italian separates. Cords, jeans, shirts, knitwear, accessories in bright colours. The junior department called '012' sizes from birth to teens.

Castlecliff of Edinburgh
25 Johnston Terr
Mollie McNelly 226 2623
Mon-Fri 9-4

Shetland wool jumpers (18"-30"), hats and scarves. Variety of patterns and colours on offer. Made-to-measure for an extra charge. Good value. This is a Youth Training Scheme venture.

Co-op (Scotmid)
See above 'Department Stores etc'.

Gifts by Design
130 Morningside Rd
447 0432
Mon-Sat 9.30-6

Beautiful sleeping bags, cotton play-boots and a variety of clothes made by 'Barley Mill' in cotton, tartan and other fabrics. Small selection in stock but can order any size. See also 'Toy Shops etc'.

Grange Handknits
6 Grange Loan, Grange
667 5846
Mon-Sat 9-5.30; Sun 10-4

This small shop only sells garments hand-knitted in 100% wool, from 22". Jumpers, cardigans, jackets with hoods, hats, scarves and gloves in Aran and colourful Icelandic wool. Good selection and will make-to-measure if required (extra long sleeves etc).

Marks and Spencer
See above 'Department Stores etc'.

Miss Richardson
139 Gorgie Rd, Gorgie
337 5050

Old fashioned drapers with dust laden window hiding incredibly cheap baby clothes, ladies' lingerie and aprons like your granny used to wear. Erratic unadvertised hours.

Mackays
St James Centre, Cameron Toll, Wester Hailes and New Kirkgate

Small ranges of 'cheap and cheerful' baby and children's wear. Inexpensive long-sleeved aprons ideal for playschool and painting.

National Childbirth Trust
Contact Office 225 9191
Mon-Fri 9.30-11.30

New and secondhand baby and children's clothes, phone office for details.

Number Two
2 St Stephen's Pl, Stockbridge
225 6257

Frame-knitted adult and children's clothing — often in bright stripey designs or with motifs. Durable babies' bootees in wool and suede, making them non-slip. Also dressed teddies.

Orphan Annie
29 Cockburn St
225 8947

First size denim jeans, and other cotton garments, Pods and Kickers shoes in small sizes.

Pine and Old Lace
46 Victoria St
225 3287
10.30-5; Closed Wed. Phone to check if making a special trip as this is a one-woman shop.

Stock usually includes antique Christening gowns and baby clothes.

Score Commotions
44 Hanover St
225 2043
Also at West Bow

Fancy dress from 4 months, around £5 to buy (no hire for children). Also helium and modelling balloons, masks, fireworks, jokes etc. Many of the goods are geared towards an 'Adult market' which may provoke awkward questions from young children.

The Scotch House
60 Princes St
226 5271

1st floor: Kilts, in a variety of tartans, for children of all ages. Waistcoats, scarves, hats etc in tartan; and berets, gloves and jumpers in 'Fair Isle'.

Seconds and Firsts
364 Morningside Rd, Morningside
447 3588;
113 St Johns Rd, Corstorphine
334 4744;
25 Raeburn Pl, Stockbridge
332 3212;
Cameron Toll Shopping Centre,
Cameron Toll
664 3026

Large selection of chain store
seconds and 'Happit' firsts. Particularly good value for pyjamas, tracksuits and dungarees. Easy access to
all stores. There are 2 Morningside
branches; this one only stocks children's wear and ladies' lingerie.

Sunday Best
13 Colinton Rd, Morningside
447 9321
Mon-Fri 9-1, 2.30-5.30; Sat 9.30-
5.50

Expensive, mostly continental baby
and children's wear with more
casuals than frillies despite its name
(eg Osh Kosh). Toys to play with and
easy access.

Viyella
128a Princes St
225 4652
Mon-Fri 9-5.30; Thurs 9-7; Sat 9-6

At the back of the shop there is a
small selection of dresses (many
smocked) and shirts in Viyella's
classic wool and cotton mix.

What Everyone Wants
South Bridge

2nd floor: Large selection of children's clothes — ends of factory runs
and seconds means that quality and
availability ranges widely. Prices
often very cheap. **Toys** on **3rd**. No
lift and often very crowded. Pushchairs and prams are not allowed.

The Young Ones
120 Gorgie Rd, Gorgie
346 0069;
and 1001 N. Saughton Rd
334 4976

Cheap children's clothes.

MAKE YOUR OWN

Edinburgh has an excellent choice of
wool and fabric shops and you
always end up with an 'exclusive'
outfit. We feel the ones listed below
have something special to offer and
you may not know about some of
the more out of the way ones. Of
the department stores, John Lewis
has the most extensive fabrics
department and a rummage box although not orientated towards
children's fabrics. Liberty, 47 George
St, and Laura Ashley, 137 George St,
often have good value remnants in
natural fibres at sale times. There
are many wool shops scattered
around the suburbs and most stock
baby wools. Pingouin have children's knitting patterns in up to the
minute, colourful designs and
usually have a toddler/baby magazine. Patons have a wide range of
knitting patterns for small babies
starting at 14". See also 'Shopping
from Home, Babies' and Children's
Clothes'.

The Cloth Shop
24 Craighall Rd, Trinity
552 8818
Mon Closed; Tues-Sat 9.30-4; Thurs
9.30-8

Excellent 'market style' fabric shop.
Rummage under bales of cottons,
cords, towelling, sheeting, Viyella,
curtaining and you're sure to come
out with a bargain. Friendly, helpful
staff provide a basket of toys to

occupy tinies. Will allow use of toilet. Wool shop next door.

The Embroidery Shop
51 William St
225 8642

Embroidery supplies, birth sampler kits. Specialist shop which also runs classes.

The Finishing Touch
134 Nicolson St, Newington
667 0914
Mon-Sat 10-5.30

A huge range of colourful and unusual buttons. Lace trimmings, greetings cards, wrapping paper, ribbons. Lots of helpful hints and advice. See 'Birthdays and Celebrations'.

Get Knitted Sewing Centre
6-8 Viewforth, Bruntsfield
228 6952
Mon-Sat 9.30-5; Wed 9-1

Specialise in stretch type fabrics, ideal for baby suits, T-shirts, pyjamas etc. Very helpful staff. Runs sewing classes.

John Smith Wools
10 Frederick St
225 2808;
27 Queensferry St
225 5327

Large wool shop which includes baby wools, soft toy kits, birth sampler kits and haberdashery.

Remnant Kings
43-45 Lothian Rd
229 5135;
88 Newington Rd, Newington
667 7210;
15 Dalry Rd, Haymarket
337 4499

Large selection of fabrics from cheap and cheerful cottons to silks. Also stocks a range of sheeting, quilting, cords, wools and remnants sold by weight — very cheaply. Lots of trimmings and motifs. Paper patterns (Vogue patterns ordered).

CHILDREN'S SHOES

Many mothers think that retailers put children's shoe departments in basements or on 1st floors, simply to irritate them and add to the hassle of a shoe-buying trip. In fact it is for safety — so that junior does not take a trip straight out of the door when asked to take a few steps to see if the shoes fit. Many shops have a ticketed queuing system — always take a ticket before you look around. Avoid Saturdays and school holidays if possible as they tend to be particularly busy.

The shops below with a ★ before their name are listed in the Children's Foot Health Register whose aims are supported by the British Medical Association, and other health, chiropody and shoe associations. The CFHR lists shops which promise to: stock children's shoes in whole and half length sizes from infants size 3 to size 5½ for boys and girls; stock 4 width fittings; employ trained staff to measure both feet and carefully fit shoes at time of sale. The list is updated annually and is available from The Children's Foot Health Register, 84-88 Great Eastern St, London EC2A 3ED, enclosing a 9″ × 6″ SAE. Some libraries keep a copy for reference. It also gives the full aims of the register, useful information on foot care and lists footwear retailers throughout Britain, who promise to abide by the register's aims.

Don't be shy where your child's feet are concerned. If you don't think a shoe fits, ask to have it checked by another fitter. Complain to management if you feel a shop's standards have dropped. Several shops which sell nursery equipment also sell soft shoes for babies and toddlers, see below 'Nursery Equipment etc', and above 'Baby and Children's Clothes, Number Two and Orphan Annie'.

The following shops sell 'good brand' names in width sizes:

Aitken and Niven
See above 'Department Stores etc'

★ **Bally Shoe Co Ltd**
123 Princes St
225 5057
Mon-Wed 9.30-6; Thurs 9.30-7.30; Fri, Sat 9-6

The children's department is downstairs and stocks Bally, Clarks and Startrite. Staff are helpful and will allow the use of their lift. Some toys to play with and a video.

★ **Bayne and Duckett**
St James Centre
556 2793

Small shop, pleasant and helpful staff. Easy access and usually quieter than Princes St stores. There are other branches throughout the suburbs but many will be closing, some may be re-opened by the owners 'Clarks' under their own name.

Co-op (Scotmid)
See above 'Department Stores etc'

A Goldberg and Sons
See above 'Department Stores etc'

K Shoes
117 Princes St
225 5459

This basement department has a large rocking horse to play on. Good selection including K's own scuff-proof shoes which seem to defy even the hardest wear. Pushchairs can be left with staff on the ground floor.

★ K Shoes
Cameron Toll Shopping Centre, Lady Rd
664 8465

Easy access from shopping mall, has a play table and somersaulting monkey to keep youngsters happy. Stock similar to Princes St.

John Lewis,
See above 'Department Stores etc'

★ Peter Lord
79 Princes St
225 3761

(Also at Cameron Toll Shopping Centre)

Children's department downstairs. Pushchairs can be left with staff on the ground floor. Good selection, mainly 'Clarks'. Ticketed queues. Climbing frame with chute and large-scale train to play on. Children may use staff toilet.

Also has an 'odd shoe service': once your child's feet have been accurately measured you select a suitable shoe (most styles are available). This information is then sent to head office and the pair is sent to the shop in approx 4-5 weeks. These shoes cost between 25-30% more than the standard pair.

★ Russell and Bromley
106 Princes St
225 7444
Mon, Wed, Fri 9-5.30; Tues 9.30-5.30; Thurs 9-7.30; Sat 9-6. Open Sun at Easter, Summer and Christmas. Open Bank Holidays

An escalator takes you to this large 1st floor department — there is no guard at the top so youngsters must be carefully watched. Stairs back down. Ticketed queuing system. Distorting mirrors and life-size lion and other soft toys to scramble over. Beware sharp edges on seats. Children are not allowed to use the staff toilet and you are usually directed to Debenhams 4th floor a few doors away! You are always asked if you would like to open an account.

NURSERY EQUIPMENT including REPAIRS
There are many shops in Edinburgh that sell selections of well known brand name equipment — they are listed below. If you decide to buy secondhand or an uncommon (usually foreign) make, you must satisfy yourself as to its safety. Secondhand equipment can be in very good condition but may not conform to current safety standards. It is also best to ask about servicing and repairs before you buy — most of the outlets we've listed will do both to the brands they sell, and most will consider lending you a temporary re-

placement if the repair will take some time. Talk to friends before you buy — you only get to know the pros and cons of your equipment once you've lived with it for a while. Shops usually keep one demonstration pram in stock and order your style and colour. This can take from 6 to 20 weeks. No shop will make you buy a pram if you suddenly don't need it (if you discover you're having twins for instance) and most will store it until the day it is needed. All other equipment is usually kept in stock. Which? magazine often has reports on nursery equipment and it's worth checking back numbers in the library, even if it's just to see what to look out for. See also 'Hiring'.

Adams Children's Wear
See above 'Baby and Children's Clothes'

As Good As New
See below 'Secondhand'

Boots,
See above 'Department Stores etc'

Co-op (Scotmid)
See above 'Department Stores etc'

The Corstorphine Pram Centre
115-117 St Johns Rd, Corstorphine
334 6216
Wed: Closes at 1

Wide selection of prams, pushchairs, cots and lots of other equipment. Premature baby clothes, soft baby shoes, and small collection of baby and children's clothes and toys. Service and repair of MacLaren and any other brands being sold in the shop. Usually takes a few days unless parts have to be sent for. Will consider a loan during repair.

The Foam Centre
163 Causewayside, Newington
667 1247
Mon-Sun 9.30-5.30. Later at Christmas

Foam cut to any size and density. Can be made to fit cots, Moses baskets (also in stock), bumpers, booster seats etc. 'Beans' to top up or make your own bags. Visiting children usually receive a balloon. Maternity wedges, lumbar rolls, brightly coloured cubes also supplied. See also 'Annual Events, December'.

A. Goldberg and Sons, Jenners, John Lewis, Marks and Spencer, Mothercare
See above 'Department Stores etc' for details of these shops

National Childbirth Trust
Contact Office 225 9191
Mon-Fri 9.30-11.30

Supply a catalogue from which you can order nappy stackers, changing bags, cat nets, cot beds etc, and leaflets on many aspects of pregnancy, birth, breastfeeding and early parenthood. Sells 'Nuk' teats, designed to be similar to breast. Secondhand equipment usually available. Phone office for details of all services.

Raeburn Pram Centre
48 Raeburn Pl, Stockbridge
332 8214
Closed 1-2 and Wed pm

Good selection of prams, pushchairs, cots, mattresses (including safety mattresses with ventilation), Snugli baby carriers and all the other equipment you need for a baby. Premature baby clothes and baby clothes and toys. Stocks, services and repairs MacLaren, Silver-cross and Cindico. Repairs usually take a few days unless parts have to be sent for. Will consider a loan interim.

Royal Blind Asylum Shop
1 Bruntsfield Pl
229 1294

Good selection of Moses baskets and children's chairs. Cot and bed mattresses. Will make basket stands to order.

Scott Brothers
40 Cockburn St
225 7788

Extensive range of prams, pushchairs, cots, car seats, and lots of other equipment. Toys, including a range of sit and ride toys for all ages, junior bikes and dolls' prams. Leather shoes for babies. Will service and repair MacLaren, Cindico,

amongst others; loan considered. Repairs only take a few days unless parts have to be sent for.

Stork Exchange,
See below 'Secondhand'

Graham Tiso
115-123 Rose St
225 9486

1st Floor: Karrimor baby carriers, will help to fit and may offer refund if uncomfortable. Toddler size backpacks. Helpful staff will carry pushchairs up and down stairs.

CHILD SEATS

FOR BICYCLES

City Cycles
87 Slateford Rd
337 2351

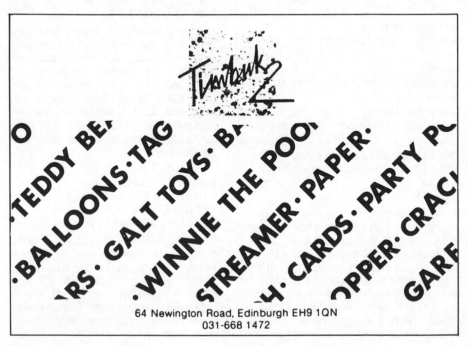

Edinburgh Bicycle Co-operative
5/6 Alvanley Ter, Bruntsfield
228 1368

Also sells protective head gear (crash helmets) for children (£35).

Robin Williamson Cycles
26 Hamilton Pl, Stockbridge
225 3268

Spokes Resources Group
53 George IV Bridge
225 6906

Mail order safety materials for bikers, eg tabards, reflective strips. See 'Shopping from Home, Miscellaneous'.

FOR CARS

Child seats are available in most chain stores selling nursery equipment and also in some car accessory shops. See 'Travel and Transport'.

TOY SHOPS, DOLL REPAIRS AND SPECIAL GIFTS

Particularly if you are buying toys from unorthodox sources, you will need to satisfy yourself as to safety. When buying for playgroups etc, it is worth asking whether discounts are available. Also refer to the specialist party shops in 'Birthdays and Celebrations', and to 'Department Stores etc', in particular Jenners, John Lewis and Menzies are recommended.

Argos
2-5 North Bridge
558 1474
Mon-Sat 9-5.30

A reasonable selection of popular toys, competitively priced, if they've got what you want. Choose from range in catalogue, they'll get it from stores.

Azteca
12-14 Victoria St
226 6695

Mexican and South American craft shop which includes some unusual toys and a few items of children's clothing. Large selection of domestic miniatures, suitable for use in dolls' houses etc.

Crafts 'n' Puzzles
within 'Scottish Crafts', Waverley Market

Will make easy jigsaws of children's names (35p per letter + 35p p + p) and send them direct to you.

Digger
35 West Nicolson St, Newington
668 1802
Mon-Sat 10-5.30

Small shop up 3 steps. A treasure trove of handmade and traditional wooden toys. Dolls' houses and furniture, wooden framed mirrors, bookends, clocks decorated with ducks, cats or anything you wish. Selection of novelty badges, including 'Maisie' badges. A few Shetland jumpers and hats.

Dolls' Hospitals
See Outdoors and Gallery Dolls

Early Learning Centre
67-83 Shandwick Pl
228 3244

Toys that are educational, safe and robust, catering particularly for younger children. Laid out in the shop under sections, eg First years, manipulative play, musical, pretend play, outdoor play, books, etc. There is a large play area for

19

children inc. a Brio train set. No customer toilet but there is a staff toilet downstairs which children may be able to use, provided staff agree and there is not any stock blocking the way! Noticeboard at entrance gives information on play-groups, etc. Catalogue available, see 'Shopping from Home'.

Edinburgh Wax Museum Shop
140 High St
225 9566
Mon-Sat 10-5.30. Longer in Summer.

Candles made while you watch, with any name, colour, etc. Also large selection of novelty candles (cats, elephants, mice, clowns etc). Will help parties of supervised children (min. 4/5 yrs) to make their own candles. You do not need to visit the wax museum to enter the shop. See also 'Places to Visit, Museums'.

Gallery Dolls and Dolls' Hospital
35a Dundas St
556 4295
Mon-Sat 9-5

Antique and reproduction dolls for sale in this basement shop. Porcelain dolls are made here, and the proprietor is hoping to start classes to pass on some of her skills. But any type of doll or soft toy can snuggle up in bed in the 'admission ward' whilst waiting for a facelift, new hair, limbs, eyes, ears or a growl! The 'theatre nurse' wears a uniform, and there's a re-cuperation bed too!

Gamesmaster
13 Forest Rd
226 3354

Mostly games for adults, but will make jigsaws from your own photo-graphs. Hand in negative and they will make wooden jigsaws from 24 pieces. Leaflet available.

Galt Toy Shop
See Jenners, in 'Department Stores etc'.

Gartons
249a St John's Rd, Corstorphine
334 4572

Small, well stocked toy shop. Friendly staff. Counter service.

Gifts by Design
130 Morningside Rd, Morningside
447 0432
Mon-Sat 9.30-6

Craft gifts including birth samplers (embroidery) with individual details, track suits, sleep bags made to order and measure in 2 weeks. Also pottery, jewellery, wooden gifts, jig-saws etc. Small selection of children's clothes which is the basic range of Barley Mill (see 'Shopping from Home'). Orders for Barley Mill clothes taken here also. Cards, wrapping paper etc.

Habitat
32 Shandwick Pl
225 9151
Mon Closed; Tues 9.30-5.30; Wed-Fri 9-5.30; Sat 9-6; Sun 10-5

The shop is on 3 floors with steps, but ask to use the staff operated lift. On the 1st floor there is a limited range of good quality toys and books — more are stocked at Xmas time. The ranges of rugs, crockery, lights, beds and textiles include many designed especially for, or suitable for children. **Toilets** are situated at the rear of the ground floor; difficult access to the rest of the shop. **Restaurant, 1st,** see 'Eating Out in Central Edinburgh (20)'.

Harburn Hobbies Ltd
67 Elm Row, Leith Walk
556 3233
Mon-Sat 9.45-6; Wed 9.45-1.30

Large collection of model railways and construction toys, eg Duplo.

Harlequin
25 Newington Rd, Newington
668 1455
Mon-Sat 9.30-5.30

Glass and gift shop which also sells wooden Christening clocks with hand painted faces with baby's weight, date, delivery time etc, to order. Children's portraits painted from photos — 10 days delivery.

Helios Fountain
7 Grassmarket
229 7884
Mon-Sat 10-6

Lots of crayons, paints, craft supplies, some handmade wooden toys (children are not allowed in this section unsupervised), alternative books and cafe. See also 'Eating Out in Central Edinburgh (21)'.

Jolly Giant Superstore
Peffermill Industrial Estate, Peffermill
661 7344

Warehouse of big name toys (Galt, Fisher Price), bikes, dolls prams, but generally no cheaper than town shops. There is a large notice by the bikes and slides asking parents to keep their children off. There are toys (which unfortunately are rather tatty) to play with near the check outs. Car park. **Toilets**.

Laverock
5 Raeburn Pl, Stockbridge
332 4605

A bathroom accessory shop which includes animal shaped soaps, towels and face flannels with de-

signs for children, eg Beatrix Potter, Winnie the Pooh etc.

You can also buy this sort of thing at Mothercare, Crabtree and Evelyn and Studio One. The Body Shop have a large range of toiletries but nothing specific for children.

The Mulberry Bush
77 Morningside Rd, Morningside
447 5145

Owned by Garvald Training Centre. Sells large wooden toys — rocking horses, puppet theatres, dolls' cribs, etc, and small wooden toys made by Campsie Village Trust. Also puzzles and dolls' house furniture. Small selection of books for young children as well as books on problem children.

Museum of Childhood
42 High St
June-Sept, Mon-Sat 10-6; Oct-May, Mon-Sat 10-5. During Festival, Sun 2-5

Small shop counter at entrance of museum. Sells 'old fashioned' small toys/gifts: wooden, tin, paper, posters etc. Details of museum in 'Places to Visit, Museums'.

Marks and Spencer
53 & 104 Princes St

Small range of books, toys and gifts at Christmas. Also children's videos. Check both shops as stock is different in both.

The National Trust Shop
Charlotte Sq
225 2160/5922

Attractive craft mobiles, badges, soaps, tins, mugs etc. Open whenever the Georgian House (see 'Places to Visit, Historic Buildings') is open, generally 1 April-31 Oct,

21

10-4 or 5. You do not need to pay admission to house to visit the shop.

A. T. Nisbet
10 Southfield Pl
669 6645

Toy making supplies.

Outdoors (and Dolls' Hospital)
28 Dalry Rd, Haymarket
337 6360
Mon-Sat 9-5.30

Climbing frames, trampolines, swings, slides, sports gear. Doll repairs also. Inflatable castle for hire, see 'Hiring, Inflatables'.

Royal Mile Miniatures
154 Canongate
557 2293

Collectors' shop selling beautifully made, hand crafted dolls' houses and miniatures, dolls' house kits and fittings (pelmets, cornices, tiles etc). Craftsmanship reflected in the prices, ie very expensive.

Scottish Pre-School Play Association
15 Smith's Pl, Leith
553 2185
Mon-Fri 10-3; Closed during school holidays

Children's stationery and craft items (crayons, paper, paints, scissors etc) at competitive prices. Cheaper still to playgroups registered with SPPA.

Studio One
10-14 Stafford St
226 5812

Down very steep steps to basement shop full of pocket money toys, stocking fillers, novelties, Xmas decorations etc. Allow use of staff toilet, but it is not close by.

The Tappit Hen
109 High St
557 1852

Scottish dolls and soldiers.

Tanya's Toys
Waverley Market
556 6359

A well-stocked toy shop, play-people, dressing up clothes, soft toys, dolls, baby toys, some larger toys and books. Like all units in Waverley Market it is small. There is a 'Playmobil' table with a few toys on it for children to play with. Situated next to Teddy's Place, see below 'Creches while Shopping'.

The Tartan Gift Shop
Princes St

Scottish dolls dressed in tartan.

Timbuk-2
64 Newington Rd, Newington
668 1472

Small shop that sells a variety of children's novelties and gifts. A good selection of mobiles and a corner devoted to 'Partywear'. Cards and wrapping paper. Friendly staff. Small supply of Galt toys.

Toucan Crafts
81 Morningside Rd, Morningside
447 1671
Mon-Sat 9-6

Craft materials, pipe cleaners, wax crayons, mobile kits, plaster casting kits etc. Orders taken of dough letters of child's name. Names painted on paper and decorated. Soft toys, bibs, baby clothes — all hand made locally. Specific orders taken for almost anything (eg lining Moses basket). Friendly staff.

Toytub
100a Raeburn Pl, Stockbridge
332 7951

Old fashioned shop, with counter service, good range of models and toys. Children must be well controlled.

Toys Galore
193 Morningside Rd, Morningside
447 1006
Mon-Sat 9.30-5.30; Sun in Dec

Good choice of toys for all ages with some to try out while you look. Includes Galt, Fisher Price, Brio, etc. 10% discount to playgroups. Active window trains running, puppets dancing etc. Difficult to manoeuvre buggy. Won the 'National Association of Toy Retailers' award in 1984.

Whichcraft
94 Raeburn Pl, Stockbridge
343 1800

An outlet for several crafts people — good quality items, many suitable for children, eg quilted jackets, patchwork cot quilts, wooden dolls' houses, etc.

Wonderland
97 Lothian Rd
229 6428
(Also at 116a Rose St 229 6428)
Mon-Fri 9-6; Sat 9-5.30; Sun 12-5

Small toy shop on basement and ground floors, specialising in model vehicles and construction kits. Large stock of Lego but no Duplo or trains. Lots of model cars and trains but range for under 5s limited. Usually working models in the window.

BUYING CHILDREN'S BOOKS

Several of Edinburgh's many book-shops include a wide range of children's books and also provide a 'play' area for children with, for example, toys, crayons, tables, chairs and books. This can make buying books a pleasant experience for both adult and child. Most bookshop staff are very helpful and computerisation means that titles and authors' names are readily accessible. Despite television and videos, books are still very popular with under fives and we have listed here the best stocked and most helpful shops as well as those too prominent to be ignored. Children's books are also available at supermarkets (Sainsbury's have their own label), most department stores, most toy shops, by mail order (see 'Shopping from Home') and of course, secondhand.

The Edinburgh Children's Book Group is a registered charity aiming to bring children, parents and books together. They will hold book evenings in your home, arrange book centred events, read to children in hospitals. News-sheet for members, also evening meetings with guest speakers, eg publishers, artists, editors. Contact: Mrs R. Knox, 17 West Savile Ter, EH9 3DY, 667 4500.

'The Good Book Guide to Children's Books', Penguin, 1986 (Annual Publication) recommends classic and modern books for children of all ages and reading stages, and its recommendations are not confined to Puffins! From bookshops or: The Good Book Guide, 91 Great Russell St, London WC1, £4.50, incl p + p.

Some books with an Edinburgh theme which appeal to young children are:

'The Tale of Greyfriar's Bobby', by Lavinia Derwent, Puffin, 1985, £1.50. A simply written but long version of the tale of the faithful dog.

'Maisie Comes to Morningside', by Aileen Patterson, Byway Books, £1.50. Detailed and glossy illustrations of identifiable places in Morningside; Maisie is a kilted kitten who visits her granny in the city.

'Songs of the Singing Street', by Doug Mann, Canongate, 1985. Words and music of traditional Scottish street songs, including one about the aforementioned dog.

'A Child's Garden of Verses', by Robert Louis Stevenson. A classic. 'The Lamplighter' lit the lamp outside RLS's home in Heriot Row, and it's still there, although it's electric now.

BOOKSHOPS

Bargain Books
Princes St
Mon-Sat 9 am-11 pm; Sun 9 am-10.30 pm

Cheap books, some children's books, mainly in the basement accessible only by spiral stairs which would be very tricky with a buggy. Staff not willing to allow a toddler to use their toilet. No facilities for children.

Bauermeisters Booksellers
19 George IV Bridge
226 5561
Mon-Sat 9-5.30

University bookshop with small children's section on the ground floor unfortunately placed next to the stairs to the basement. No special facilities for the young.

Church of Scotland Bookshop
117-119 George St
225 2229
Mon-Sat 9-5.30; Tues 9.30-5.30

The children's bookshop is next door to the main bookshop. It has a wide range of attractively displayed books including religious books. The shop also has cards, stationery, videos, records and cassettes, posters, jigsaws and a few gifts. Friendly staff will allow the use of their toilet.

The Edinburgh Bookshop
57 George St
225 4495
Mon-Sat 9-5.30; Sun 11-5

Spacious children's book section at rear of shop (up a few steps). Children's table and chairs and toys. **Toilets** in the basement (no lift) with no facilities for mother and baby. **Cafe**: see 'Eating Out in Central Edinburgh (15)'.

First of May
Left Bookshop and Meeting Place, 43 Candlemaker Row
225 2612
Mon-Sat 10-6

Co-operative bookshop stocking radical books (feminist socialist/anti-racist/libertarian non-sectarian) and magazines. Small kids section at rear with a box of toys. Toilet available (upstairs).

Glowworm
7 Main St, Balerno
449 4644
Mon-Fri 9-5, closed 1-2; Wed 9-1; Sat 9-5

Out of town but worth a visit. Children's and adults' books, stationery, cassettes, art and craft supplies, gifts. Children's play area, Klik coffee corner for adults. Puffin computer programme will give each child a booklist based on age and interest. Discount for schools and playgroups. Staff toilet available.

Stockbridge Children's Bookshop
26-28 NW Circus Pl
225 5355/1035
Mon-Sat 9-6; Thurs 9-8; Sun 12-4.30. Longer during Festival
(Also a small branch in Waverley Market)

Good selection of children's books in separate shop next door to main shop. Books and toys for children to play with in both shops. The bookshop put out a newsletter and run some competitions. Friendly staff will allow the use of their office to breastfeed and have a toilet one can use (although rather inaccessible).

James Thin
53-59 South Bridge
556 6743
Mon-Sat 9-5.30; Children's Saturday Club 10-11.30
(Also a small branch in Waverley Market. Paperbacks only)

University bookshop. There is a large, pleasant children's section downstairs (long flight of steps, no lift), with little table and chairs, toys, blackboard, books to read and beanbags in the Ladybird corner. The Saturday Club includes quizzes, competitions, games and storytelling (which will be geared to the ages of the children present). Friendly staff will allow use of their toilet.

Waterstones Bookshop
114-116 George St
225 3436
Mon-Fri 9.30 am-10 pm; Sat 9.30-7; Sun 12-7

A large, high quality bookshop with a vast range of books for both adults and children. Its emphasis is on 'fun for all the family' with live music events and long opening hours. The children's section is at the back of the shop with mini seats and table, blackboard, beanbag and toys. It has a large selection of books but is rather crowded. No public toilet but the staff toilet is right next to the children's department, children are welcome to use it. Tight squeeze to change a nappy.

SECONDHAND GOODS

As Good As New
50 Rodney St, Canonmills
343 3382 (evenings)
Tue, Wed 10.30-2.30; Thurs-Sat 10.30-4

Small shop with large selection and rapid turnover of good quality secondhand baby and children's clothes, toys, books and occasionally equipment. Prices are relatively high for secondhand goods. Purchases items in good condition for 50% of their selling price. Toys for children to play with whilst you look.

Hand-in-Hand
3 NW Circus Pl, Stockbridge
226 3598

Antique christening gowns, Shetland lace shawls and some children's clothes, as well as clothes and textiles.

National Childbirth Trust
225 9191 ext 51
Mon-Fri 10-12 noon

Fund-raising events usually have a secondhand clothes stall, check press for details.

25

Second Time Around
129 Easter Rd
Mon-Sat 10-5

Sells a variety of secondhand goods including babies and children's wear, also a few toys. Reasonable prices.

Stork Exchange
49 Comiston Rd, Morningside
447 5434
Mon-Sat 10-4.30; Closed Wed

Buys and sells good quality modern nursery equipment and maternity clothes. See also 'Hiring Children's Items'.

Charity shops throughout the city (Oxfam, Dr Barnardo's, Beauty without Cruelty, St Columbas Hospice, ECSS, RNLI, YWCA Nearly New Shops) are worth keeping an eye on for children's clothes. See under 'Charitable and Benevolent Organisations', in the Yellow Pages for

as good as new
buy & sell
clothes Books TOYS
for children up to 8yrs

Open: Tues-Sat 10·30 - 4pm
Wed 10·30 - 2·30pm
50 Rodney Street
(canonmills)
Tel : 343 3382 (eve)

addresses of their shops. Most are voluntarily staffed so opening hours tend to be short with lunch time closing.

Other suggestions: Evening News, Edinburgh Advertiser, Jumble Sales, YWCA Toy Fairs and other local festivals and fairs throughout the year — see 'Annual Events'. Notices in newsagents, supermarkets, playgroups etc. You could also put up a 'wanted' notice.

FOOD

Casey's
52 St Mary's St; and at cnr Easter Rd/London Rd

An old-fashioned confectioners with traditional sweets in jars behind the counter. Also decorated and named Easter eggs.

Real Foods
8 Brougham St
228 1651;
and at 37 Broughton St
557 1911

Although there are health food shops in nearly all areas we know of none that rival this one for range and price. There is a dauntingly large range of grains, pastas, beans, rices, herbs, spices, soya products, etc. Also organically grown baby foods, alternatives to cows' milk, gluten free products, ranges of leaflets on weaning babies on to wholefoods, children's wholefood party recipes, hyperactivity and diet, etc. Will deliver within the Edinburgh area on Friday (COD £1.50 charge for orders under £50), or phone in large orders 24 hours in advance to collect personally, or use mail order service anywhere in the country.

Quantity from 1 oz upwards, carriage rate for orders less than 300 kg. The only problem at both shops is escaping the traffic wardens as you try to lug your sack full of good health without dropping the baby or letting the toddler get run over. Catalogue available.

Supermarkets

Nearly all supermarkets now provide trolleys with child seats. Many of the larger ones, such as Asda, sell children's clothes, books and toys, as well as their own brand of toiletries and disposable nappies. Most are currently removing unnecessary sugar and many additives from their ranges (Sainsbury's is the original home of the additive-free fish finger!). However, despite this apparent concern to market good health, most persist in arranging sweets at exactly child's eye height at the check outs. Thus

we could not award "We welcome small children" symbols to otherwise good supermarkets. If you ask, Safeway will carry parcels to your car, help you pack and unpack, and let locals borrow their trolleys to wheel shopping home. Safeway have now introduced child restraint safety belts on their shopping trolleys, so you can concentrate on your shopping rather than the safety of your child. Marks and Spencer has a collect-by-car service.

We know of a few places where toddlers are allowed to use the staff toilets — several branches of Safeway and William Low in Canonmills. If you ask for the use of a toilet in Savacentre at Cameron Toll you will be directed to the public toilets, out of the supermarket, off the central aisle of the shopping complex. There is a children's leisure centre, with videos, books, play area and snacks, for 4-12 year olds at Asda. Qualified staff. £1.50 whilst shopping in the store. See also 'Birthdays and Celebrations' for special party food.

CRECHES WHILE SHOPPING

Finally, if it's all just too difficult to shop with tinies in tow, here are some places (other than Granny's!) to leave them:—

Asda
The Jewel, Duddingston. See above 'Food, Supermarkets'.

Little Marco's
51/95 Grove St
228 2341
Mon-Fri 9.30-4.30
3-5 yr old £2/hr; under 3 £4/hr.
Book in advance.
See also 'Activities for Children'.

Shopper's Creche

Organised by Edinburgh District Council Women's Committee in one of the shopping centres over the Christmas period. Phone 225 2424 ext 5090 or 5091 for details.

Teddy's Place

Waverley Market (upper floor, near lift)
Mon-Sat 9.30-5.30; Thurs 9.30-7; Sun 11.30-4.30

Open to all children between 18 months and 5 years. 2 hours is the maximum length of any one visit. Qualified childminders and good play equipment and toys. £1/hr/child.

CHEMISTS WITH EXTENDED HOURS

The Lothian Health Board Primary Care Division, 14 Drumsheugh Gardens EH3 7UJ (225 1341) keep a list of chemists and operate a rota to provide pharmaceutical services outside normal shop hours. There is also an Emergency Prescription Dispensing Service. This operates through local police stations so that if you have a prescription that has been marked "Urgent" by your doctor you should call at, or phone, your local police station who will advise you how to contact a chemist participating in the scheme.

OPEN SUNDAY:

Black, John
146 Gorgie Rd
337 1659
10 am-12.30 pm

Boots The Chemists Ltd
48 Shandwick Pl
225 6757
11 am-4.30 pm

Ferguson, James
22 Hillhouse Rd
332 3602
12.45-1.30 pm

Iqbal, Mohammed
9 West Richmond St
12 noon-5 pm

Safeway Food Stores Ltd
33 Cameron Toll Shopping Centre, 6 Lady Rd, Livingston 30449
11 am-5 pm

OPEN AFTER 6 pm

Allan Ltd, G W
102 Ferry Rd
554 1394
Mon, Tues, Thurs, Fri 7 pm

Boots The Chemists Ltd
14 Cameron Toll Shopping Centre, 6 Lady Rd
666 1111
Weekdays 8 pm;

101-103 Princes St
225 8331
Thurs 7 pm;

5-7 St James Centre
556 1062
Thurs 7 pm;

48 Shandwick Pl
225 6757
Weekdays 9 pm

Lindsay & Gilmour
11 Elm Row
556 4316
Weekdays 6.30 pm

McInnes, Peter M
50 Restalrig Rd Sth
Weekdays 6.30 pm

Morningside Pharmacy
207-209 Morningside Rd
Weekdays 8 pm

Rutherfords (Chemists) Ltd
153 Morningside Rd
447 2041
Weekdays 8 pm

Safeway Food Stores Ltd
33 Cameron Toll Shopping Centre; 6 Lady Rd, Livingston 30449
Mon, Tues, Weds, Thurs 8 pm; Fri 9 pm

Wade, Hubert O
162 Easter Rd
661 4195
Mon, Tues, Thurs, Fri 6.30 pm

Toilet Stops

Public toilets are run by Edinburgh District Council. Many are under street level with a long flight of steps, most are very old with tiled walls and floors. Generally they are very clean and staff most helpful.

The following toilets have a mother's room facility:—

Waverley Market

Open 24 hours, down a long flight of steps from Waverley Bridge or during Waverley Market opening hours from the lowest level (to the left of Café Noir).

Mound

Princes St. 9 am-11 pm. East of the Royal Scottish Academy, underground next to the police box.

Bath St

Portobello. 9 am-11 pm

There are no plans to include facilities for feeding or changing in any other EDC toilets, due to lack of money and space in some locations. No gent's toilets have any provision for feeding or changing.

The following toilets are open 7 days per week. Those with a star before them are shown on the map.

24 Hours

★Waverley Market.

9 am-11 pm

★Mound; Hamilton Pl, Stockbridge; ★Hunter Square; ★Castle Terr Car Park; Canonmills; Joppa; Hope Park; Haymarket; Ardmillan Terr, Gorgie; Nicolson Square; Bath St, Portobello; ★West End, Princes St; High St, South Queensferry; Bruntsfield; ★Canongate; ★Castlehill; Tollcross; ★Middle Meadow Walk; London Rd; Taylor Gdns, Leith.

9 am-7.30 pm

Wester Hailes; Canaan Lane, Morningside; ★St James Centre; Vanburgh Pl, Leith; St John's Rd, Corstorphine.

10 am-5 pm

Colinton Rd; Granton Square, Granton; Liberton Gdns, Liberton; Currie; Silverknowes (see below); Fairmilehead; Juniper Green; Newhaven (gents only); Albert St (gents only); Hawes Pier (see below).

Seasonal Opening — May-Sept 9 am-11 pm

Cramond; Pipe St, Portobello; Silverknowes; ★Ross Bandstand, Princes St Gardens; Pittville/Bellfield, Portobello; Promenade West, Portobello; Hawes Pier.

If you have any comments on Edinburgh District Council public conveniences and their provision (or lack) of facilities for parents with babies and young children write to The Director of Cleansing, Department of Cleansing, King Stables Rd, Edinburgh EH1 2JZ.

For details of toilets and mother's rooms in shops see 'Shopping'.

Shopping from Home

How often have you thought 'there must be an easier way to shop!' rather than battling through crowds with buggy and complaining kid(s). Shopping with small children is NOT easy. Mail order firms have responded to this in quantity, quality and variety. Increasingly more people are shopping from home. Listed below are some of the smaller and more popular mail order firms, some of which have been personally recommended to us (marked ★). They usually require a stamped addressed envelope in which to return their catalogue. There are a few things to bear in mind when ordering through the post:—

1) Check your information is up-to-date;

2) Read the advertisement carefully, including the small print;

3) Don't send money (never send cash) in advance unless asked to do so and keep a note of this;

4) Set a time limit for delivery (eg 28 days) and add "Time is the essence of the contract";

5) Keep a copy of the advertisement, your order and date sent;

6) Make sure you always include your home address with all your correspondence.

The Office of Fair Trading produce a leaflet called 'Buying by Post'. This is available from many public libraries, the Citizens' Rights Office and the Citizens' Advice Bureau, who can assist should problems arise — see 'Welfare'.

BABIES' AND CHILDREN'S CLOTHES

Bambini
Lilac Cottage, Matlaske, Norwich NR11 7AQ
026 377 467

Babies and small children's (up to 110 cm) dresses, trousers, shirts, quilted jackets, fancy jumpers. Also willow cribs and Moses baskets with a selection of linings, or will make up with your own material.

Barley Mill
Glenfarg, Perth PH2 9QL
033 76686

Children's clothes in cotton cord. Their basic range is stocked at Gifts by Design (see 'Shopping, Toy Shops etc') where you can also place an order.

Blooming Kids
(Blooming Marvellous Ltd), PO Box 12F, Chessington, Surrey
01-391 4822

Children's clothes, 0-5 yrs.

The Children's Clothing Company
52 Shandon Rd, London SW4 9HR
01-675 4226/0206

Designer clothes for the under 5s aimed primarily at the average to tall child who often has to wear clothes for an older age range.

Childs Play Collection
Essy Roberts, 10 Rutland Sq, Edinburgh EH1 2AE
229 4374

Tartan clothes for children for special occasions in kit form or ready made.

★ **Clothkits**
24 High St, Lewes, Sussex
Lewes 77111

Clothes for all the family to be cut out and sewn or ready made.

★ **Cotton-On**
29 North Clifton St, Lytham FY8 5HW
0253 73611

Specially for those with sensitive skins, 100% cotton garments (from 1 yr up), mainly underclothes, sleep wear with scratchmits.

Dollycare
13 Elmtree Rd, Cosby, Leics
0533 773013

Clothes made especially for small babies, 3 sizes: 3-8 lbs, 5-8 lbs, and 8-12 lbs. Reasonably priced. Available locally at Corstorphine Pram Centre, Raeburn Pram Centre — see 'Nursery Equipment etc', — and Jenners and John Lewis — see 'Department Stores etc'.

Hand Smocked Frocks
Angela Master, 2 Shubbery Grove, Royston, Herts SG8 9LJ
0763 47277

Dresses readymade or kit form, smocked, or not, from £10.

Jellybeans
Malthouse, Elmsted, Ashford, Kent TN25 5JZ
Elmsted 220/326

Kit form or readymade in a choice of fabrics at reasonable prices. Dresses, trousers, shirts 0-9 yrs.

★ **Kangaroo**
91 Ewart St, Brighton BN2 2UP
0273 674512

Sailing gear — including buoyancy aids (smallest size 0-2 yrs £20), guardrail netting for boats or stairs, 100% waterproof jackets, trousers, coats from 90 cm to teens and clothes: jumpers, trousers and swimsuits.

★ **Kidstuff**
10 Hensman Hill, Clifton BS8 4PE
0272 734980

Mainly dungarees, pinafores and woollen jumpers. Hardwearing and attractive. Responds quickly to orders.

Knitwise
42 Mayflower Rd, Park Street, St Albans, Herts AL2 2QW
0727 74055/72086

Kit knits or readymade picture sweaters for children from size 22" from around £10. Also offer a hand knitting service.

★ **Rich Knits**
33 Couston St, Dunfermline KY12 7QW
3 722065

100% pure Shetland wool jumpers in stripes, checks or all-over Fair Isle in 17 colours for you to choose your own combination. Pinafores and dungarees in cord. Excellent value and good quality. Send for a small brochure.

Smock — Frock
8 Strathearn Rd, Edinburgh EH9 2AE
447 7843

Hand smocked dresses.

Snap Dragon
The Glebe, Nash Rd, Whaddon, Milton Keynes MK17 0NQ
0908 501928

Dungarees and reversible dresses in bright colours.

★ **Sproggies**
59 Fisher Rd, Diss, Norfolk 1P22 3JR
0379 51558/3432

Trousers and dungarees of various styles up to 110 cm (less than £10 pair).

★ **Young Classics**
The Workshop, 7A Laburnum Ter, Ashington, Northumberland NE63 0XX

Jackets, jumpers, trousers, shirts up to age 6/7. Reasonably priced.

PARTY-PLAN

There are a few local companies which make children's clothes and distribute through party-plan. You can sometimes end up with an individually designed garment.

Baggins
Local shop in Stockbridge, but also sells through party plan. See 'Shopping, Babies' and Children's Clothes'.

Millikids
38 Lamburton Court, Pencaitland
Pencaitland (5) 3400687

Made-to-measure clothes (birth-10 yrs). Choose your own style from basic patterns and materials.

Scallywags
19 Rosevale Pl, Edinburgh EH6 8AP
553 5622

Applique tops, tracksuits, cord trousers, pinafores and blouses.

Woolly Minded
5 Tyler's Acre Rd, Edinburgh EH12 7HY
334 4266/667 9520

Jumpers, skirts, dungarees.

CHILDREN'S BOOKS

Books for Children
Farndon Rd, Market Harborough, Leics LE16 9NR
0858 34567 (2-4 pm)

Hardback book club, under 5s to over 10s. Monthly catalogue.

Letterbox Library
Box 38, 5 Bradbury St, London N16 8JN
01-254 1640

A non-sexist children's book club.

★ **The Red House Children's Book Club**
Witney, Oxford OX8 6YQ
0993 71144/74171

Discount is usually on hardback books. Quarterly catalogue.

MATERNITY CLOTHES

Arabella — Fashion Feeders
Mrs C Bell, The Studio, Lundie, Angus
08286 237;
or
Mrs C H Rowan, Olimmuir, Kirriemuir, Angus
0575 73116

Garments designed for discreet breastfeeding with concealed zips etc. Shirt around £17, dress for £27.

★ **Blooming Marvellous**
PO Box 12F, Chessington, Surrey KT9 2LS
01-397 5954

Maternity wear: shirts, dungarees, dresses, T-shirts (some with slogans), tracksuits, shorts, nightdresses, bras, swimsuits.

★ **NCT (Maternity Sales) Ltd**
9 Queensborough Terrace, London
W2 3TB
01-221 3833

MAVA bras, maternity nightdresses, tracksuits, swimsuits, baby mat and holdall (all profits covenanted to the NCT). Also books, leaflets, breast shields, pads and pumps. Contact local NCT Office: Stockbridge Health Centre, India Pl, Edinburgh EH3 6EH; 225 9191, Mon-Fri 9.30-11.30, for local sales agent (fitting service available too).

SHOES

Adams and Jones
Crispin Hall, High St, Street, Somerset BA16 0EZ
0458 45441

Handmade leather footwear for adults and children.

Clarks and Peter Lord

Also have an 'odd shoe' service through many branches. Charge 30% extra for specially made shoes. See 'Shopping, Children's Shoes'.

SOFA
17 Deva Close, Poynton, Cheshire SK12 1HB

Send a stamped addressed envelope for information on where to get odd sized shoes.

Start-rite Shoes Ltd
John Peach, Customer Liaison Officer, Crome Rd, Norwich NR3 4RD
0603 43841

Start-rite's 'odd shoe' service, offers shoes specially made at around 25% less than the price of two pairs of shoes.

TOYS

★ **Croglin Toys**
1 Mulcaster Pl, Croglin, Nr Carlisle, Cumbria CA4 9RX
076-886 405

Solid, lasting, wooden toys from baby toys to trikes, farms and garages. Also larger items (climbing frames, easels, dolls' houses), unsuitable for posting.

★ **Discovery Toys**

Educational toys from birth to adult. An agent will demonstrate toys in your home. For your local agent contact the regional co-ordinator, Anne Dall, 18 Primrose Bank Road, Trinity, 552 2105.

Early Learning Centre
Hawksworth, Swindon SN2 1TT
0793 610171

Order from their catalogue by post or phone, carriage charge. Wide range of educational toys, also outdoor play equipment. Local shop: 67-83 Shandwick Pl. See 'Shopping, Toy Shops etc'.

★ **Montrose Play Equipment**
Montrose Products, 28-34 Fortess Rd, London NW5 2JH
01-485 6751/2

Climbing towers, slides, swings, trampolines, sand and water play, bikes, all at very reasonable prices. Distributors of well known brand names.

★ **Tridias**
124 Walcot St, Bath

Very wide range of toys, expensive dolls' houses to cheap party presents.

Wrencraft
Liz Wight, 75 Clermiston Rd, Edinburgh EH12 6UU
334 2812

Custom-made toys and mascots. Makers of 'Maisie' toys (characters from Aileen Paterson's books), and 'Little Marco' cuddly bear. They will design a soft toy or mascot of your choice from a picture or motif.

MISCELLANEOUS

Heather Quilts
84 Gilmore Pl, Edinburgh EH3 9PF
229 3652, afternoons and evenings

Individually made cotton quilts from £30, cot size.

Heinz Baby Club
Vinces Rd, Diss, Norfolk IP22 3HH
0379 51981

Co-ordinating nurseryware including fabric, wallpaper and equipment. Also a wide range of toys and outdoor equipment at reasonable prices. Discount for members but don't need to be a member to order.

Hushabybaby Productions Ltd
39 Ranmoor Cres, Sheffield S10 3GU
0742 307010

Womb noises tape to calm fretful babies and induce sleep naturally (£4.99).

Jaygee Cassettes
19 Golf Links Rd, Burnham-on-Sea, Somerset TA8 2PW

Baby soother cassette (£4.99 inc p & p). Must be started within 10 weeks of birth.

Laura Ashley
Box No 1, Mail Order Dept, Carno, Powys, Wales

Ladies' and children's clothes, home furnishing. Local shops: 126 Princes St (clothes); and 137 George St (furnishing).

★ Loveseat
In-Car Safety Centre, Freepost, Luton LU2 0BR
0582 22129

Baby car seat from birth to approx 9 mths. Designed to ride either in front (facing rearwards) or back secured with car safety belt. Free standing. Around £42.

★ Mothercare-by-post
PO Box 145, Watford, Herts
0923 25635

Order from the catalogue of Mothercare products, maternity wear, baby and children's clothes and equipment. Local shop: 84a Princes St.

Oh/One/Oh
Bradford, West Yorkshire BD99 4BR

Maternity clothes, baby and children's clothes (up to age 10), equipment and children's furniture.

Real Foods
Health foods including baby foods and special dietary food delivered to your home. See 'Shopping, Food'.

SPOKES Resources Group
53 George IV Bridge, Edinburgh EH1 1EJ
225 6906

Safety materials for bikes and riders or even pushchairs! Tabards £3.50, reflective strip 15p.

Winganna Natural Products
Sandy Hill Cottage, St Ishmaels,
Haverfordwest, Dyfed SA62 3DL
06465 403

Natural fleeces for baby (£23-£30),
wind-cheaters for the family, baby
blankets and shawls, rugs and soap.
Research shows babies sleep better
on natural fleeces. Order through
NCT Office, see above 'Maternity
Clothes', for % to go to the NCT.

Hiring

Please phone in advance to make
sure that what you require is available and, particularly when the
business is run from home, that
someone will be available to see
you.

CLOTHES

Fabric Care
50 Ashley Ter
337 1344
Mon-Fri 8-1, 2-5; Sat 9-12

Jumper shop which has christening
gowns for hire. £7.50/dress, £1.50/
shawl.

Fancy Dress Hire Shop
21 Castle St
226 5457
Mon-Fri 9.30-5.30; Sat 9-5

The major stockist of children's
fancy dress in Edinburgh. Prices
around £5/outfit.

**Flamingo Ballgown and Cocktail
Dress Hire**
5 Gloucester Sq
226 3669

About 120 unique designer dresses
available for hire, including about
30 suitable for maternity wear. Sizes
8-16. Small alterations can be made.
Can deliver to and collect from your
home. A new company run from the
proprietor's home. About £20-£30,
and £30 returnable deposit.

EQUIPMENT

Babyhire
12 Inverleith Pl
552 3786

Babyhire is run from the proprietor's own home. Large range of
items for babies and toddlers at
reasonable rates. Hire for up to 3
mths. Major items include carrycots,
prams, buggies, high chairs, babydiners and fireguards. No car seats.
Friendly and helpful service. Will
deliver within city boundary (75p
charge).

Cots Galore
447 1551/5328

Hire of baby and toddler equipment
run from the proprietors' own
houses in Morningside. Large range
of items at reasonable rates (similar
to above). Double buggy £1/day,
£18/3 mths, travel cot £3/wk. Considering stocking car seats. Have
bed wetting alarms.

Hamilton Hire
13 Fox Spring Cres, Fairmilehead
445 2814

A new hire company run from proprietor's home. Travel cots, buggies,
stairgates, etc. Hoping to stock car
seats once business is built up a bit.
Rates not finalized but no doubt will
be competitive.

National Childbirth Trust
Stockbridge Health Centre, India Pl, Stockbridge
225 9191
Mon-Fri 9.30-11.30

Hire of Egnell breast pumps. Contact the office for your local agent.

Stork Exchange
49 Comiston Rd, Morningside
447 5434
Mon-Sat 10-4.30; Closed Wed

A secondhand baby equipment shop which hires goods as well. Hire up to 4 weeks, £10 deposit. Only hires the major items ie cots, travel cots, high chairs, buggies, pushchairs and playpens. Rates: cots £5/wk, £2.50/weekend; travel cot £3/wk, £1.50/weekend.

SKIS

Ski-sport and Sun
5/6 Barclay Ter, Bruntsfield
229 9599
Mon-Fri 10-6, Sat 9-5

During season hire of skis, ranging from 80 cm, size 23(4) boot for £6/day. Also have plastic toddler skis. Sell off equipment at end of season.

As far as we could tell this is the only shop which hires skis for the under 5s. Hillend Ski hire is only for 6+. Equipe Ski Hire starts at 1.50 m skis. Out-of-town under 5s ski hire is available at Badenoch Ski School, Kingussie and the Day Lodge, Cairngorm, Aviemore.

INFLATABLES

Outdoors
28 Dalry Rd, Haymarket
337 6360
Mon-Sat 9-5.30

Large inflatable castle (13'×7') for hire. £30/day inc delivery and collection. £25/day, collect it yourself.

Theatre Workshop
34 Hamilton Pl
225 7942

Hires out large inflatables, suitable for bouncing and sliding for disabled and young children, for £10/day to a community group, £20/day to a private individual plus £20 deposit.

Cake Tins. See 'Birthdays and Celebrations'.

Eating Out

When we began research for this section we all felt that there were all too few places where children were really welcome. This is still true to a certain extent but, through our questionnaire, we hope we can reveal to you the facilities provided by Edinburgh's eating establishments and broaden your choice of where to enjoy a meal with your children away from home. The 'We Welcome Small Children' symbol is used to show those of special note.

We surveyed over 150 hotels, restaurants, pubs and coffee shops by questionnaire and have added personal experience where possible. Some, despite being reminded, did not reply and we can only assume that children would not be welcome. Others used the opportunity to vent their feelings on the dangers of hot food and drink, unsupervised children and the mess and annoyance they caused. Invariably these

places did not provide high chairs which can confine these hazards to a limited area. We have included all premises surveyed which have a high chair and many others besides. Some, although well frequented by junior patrons indicated that they did not in fact welcome children and we have respected their wishes not to be included. Unless mentioned, all premises provided half portions or were willing to give you an extra plate to share food. We have stated where special children's menus are available. Toilet access should be reasonable, we've said if there are stairs or other hazards on the way.

Each establishment entry has a line beginning with a '£'. This list shows the facilities provided. The terms used are explained below.

£ This symbol represents the approximate price of an adult main course. £ — under £2.50, ££ — £2.50-£5, £££ — over £5.

High Chair This is used as a general guide to child seating, a few premises use 'clip-ons' or have booster cushions. Unless otherwise stated you can use your own 'clip-on'. Remember reins!

Breastfeeding Permitted This applies only to the eating area. If there is a private facility it is mentioned in the text — try to be discreet as other guests can be easily embarrassed.

Bottles Heated This also applies to baby food. If you are using your own food and drink it is courteous to ask permission.

Feeder Beakers Some establishments provide these but we all know how tricky they are to keep clean.

Nappy Change Surface What constitutes a 'good changing surface' to an experienced Mum and that of a Manager with no children is very different. A shelf with a rim is so easy to install and doesn't take up much space, and yet is such a back-saving, tights-saving asset to a Mum that we hope more proprietors will consider providing one.

Family Room Scottish Law does not permit pub landlords to allow children into a 'bar'. This is an area where alcohol is served. Many get around this by providing a 'family room'. This is often the function or dining room which is not used during the day; it rarely has any facilities for families and most don't feel very welcoming.

Garden Most pub gardens are very busy in good weather. Mum and Dad can relax and the children can run about. However if it does rain, unless there is a family room, you cannot go inside.

Parties Hosted Contact management for details, see also 'Birthdays and Celebrations'.

We hope we've covered everything to help you choose the most suitable venue for your meal.

Some places cannot allow prams or pushchairs. If there is a covered area nearby we've said so, but remember, your pram etc is your responsibility — invest in a bicycle chain for only a few pounds and this should deter most thieves.

Try to keep your child under control, for their safety as well as staff and other guests' peace of mind. The more pleasant experiences proprietors have with young children, the more they will encourage families to frequent their restaurants and the more they will provide the appropriate facilities.

The establishments have been split into five areas: Centre (C), where the restaurants have been numbered to correspond to the locations indicated on the map, and North (N), South (S), East (E) and West (W). Suburban locations have the area included in the address, and your 'Thompson Local Directory' has a good map of the Edinburgh area on page 11 which shows these clearly.

The following list may help if you're not familiar with Edinburgh's 'restaurant scene' and want to plan a family Sunday lunch or evening meal.

Sunday Lunch
Bar Italia (C3), Bar Roma (C4), Caledonian Hotel (C6), George Hotel (C18), L'Auberge (C26), New Edinburgh Rendevous (C33), North British (C34), Dragonara Hotel (N), Kavio (N), The Peacock Inn (N), The Iona Hotel (S), The Fairmile Inn (S),

Glenburn Hotel (S), Hunters Tryst (S), Johnsburn Hotel (S), Marchbank Hotel (S), Lady Nairn Hotel (E), The Commodore (W), Cramond Brig Hotel (W), Crest Hotel (W), Ellersly House Hotel (W), Lauriston Farm Restaurant (W), The Pride of the Union (W), Post House (W).

Evening Meal
Bar Italia (C), Bar Roma (C) New Edinburgh Rendevous (C), Pizza Hut (C), Pizzaland (C), Kavio (N).

Please let us know of any other places where you and your children have enjoyed a meal and any good or bad experiences in those included in the book — comments please to the address at the front of the book.

EATING OUT IN CENTRAL EDINBURGH

(1) **Aitken and Niven**
79 George St
225 1461
Mon-Sat 9-5
£, High chair (1), bottles heated, feeder beakers.

Up steep flights of stairs to this 2nd floor self service cafe, sells home-made soup and light meals. Too small to allow pushchairs and prams but there is room to secure nearby. See also 'Shopping, Department Stores etc'.

(2) **Austin Reed**
124 Princes St
225 6703
Mon-Sat 9.30-4.30; Thurs 9.30-5
££, Breastfeeding permitted.

Entry to this basement restaurant by lift at rear of ground floor (or stairs). Quiche, salads etc.

(3) **Bar Italia**
100 Lothian Rd
229 0451
Mon-Sun 12 noon-3 am
££, High chairs (2), breastfeeding permitted, bottles heated.

Italian restaurant. Friendly waiter service. Not enough room for prams, pushchairs at a pinch.

(4) **Bar Roma**
39a Queensferry St
226 2977
Mon-Sun 12 noon-2.30 am
££, High chairs (4), breastfeeding permitted, bottles heated.

Children are made very welcome in this Italian restaurant. A bit of a squeeze for pushchairs between tables. Toilets upstairs with feeding chair.

(5) **British Home Stores**
64 Princes St
226 2621
Patio Restaurant
Mon-Thurs 9-5.30; Fri 9-6; Sat 8.30-6; Sun 12.30-5
£, High chairs (8), bottles heated.

Large spacious self-service restaurant. Level access from Rose St entrance but up from main store escalator to centre of eating area — beware! Extensive choice from snacks to lunches. Each high chair comes with a disposable bib — very handy if you find you've forgotten yours. Children's menu. Toilets upstairs (see 'Shopping, Department Stores etc'.)

(49) **Cafe Noir**
Waverley Market (lowest level)
Princes St/Waverley Bridge
556 1374
Food, coffee, snacks Mon-Sat 8-6 (meals from 11.30); Thurs 8-8; Sun 12 noon-6
£.

Children are only allowed on the terraced area of the bistro-style bar. Water and fountains to watch. Table service, coffee, snacks, self-service salads.

(6) **The Caledonian Hotel**
Princes St, West End
225 2433
Mon-Sun 12 noon-2.30, 6.30-10
£££, High chairs (3), breastfeeding permitted, bottles heated, courtyard garden, parties hosted.

The Gazebo is a spacious informal restaurant serving hot and cold buffet, à la carte and children's menu in this large hotel.

(49) **Caravelle**
Waverley Market (middle level), Princes St/Waverley Bridge
558 1138
Summer 11-8.30; Winter 11-11
££, High chairs (3), breastfeeding permitted.

Italian restaurant within Waverley Market. Access by lift during day but half way down Waverley steps in evening.

(7) **Circles Coffee House**
324 Lawnmarket, High St
225 9505
Mon-Sat 10-5. Longer in Festival
£, bottles heated.

Self-service restaurant near the castle. Home baking, salads.

(8) **City Art Centre**
2 Market St
225 2424
Mon-Sat 8.30-4.30
£, Breastfeeding permitted, bottles heated.

Easy access to airy self-service cafe. Salads, quiche, lasagne, baking etc. Toilets ground floor. See also 'Places to Visit'.

(9) **The Cornerstone**
St John's Church Vaults, Lothian Rd (corner with Princes St)
229 4541
Mon-Fri 10-4; Thurs 10-5; Sat 10-3 approx. Usually later in summer
£, High chairs, breastfeeding permitted, bottles heated, parties hosted.

Basement restaurant under church serving mainly organically, locally grown produce. Campaign coffee. Toilets up steps.

(10) **Country Kitchen**
4-8 South Charlotte St
226 6160
Mon-Sat 8-6.30. Later in summer
£, High chair (1), breastfeeding permitted, bottles heated, nappy change surface.

Very spacious self-service restaurant. Two service counters at busy times. Large choice of vegetarian, meaty wholefoods, salads, high fibre, low sugar, fresh fruit. Good for finger feeders. Advice on dishes suitable for special diets. A small raised fountain could entertain youngsters and there is often a piano player in the afternoons. Access to toilets difficult, through doors and down one floor.

(11) **Crawfords**
217 High St
225 4330
Mon-Fri 8-5; Sat, Sun 9-5. Later in summer
£, High chairs (3), breastfeeding permitted, bottles heated.

Family restaurant with table service. Small children's menu, fish fingers, sausages, chips etc. Toilets downstairs.

41

(12) **Crawfords**
122 Rose St
225 4204
Mon-Sat 9-6. Later in summer
£, High chair (1), breastfeeding permitted, bottles heated.

Very spacious restaurant in pedestrian precinct. Small children's menu includes fish fingers and sausages with chips. Friendly table service.

(13) **Crawfords Country Kitchen**
90 Princes St
Jan-June Mon-Sun 8-7; June-Oct Mon-Sun 8-10.30; Oct-Dec Mon-Sun 8-8
£, High chairs (4), breastfeeding permitted, bottles heated.

A few steps down and along a corridor into large self service restaurant. Varied menu, salad bar, chair suitable for feeding in cloakroom.

(47) **Crawfords Country Kitchen**
26 St James Centre
556 3113
Mon-Sat 8-5.15
£, High chairs (3), breastfeeding permitted, bottles heated, nappy change surface.

Self service 'country kitchen' restaurant with very easy access.

(14) **Debenhams**
Freebody's Restaurant (4th floor)
109-112 Princes St
225 1320
Mon, Tues 9-5; Wed, Fri, Sat 9-6; Thurs 9-8
£, High chairs (2), breastfeeding permitted, bottles heated, feeder beakers.

Large traditional style restaurant with excellent views of Edinburgh Castle. Waitresses serve large varied menu including hot croissants and delicious cream cakes. Toilets and Mother's room nearby. See 'Shopping, Department Stores etc'.

(15) **The Edinburgh Bookshop Cafe**
57 George St
225 4495
Mon-Sat 9.15-5; Sun 11-4.30
£, High chair (1), breastfeeding permitted, bottles heated, feeder beakers.

Substantial snacks and lovely cakes and biscuits in this first floor cafe. No child portions. Clip on seats not permitted. Toilets, basement. See 'Shopping, Buying Children's Books'.

(16) **Fat Sams**
The Old Meat Market, Fountainbridge
228 3111
Sun-Thurs 12 noon-1 am; Fri, Sat 12 noon-3 am
££, High chairs (3), breastfeeding permitted, bottles heated, nappy change surface, toys, parties hosted.

Waiter service restaurant with a 'carnival' atmosphere. The large automated puppets that hang from the ceiling dance and sing. Pizza, burgers etc. See 'Birthdays and Celebrations'.

(17) **Frasers**
Princes St, West End
225 2472
Mon-Sat 9-5.30; Thurs 9-7
£, High chairs (4), bottles heated.

5th floor self-service restaurant with easy access from lifts. Spacious eating area, children's menu. Toilets nearby. See 'Shopping, Department Stores etc'.

(18) **The George Hotel**
21 George St
225 1251

£££, High chairs (2), breastfeeding permitted, bottles heated, parties hosted.

Large, spacious hotel at the east end of George St. No children's portions so might be better as a treat for morning coffee or afternoon tea.

(19) Gennaro
64 Grassmarket
226 3706
Mon-Sat 12 noon-12 m'night
££, High chairs (2), bottles heated.

Table service, Italian restaurant. Half portions in pasta only.

(20) Habitat
32 Shandwick Pl
225 9151
Tues-Sun 11-4.30
£, High chairs (2), breastfeeding permitted, bottles heated, feeder beakers.

Airy self-service coffee shop on 1st floor. Quiche, salads, snacks, delicious coffee. Large windows give good views along Princes St and towards Haymarket Station. Staff lift available. Toilets on the ground floor. See 'Shopping, Toy Shops etc'.

(21) Helios Fountain
7 Grassmarket
229 7884
Mon-Sat 10-6; summer 10-8
£, High chair (1) (no centre strap), breastfeeding permitted, bottles heated, feeder beakers, nappy change surface.

Friendly self-service, wholefood, vegetarian restaurant using mainly organically grown produce. Stools for seating may be tricky for toddlers or feeding, but privacy for the latter would be given on request. Also a craft shop (see 'Shopping, Toy Shops etc'). Children are not allowed in this area alone.

(22) Hendersons
94 Hanover St
225 2131
Mon-Sat 8 am-10.45 pm; Sun all day in summer
£, High chairs (2), breastfeeding permitted, bottles heated, parties hosted.

Basement, self-service restaurant serving broad range of vegetarian and vegan food. Half portions in hot food only but lovely snacks for finger feeders. Quiet alcoves make pushchair access tricky, but good for breastfeeders.

(23) Jenners
Rose St Restaurant (2nd Floor)
225 2442
Mon-Sat 9.30-5
££, High chairs (2) (no centre strap), bottles heated, feeder beakers, parties hosted.

There are 4 cafes in Jenners and management suggested that this one would be the most suitable for children. Large self-service restaurant with no smoking area. Easy access from Rose Street lift. Toilets on 1st or 3rd floors. See 'Shopping Department Stores etc'.

(24) King George
45/50 George IV Bridge
225 1681
Mon-Fri 9-5; Sat 9-4. Summer: Mon-Sat 9-7; Sun 11-6
£, Breastfeeding permitted, bottles heated, nappy change surface, family room, parties hosted.

Bistro style pub with large varied menu.

(25) Lachana
3 Bristo Pl
225 4617
Mon-Thurs 12 noon-2.30, 4.30-7; Fri 12 noon-2.30 pm
£, High chair (1), breastfeeding permitted.

Small, casual, vegetarian restaurant. Popular with students as it is near the University and has a good value 'eat as much as you like' buffet from £1.99. Chair suitable for feeding in cloakroom.

(26) L'Auberge
56-58 St Mary's St
556 5888
Mon-Sun 12.15-2.45, 6.45-9.45
£££, no clip-on chairs permitted, no pushchairs or prams.

Over 3s are welcomed to this restaurant for a family lunch on Sundays (weekdays tend to attract business people). French menu with vegetarian options. Toilets downstairs.

(47) John Lewis
St James Centre
556 9121
Tues, Wed, Fri 9-5.30; Thurs 9-7; Sat 9-6
£, High chairs.

Excellent restaurant, menu with a dish of mashed vegetables for infants. Spectacular views across Edinburgh and the Forth to Fife on clear days. Waitress service restaurant and snack bar which sells delicious cream cakes. Pushchairs and prams are not allowed inside but there is room for you to secure at door. Toilets nearby. See 'Shopping, Department Stores etc'.

(27) Lilligs
30 Victoria St
225 7635
Mon-Sun 11-11
££, High chair (1), breastfeeding permitted, bottles heated, parties hosted.

1st floor restaurant with plenty of room at foot of stairs to secure pushchairs. Bistro style, vegetarian and children's menu. Self-service, friendly staff.

(28) Littlewoods
91 Princes St
225 1683
Mon-Wed 9-5; Thurs 9-7; Fri, Sat 9-5.30
£, High chairs (4), bottles heated.

Spacious and popular, self-service, basement restaurant. 'Traditional food', no smoking area. Can only be reached by long flight of stairs or escalators. Toilets ground floor. See 'Shopping, Department Stores etc'.

(29) Lower Aisle Restaurant
Under St Giles Cathedral, Parliament Sq, High St
225 5147
Mon-Fri 10-4.30; Sun after services; Sat in summer
£, High chair (1), breastfeeding permitted, bottles heated, feeder beakers, nappy change surface.

Very easy access in Parliament Sq to this spacious self-service restaurant. Soup, rolls, light snacks. Fraternised by the legal profession. It often gets very busy, especially after services and with tourists visiting the Cathedral. Friendly staff. See also 'Places to Visit, Historic Buildings'.

(30) Mama's
30 Grassmarket
225 6464
Mon-Thurs 12 noon-12 m'night; Fri, Sat 12 noon-1.30 am
£, breastfeeding permitted, bottles heated.

Children invited during the day to choose topping for spicy-tomato-sauced pizza. Will deliver pizzas (from 6" dia) with your choice of topping for parties or nights when babysitters cannot be found. No clip on seats permitted.

(31) **The Mount Royal Hotel**
Princes St
225 7161
Lounge and light snacks Mon-Sun 10-8.30; Lunch Mon-Sun 12-5; Dinner Mon-Sun 6-9.15
££, High chairs (3), bottles heated, feeder beakers, parties hosted.

Restaurant and lounges in this large hotel. Children's menu available.

(32) **The Netherbow Arts Centre**
High St (near Museum of Childhood)
556 9579
Mon-Sat 10-4. Closed first fortnight in Sept
£, Breastfeeding permitted, bottles heated, feeder beakers.

Pleasant cafe which opens onto a small enclosed courtyard with seating. There is usually an exhibition around the walls. Snack lunch and excellent home bakes, salads for finger feeders. Toilets on 1st floor are small but if you ask at the box office you may use the theatre dressing room for changing nappies. See also 'Places to Visit, Art Galleries' and 'Theatres and Cinemas'.

(33) **The New Edinburgh Rendezvous**
Queensferry St (above Sibbald Travel)
225 2023
Mon-Sat 12 noon-2, 5.30-11.30; Sun 1-11.30
££, High chair (1) plus 3 babydiners, bottles heated.

1st floor licensed Chinese Restaurant, there is a lift but it often doesn't work. Quite a few dishes which might suit junior's tastes but unfortunately no children's portions — even if they are prepared to try with chopsticks! Nice to find a restaurant with facilities for children whilst giving them a taste of another land and Mum and Dad a change from fast food!

(34) **North British Hotel**
Princes St, East End
556 2414
Mon-Sun 12 noon-2.30 pm, 6.30-9.30
££, High chairs (3), breastfeeding permitted, bottles heated, nappy change surface.

Children are welcome in this large traditional restaurant within hotel. Lovely views towards castle. Cloakroom has chair suitable for feeding.

(35) **The Pancake Place**
126 High St
225 1927
Mon-Fri 9.30-6; Sat 10-6; Sun 10.30-6. Evenings in summer
£, High chairs (4), breastfeeding permitted, bottles heated, feeder beakers, parties hosted.

As the name suggests, specialists in pancakes, savoury (meat and non meat), sweet fillings, baking. Ground and lower eating areas. Toilets: ladies ground floor, gents lower floor. Families warmly welcomed.

(36) **The Pancake Place**
35 Shandwick Pl
226 6322
Mon-Sat 8-6; Sun 10-6
£, High chairs, bottles heated.

Well-behaved children only welcomed in this table-service restaurant.

(37) **Pizza Hut**
36 Hanover St
226 3652
Also Princes St and Cockburn St
July-Sept, Mon-Sun 11 am-2 am; Oct-June 11 am-11 pm
£, High chairs (3) and booster

cushions, breastfeeding permitted, parties hosted.

Easy access to spacious waitress service restaurant. Pizza, pasta, salads and full children's menu. 'Care Bears' theme for parties and on menu. Crayons and pictures to colour in whilst restless youngsters await their meal. Phone in your order and it will be freshly made and ready to take away in 20 minutes. See also 'Birthdays and Celebrations'.

(38) **Pizza Plaza**
North Bridge (foot)
Winter 10 am-11 pm; Summer 8 am-3 am
£, Breastfeeding permitted, bottles heated, feeder beakers.

Table service, large range of pizzas and varied children's menu. Fairly small but chairs can be removed to allow pushchairs to 'sit' at table. Toilets upstairs.

(39) **Pizzaland**
15 Castle St
225 2081
Mon-Sat 11-11; Sun 12 noon-10
£, Breastfeeding permitted, bottles heated, nappy change surface, parties hosted.

Table service restaurant — pizza, pasta and vegetarian food. Children's menu. Ladies' toilets up one flight of steps, chair suitable for feeding. See 'Birthdays and Celebrations' for all branches.

(40) **Pizzaland**
5 Frederick St
Mon-Sat 11-11; Sun 12 noon-10
££, High chairs (3), bottles heated, feeder beakers, parties hosted.

Table service, pizzas, pasta, salad bar. No prams and a bit of a squeeze for pushchairs. Few steps at entrance. Toilets down many stairs.

(41) **Pizzaland**
7/9 Hanover St
225 4808
Mon-Sat 11-11; Sun 12 noon-10. Later in summer.
£, High chair (1), breastfeeding permitted (in an alcove if possible), bottles heated, parties hosted.

This Pizzaland is between Rose St and Princes St. There is another between Rose St and George St but it is down a steep flight of steps and as both have the same menu we recommend this one which has a ground and upper floor eating area. There is a small fountain on the ground floor which will keep children amused. Children's menu, hats and badges sometimes given out. Toilets upstairs.

(42) **Pizzaland**
46/56 North Bridge (on corner of High St)
225 2044
Mon-Sat 11-11; Sun 11-10. Later in summer.
££, High chair (1), breastfeeding permitted, bottles heated, novelties provided, parties hosted.

Friendly pizza restaurant also suitable for vegetarians. Salad bar, children's menu, easy access to spacious eating area but toilets downstairs.

(43) **Pizzaland**
65 Shandwick Pl
Mon-Sat 11-11; Sun 12 noon-10
£, High chairs (4), breastfeeding permitted, bottles heated, nappy change surface, parties hosted.

Easy access to table-service pizza restaurant. Small children's menu, also baked potatoes etc. Toilets downstairs.

(44) Rock Bottom
9 Shandwick Pl
228 6606
Mon-Wed 11.30-12 m'night; Thurs 11.30-1 am; Fri, Sat 11.30-2 am; Sun 4-12 m'night
££, High chair (1), bottles heated, feeder beakers, nappy change surface, parties hosted.

Basement, licensed 'de-luxe' fast food restaurant. Loud music, stone floors — beware. A room could be made available for breastfeeding. Friendly staff welcome young children. See 'Birthdays and Celebrations'.

(45) Royal Museum of Scotland. See 'Places to Visit'.

(46) St Andrews Square Bus Station Cafe. See 'Travel and Transport'.

(47) St James Centre. See above for 'Crawfords Country Kitchen' and 'John Lewis Restaurant'.

(48) Top Shops Restaurant
Top Shop
30 Princes St
556 0151
Mon-Sat 9-5; Thurs 9-7
£, High chairs (3), bottles heated, feeder beakers.

Fairly easy access through racks of clothes to lift and up to self-service restaurant with varied menu.

(49) **Waverley Food Court**
Waverley Market (lowest level), Princes St/Waverley Bridge
Winter: Mon-Sat 9-6, Thurs 9-8, Sun 11-5. Summer: Mon-Sat 9-8; Sun 11-5
£, High chairs (10), breastfeeding permitted, bottles heated.

A very exciting place for children, pools and fountains all keep youngsters amused and parents on their toes! Nine self-service fast food counters sharing a common eating area. Many do half portions and you're sure to find something your child will eat. Toilets. See 'Shopping, Shopping Centres and Markets'.

(49) **Waverley Market.** See above for 'Cafe Noir', 'Caravelle' and 'Waverley Food Court'.

(50) **Waverley Station.** See 'Travel and Transport'.

(51) **Wimpy**
118 Princes St/Castle St
Mon-Thurs 8-12 m'night; Fri, Sat 8-1 am; Sun 10-12 m'night
£, High chairs (4), breastfeeding permitted, no children's portions, parties hosted.

Counter service, fast food restaurant, ground and 1st floor seating. Toilets upstairs. Hostess on hand to help mothers with children. Hats given to children. See 'Birthdays and Celebrations'.

EATING OUT IN NORTH EDINBURGH

The Breadwinner
1 Raeburn Pl, Stockbridge
332 3864
Mon-Sat: Winter 9.30-5.15; Summer 9.30-7.30

£, Breastfeeding permitted, bottles heated, feeder beakers.

Shop selling wholefood quiche, cakes etc fronts this small self service cafe. Vegetarian food and rich cakes served by friendly staff. Door narrow and space limited.

Copper Kettle
96 Raeburn Pl, Stockbridge
332 4247
Mon-Sat 10-4.30; Wed 10-3
£, bottles heated, feeder beakers.

Small coffee shop, snacks, cakes etc. Too small for prams, pushchairs at a pinch.

The Dragonara
Belford Rd
332 2545

Restaurant: Mon-Sun 12.30-2, 7-10
The Granary (Food): Mon-Sun 12 noon-2, 6-9
£££ (Restaurant), ££ (Granary), High chairs (3), bottles heated, nappy change surface.

A la carte, self service and pub food are all served in different areas of this large hotel. The Granary is a pub therefore children are not allowed into the bar. Keep a close eye on junior as there is an open fire, indoor and outdoor water features with goldfish, and the Water of Leith nearby to entice tiny eyes. A private facility would be given for breastfeeding on request. See 'Walks and Country Places, (Water of Leith)'.

Gallery of Modern Art
Belford Rd
Mon-Sat 10.30-4.30; Sun 2-4.30.
Lunch 12-2.30
£, High chair (1), bottles heated, feeder beakers, nappy change surface.

Access by lift to licensed self service restaurant in basement. Delicious home cooked soups, quiche, cakes. Chair for feeding in cloakroom.
See also 'Places to Visit, Art Galleries'.

👫 Kavio
1 Commercial St, Leith
554 5272
Mon-Sun 12 noon-2.30; 6-11.30
£££, High chairs (2), breastfeeding permitted, bottles heated, nappy change surface, parties hosted.

Exciting restaurant where children are warmly welcomed. Mainly Italian but also serves burgers and kebabs complete with sparklers! Children can make their own pizza between 6 and 7 pm and there is a bubble making machine and 'message in lights' to keep them amused.

Peacock Inn
Lindsay Rd, Newhaven
552 8707
Mon-Sat 11-2.30, 5-11; Sun 12.30-2.30, 6.30-11. Food served 12 noon-2, 6-10.
£, High chairs (5), breastfeeding permitted, bottles heated, feeder beakers.

Large table service family room in this 'inn' on the Forth. Extensive bar menu including soup, salads, fish steak. Children's menu.

Raechels Tearoom, Royal Botanic Garden, see 'Walks and Country Places'.

Raeburn House Hotel
112 Raeburn Pl, Stockbridge
332 1707
Mon-Sun 11 am-12 m'night. Lunches 12 noon-2 pm
£, High chair (1), breastfeeding permitted, bottles heated, nappy changing surface.

This is a pub so children are only allowed in the garden — sunny days are busy. Varied pub lunches. No pushchairs inside but covered area to secure.

Royal Botanic Garden Tearoom,
see 'Walks and Country Places'.

Theatre Workshop
Hamilton Pl, Stockbridge
225 7942
Mon-Sat 10-5. Later during Festival
£, High chair (1), breastfeeding permitted, bottles heated.

Unpretentious, self service cafe. Varied menu including vegetarian. No smoking from 12-2.

The Waterfront Wine Bar
1c Dock Pl, Leith
554 7427
Mon-Thurs 11-11; Fri 11 am-1 am; Sat 11 am-12 m'night. Food 11 am-10ish
££, Breastfeeding permitted, bottles heated, garden.

Continental cuisine served. The 'garden' is alongside the docks, there is a fence but it may not prevent a determined toddler taking a dip.

EATING OUT IN SOUTH EDINBURGH

Braid Hills Hotel
134 Braid Rd, Morningside
447 8888
Hotel Food: 7.30-10.30 am; 12.45-2 pm, 6.45-8.45 pm.

Restaurant within large hotel not too far up a steep hill from the Braidburn. The Buckstone is a bar within the hotel grounds, it cannot allow children but serves a variety of bar meals which can be eaten in the large garden.

Brattisani
85/87 Newington Rd, Newington
667 5808
Mon-Sun 9.30 am-12 m'night (teas and coffees), 11.30 am-12 m'night (meals)
£, Breastfeeding permitted, nappy change surface, parties hosted.

A fish and chip shop fronts this friendly restaurant and this is reflected in the menu. Waitress service. Chair suitable for feeding in the cloakroom. Near to the Royal Commonwealth Pool.

The Breadwinner
47a South Clerk St, Newington
667 9091
Mon-Sat 9-5. 8.30 am-8 during Festival
£, High chair (1), breastfeeding permitted, bottles heated, feeder beakers, nappy change surface.

Shop selling wholefood quiche, cakes etc, fronts vegetarian self service coffee shop. Chair suitable for feeding in cloakroom.

The Bruntsfield Hotel
69 Bruntsfield Pl, Bruntsfield
229 1393
Mon-Sun 11-11
£££, High chairs (4), breastfeeding permitted, bottles heated, nappy change surface, toys.

Large hotel overlooking Bruntsfield Links with two table-service restaurants. Children's menu. Chair suitable for feeding in cloakroom.

The Cappuccino
15 Salisbury Pl, Newington
667 4265
Mon-Sat 9-8.30
£, bottles heated.

Children are made very welcome in this traditional Italian cafe. The ice cream, as you might expect, is delicious with many varieties to choose from. Toilets downstairs.

The Coffee Cup
210 Morningside Rd, Morningside
447 4737
Mon-Sat 9.30-5.30
£, breastfeeding permitted, bottles heated, feeder beakers, nappy change surface.

Friendly table service restaurant with varied menu.

Dell Inn
27 Lanark Rd, Craiglockhart/Longstone
443 9991
Food: Mon-Sun 12 noon-2, 7.30-10
£, High chairs (2), breastfeeding permitted, bottles heated, family room, garden, parties hosted.

Self service pub food can be taken outside to bench seating on large patio overlooking river — beware. Busy on sunny days. The family room hosts a 'kiddies club' on Sat and Sun where cartoons and videos are shown and the 'bar' sells sweets.

The Fairmile Inn
Biggar Rd, Fairmilehead
445 2056
Mon-Sat 11 am-12 m'night; Sun 12.30-2.30, 6.30-11. Food: 12 noon-10 pm.
£, High chair, breastfeeding permitted, bottles heated, nappy change surface, family room, toys, parties hosted.

Self service bar food and table service restaurant situated at the foot of the Pentland Hills.

The Grange
8 Whitehouse Ter, Morningside
667 5681
Mon-Sat 11-2.30, 5-11; Sun 12.30-2.30, 6.30-11. Bar food: 11-2, 5.30-7.45
£, High chair (1), bottles heated, garden.

Small hotel with patio through bar to rear and large enclosed lawn with bench seats on good days to front. No clip-on seats permitted.

The Glenburn Hotel
Currie
449 3236
Daily 12-2.30, 6-11
Food: Mon-Sat 12-2; Sun 12.30-2
££, High chairs (2), bottles heated, nappy change surface, parties hosted, garden.

Small country hotel, clearly sign-posted from Lanark Rd West. Garden. Children's menu. Crayons and pictures to colour.

The Hunters Tryst
Oxgangs Rd, Fairmilehead/Oxgangs
445 3132
Food: Mon-Sun 12 noon-2.30, 6-10. Summer all day from 12 noon
£ (Bar), high chair, breastfeeding permitted, bottles heated, nappy change surface, family room, garden, toys, parties hosted.

Carvery in restaurant and bar meals with vegetarian options. Under 10s menu includes fish finger or burger with chips, milk or cola for 85p.

The Iona Hotel
17 Strathearn Pl, Bruntsfield/Morningside
447 5050
Mon-Sun 11-11. Bar meals 12 noon-2 pm
£, High chair (1), bottles heated, no clip-on seats permitted.

Good value bar food served in family lounge.

Johnsburn Hotel
Balerno
449 3847
Mon-Sat 12 noon-3, 5-12 m'night. Food: 12 noon-2, 7-10
£, High chairs (2), bottles heated, family room, garden, parties hosted.

Salads, home cooking served in this country hotel. Well behaved children are welcome. Large garden but beware of the burn running through.

Marchbank Hotel
Balerno
449 3970
Bar lunches 12.30-2
£, Garden.

Well behaved children allowed in the comfy lounges of this country hotel. Open fires to enjoy in winter and extensive grounds in summer. The Red Moss Nature Reserve is close by, see 'Walks and Country Places'.

Mr Boni
4 Lochrin Buildings, nr Kings Theatre
229 5319
Mon-Wed 10.30 am-10.30 pm; Thurs 10.30 am-11 pm; Fri, Sat 10.30 am-12 m'night; Sun 12.30-9.30 pm
£, High chair, breastfeeding permitted, bottles heated, parties hosted.

Ice cream parlour which also sells burgers etc. Monumental ice cream sweets will have toddlers eyes huge with wonder. Toilets downstairs. Shop at front sells take away sizes. See also 'Birthdays and Celebrations'.

Pentland Hills Hotel
44 Camus Ave, Fairmilehead
445 4444
Mon-Wed 11-2.30, 5-11.30; Thurs 11-2.30, 5-12 m'night; Fri, Sat 11 am-1 am; Sun 12 noon-12 m'night.
Food: Mon-Sat 12 noon-2 pm; Sun 12.30-2.30 pm
£, Breastfeeding permitted, bottles heated, family room, garden.

Table service bar meals in this small hotel. Prams not permitted inside. Chair available for feeding in the cloakroom.

Queens Hall
Clerk St, Newington
668 3456
Mon-Fri 12.15-2 pm (except during Festival, Christmas and New Year)
£, Breastfeeding permitted, bottles heated, parties hosted.

Well behaved children tolerated in this self service restaurant attached to the Queens Hall, which has occasional lunch time concerts. Soup, baked potatoes, quiche, salads etc. No child portions.

The Riccarton Arms Hotel
Lanark Rd West, Currie
449 2230
Mon-Sat 11-11; Sun 12.30-10.30 pm. Food lunchtime only except Sun
£, Breastfeeding permitted, bottles heated.

Small hotel with varied menu. Popular with students from the nearby university.

Sherry's
372 Morningside Rd, Morningside
447 9217
Mon-Sat 9.45-4.45
£, Bottles heated, feeder beakers, no clip on seats permitted.

Very pleasant, friendly self service coffee shop. Home baking and cooking, salads. Pushchairs allowed inside but prams must be left outside large windows near tables (for easy viewing). Toilets downstairs.

EATING OUT IN EAST EDINBURGH

Asda Superstore
The Jewel, Duddingston North
669 9151
Mon 9-5; Tues 9-6; Wed, Thurs, Fri 9-8; Sat 8.30-8; Sun 10-5
£, high chairs (2), bottles heated, nappy change surface.

Self service, substantial snacks, restaurant within store. Cloakroom has chair suitable for feeding. Plenty of parking! See also 'Shopping, Supermarkets'.

The Brunstane
The Jewel, Duddingston North
Mon-Sat 10 am-11 pm.
Food 10-8; Sun 12.30-2.30, 6-11.
Food lunchtime only on Sun
£, Bottles heated, family room, parties hosted.

'Pub' food served all day in this bar next door to Asda.

Kennedy's
20 Portobello High St, Portobello
669 7570
Mon-Sat 9.30-6
£, High chair (1), breastfeeding permitted, bottles heated.

Self service restaurant, home made soup, salads, fish, chips etc with some vegetarian dishes. Toilets through function room.

Lady Nairn Hotel
Willowbrae Rd, Duddingston
661 3396
Lunch 12 noon-2; dinner Mon-Thurs 6-10.30; Fri-Sun 6-11

££, High chairs (3), bottles heated, parties hosted.

Steak House, restaurant within hotel. Range of special children's drinks, colouring books and crayons to keep youngsters amused.

Meadowbank Stadium Cafe. See 'Activities for Parents'.

Portobello Pool Cafe. See 'Activities for Children, Swimming'.

Proms Wine Bar
Promenade (Bellfield St), Portobello
669 4432
Mon-Sat 11-11; Sun 12.30-2.30, 6.30-11.30. Winter closed Mon, Tues, Wed afternoons. Food 12 noon-3.
£, bottles heated, nappy change surface, family room, garden, toys, parties hosted.

Home made food. There is a kiosk at the foot of the garden (on the promenade) selling burgers, drinks, sweets etc.

Royal Commonwealth Pool. See 'Activities for Children, Swimming'.

St Andrews
Portobello High St, Portobello
669 2850
££, High chair (1), breastfeeding permitted, bottles heated.

Very welcoming to young children. Table service Italian restaurant. No pushchairs but covered area outside to secure.

The Terrace
Cameron Toll Shopping Centre, Lady Rd
Mon-Wed, Sat 9-7; Thurs, Fri 8-8; Sun 10-5
£, High chairs (10), bottles heated, parties hosted.

Large spacious eating area on 1st floor shared by several self service units, baked potatoes etc. One side of this area overlooks the shopping mall so there is plenty to occupy youngsters — throwing chips to the crowd below! There is sometimes a guitar player to entertain you. Easy access by small lift, tucked away behind the stairs near Savacentre means you can take your overflowing trolley upstairs with you. Toilets: See 'Shopping Centres and Markets'. See also 'Birthdays and Celebrations'.

Windsor Leisure Centre. See 'Activities for Children, Trampolining'.

EATING OUT IN WEST EDINBURGH

The Barnton Hotel
Queensferry Rd, Barnton Roundabout, Barnton
339 1144
Mon-Sun 12 noon-2.15, 6-10
££, High chairs (2), bottles heated, nappy change surface, family room, parties hosted.

Table service, varied menu. Beware opening on to car park.

Brattisani
272 Morrison St, Haymarket
229 7788
Mon-Sun 11.30-11.30
£, Bottles heated.

Fish restaurant near to Haymarket Station. Toilets down steps.

The Commodore
Marine Dr, Silverknowes
336 1700
Mon-Sun 12 noon-2 (meals), 6.30-11
££, High chairs (4), breastfeeding

permitted, bottles heated, feeder beakers, nappy change surface, family room, garden, parties hosted.

Table service in this Stakis Hotel overlooking the sea. Chair in cloak-room suitable for feeding.

The Cramond Brig Hotel
Queensferry Rd
339 4350
Mon-Sun 11 am-12 m'night. Food: 12 noon-9 pm
£, High chair, breastfeeding permitted, bottles heated, family room, no prams.

Large family room in pub. Self service, varied menu, vegetarian options. On the banks of the River Almond, see 'Walks and Country Places, Cramond'.

⛄Crest Hotel
Queensferry Rd, Blackhall
332 2442
Mon-Sun 7 am-9.45 pm. Play lounge open 5 pm Fri-5 pm Sun
££ (Lunch), high chairs (6), bottles heated, nappy change surface, garden, toys, parties hosted.

Large children's menu includes fish fingers, beans, melon, lovely sweets, also junior drinks menu! Special diets catered for. There is a children's play area in the entrance, with climbing frame, chute, tunnel, etc. Collages round walls. Jazz Sunday afternoons. Breastfeeders would be given a private facility on request. Helpful staff.

Edinburgh Airport. See 'Travel and Transport'.

Edinburgh Zoo. See 'Places to Visit, Animals in the City'.

Ellersly House Hotel
Ellersly Rd, Corstorphine
337 6888
Mon-Sun 12.15-2, 6.30-9
£ lunch, £££ dinner, High chair (1), breastfeeding permitted, bottles heated, nappy change surface, garden.

Hotel set in two acre garden with play area (chute, swings). Table service and bar lunches. Welcomes young children.

Harp Hotel
St John's Rd, Corstorphine
334 2857
Lunch 12 noon-2, dinner 6.30-9
£, High chairs (4), breastfeeding permitted, bottles heated, nappy change surface, parties hosted.

Table service restaurant within this hotel in the centre of Corstorphine's main street. Chair suitable for feeding in the cloakroom.

Lauriston Farm Restaurant
Lauriston Farm Rd, Cramond/ Silverknowes
Tues-Sat 11-11; Sun 12.30-2.30. Food: Tues-Sun 12 noon-2.30, 6-10
££, Nappy change surface, family room, garden, parties hosted.

Broad range of dishes from snacks to steaks served in this large restaurant near the sea and Lauriston Castle.

Marco's Leisure Centre. See 'Activities for Children, Playcentres'.

The Pride of the Union
From The Bridge Inn,
27 Baird Rd, Ratho
Food and hours: Mon-Sat 12 noon-2, 7-10
£, High chairs (2), breastfeeding permitted, bottles heated, family room and garden at the Inn, parties hosted.

An unusual setting for a meal — on board a barge. If junior's appetite can surmount the excitement, there is a children's menu. The barge is very popular and you are best to book. If you need a high chair, try to mention it beforehand so that it can be taken on board. See 'Birthdays and Celebrations'.

The Post House Hotel
Corstorphine Rd, Corstorphine
334 8221
Mon-Sun 12 noon-10.30
££, High chairs (6), bottles heated, feeder beakers, toys, parties hosted.

Large hotel with a coffee shop restaurant. Pushchairs are not allowed into the eating area but there is room to secure nearby. Children's menu. Sun lunches can be booked for the whole family, children are half price and there is entertainment for them afterwards including cartoons.

The Royal Scot Hotel
111 Glasgow Rd, Corstorphine (at Maybury roundabout)
334 9191

Mon-Sun 12 noon-2, 6.30-10
£££, High chairs (5), bottles heated, parties hosted.

Restaurant within large hotel. Chair suitable for feeding in cloakroom. Swimming pool free to residents.

Sighthill Hotel
Calder Rd, Sighthill
453 6051
Mon-Sat lunch 12 noon-2 pm, dinner 6-10
£, High chairs (3), breastfeeding permitted, bottles heated, family room, garden.

Table service, pub food in this small hotel. Garden opens on to car park.

St John's Restaurant
259 St John's Rd, Corstorphine
334 2857
Mon-Sun 11-2, 5-10
£, High chair, breastfeeding permitted, bottles heated, nappy change surface.

A fish and chip shop is adjacent to this table service restaurant. Italian food also served. Chair suitable for feeding in cloakroom.

Birthdays & Celebrations

THE VENUE

Several venues specialise in organising parties and the 'Eating Out' section identifies those restaurants willing to host parties. Contact the management for details of numbers, food and facilities available. Many church halls, public halls, community centres and sports clubs will hire out their premises for an afternoon; it's always worth asking in your area. The following have something special to offer — see the relevant section for full addresses and phone numbers. Phone management for full details. Remember Sat afternoons tend to be very busy — youngsters can be quite frightened if it's too crowded especially in the more energetic venues and you may have to book a long time in advance.

Fat Sams

A fun setting for a party. Entertaining and helpful staff provide hats, balloons, etc, and will help to organise games. Large automated puppets will sing 'Happy Birthday' to your child. See 'Eating Out in Central Edinburgh (16)'.

Little Marco's

An unforgettable party for most children. All parties include invitation/acceptance cards and envelopes, 'Happy Box' containing juice, crisps, sweets, blowers, etc, party hat, take home 'Happy Bag' containing novelties and sweets, helium filled balloon. The birthday child receives a badge, a special 'announcement', special song and a photograph taken with 'Little Marco' to take home. Prices vary depending on time of day and week. Recommend midweek parties for under fives. A hostess to help can be arranged in advance. Can provide a special 'Marco Bear Cake' or arrange to bring your own. Party leaflet available. See also 'Activities for Children, Playcentres'.

Mr Boni

Will give your party a private corner in the restaurant and can arrange entertainment. Further details of their amazing ice cream cakes in 'Catering and Cakes.' See 'Eating Out in South Edinburgh'.

Pizza Hut

A hostess will meet the birthday child and guests at the door and show them to a reserved table decorated with hats, banners, placemats, crayons, balloons, etc. Sun-Fri 2.30-5.30. 'Care Bears' theme throughout. Free cake if more than 12 children. Leaflet available. See 'Eating Out in Central Edinburgh (37)'.

Pizzaland

Most Pizzalands will provide a private area within the restaurant. Hats, balloons, badges and a cake. Individual management varies. See 'Eating Out in Central Edinburgh (39-43)'.

Portobello Pool Refreshment Room

Friendly staff will decorate the cafe, and have three flexible menus to suit your child's needs. There will be a sign above the pool saying 'Happy Birthday . . .' and each child receives a balloon. See 'Activities for Children, Swimming'.

The Pride of the Union

A floating party aboard a barge. This must be one of Edinburgh's more novel ideas for a party. Will obviously take more supervision than other venues but rewarded with a half hour trip along the canal and an old tractor to play on afterwards. See 'Eating Out in West Edinburgh'.

Rock Bottom

Free birthday cake, hats, balloons etc. Licensed for worn out parents. See 'Eating out in Central Edinburgh (44)'.

Royal Commonwealth Pool

Will reserve tables for your party guests and you are welcome to bring your own decorations and cake. Four menus to choose from. Leaflet available. See 'Activities for Children, Swimming'.

The Terrace, Cameron Toll Shopping Centre

Each child is given a card with the amount you wish to spend on it. They can then spend it at any of the self service units. 'Doughnut the Dog', a dressed up member of staff, often visits. Balloons provided. See 'Eating Out in East Edinburgh'.

Wester Hailes Education Centre

A 'Birthday Tea' of sausage roll, sandwiches, crisps, juice, ice cream and jelly can be supplied for your swimming party. See 'Activities for Children, Swimming'.

Wimpy

A hostess is on hand to help with each party. Reserved area where games can be played. Hats, balloons, badges, etc. See 'Eating Out in Central Edinburgh (51)'.

Windsor Leisure Centre

Specialists in parties, half-an-hour trampolining, half-an-hour cartoons followed by a birthday tea. Max 20 children. See 'Activities for Children, Trampolining.'

CHILDREN'S PARTIES AT HOME

There's a lot to remember if you decide to hold your child's party at home. We hope the following pages will help. A useful book with lots of super ideas is 'Children's Parties' by Angela Hollest and Penelope Gaine, published by Piatkus. It's also available in libraries.

This may serve as a checklist:—

Banners	Ballons
Bangs	Cakes & Tins
Candles & Holders	Cups
Fancy dress	Hats
Indoor Fireworks	Invitations
Masks	Mats
Plates	Prizes

Serviettes	Straws
Streamers	Stocking Fillers
Swag Bags	Table Cloths
.................................anything else?	

A wide range of the items listed above is available at two specialist party shops.

The Finishing Touch
134 Nicolson St, Newington
667 0914

A wonderful shop, especially for cake decorating — see 'Cakes and Catering' below — but with lots of other party paraphernalia.

Partytime
63 Raeburn Pl, Stockbridge
332 2261

If you need it for a party this shop should have a selection of it!

Also recommended when planning your party are the following, described in 'Shopping'.
Jenners — see 'Department Stores, etc', good selection of hats, masks and other dressing up requirements also lots of small gifts; John Lewis — see 'Department Stores, etc', large choice of tablecloths, serviettes, cups, plates — all in paper; Score Commotions — see 'Baby and Children's Clothes', hats, masks, streamers, etc (although many are too sophisticated for under 5s); Timbuk 2 — see 'Toy Shops, etc', small shop with 'party corner'. For more ideas see 'Shopping from Home, Toys'.

You can also send away for balloons and stationery:—

Folkdean
Lydney Industrial Estate, Harbour Rd, Lydney, Glos GL15 4EJ

Your own message printed on a balloon eg 'Happy Birthday . . .' Up

57

to 5 words or dates on to a round balloon (10" when inflated). Minimum quantity 25, but cheaper in larger numbers. Send SAE for leaflet and sample.

Baby Stationery (NCT)
33 Hyde Close, Winchester, Hants SO23 7DT

A complete range of charming and unique personalised stationery. Invitations for all occasions, Birthdays, Christenings, etc. Personalised birthday cards, congratulation cards. Send 1st class stamp or phone 0692 51749 for free catalogue. Trading in support of the NCT.

NCT Leeds Branch
5 St Chads Grove, Leeds LS6 3PN

A pad of 30 red and white party invitations for only 30p! Plus SAE.

CATERING AND CAKES

Most parents provide their own food for 'Home hosted' parties and there are books in the library to inspire you. We only found one catering company that specialised in children's parties:—

Party Snax
343 1246

Will provide a huge variety of snacks from sandwiches to fruit and mallow kebabs. From £1 per head, min £10.

The **Edinburgh Advertiser** always has plenty of names in their **Catering Services** column, or try Yellow Pages and your local 'Carry Out' for baked potatoes, fried chicken, pizza, etc as some will deliver. See 'Mamas', 'Eating Out in Central Edinburgh (30)'.

Cakes are usually the centrepiece of any party and again the library often has books with easy to follow recipes and ideas, however if you don't feel ambitious enough to tackle one, the following have been recommended, but do remember to give plenty of notice.

Lynda Anderson
445 4700

Will tackle any cake! Choose your child's favourite TV character and have it made in cake. Also makes cakes to special diet (eg flourless) or recipe.

Cakes by Cadien
332 3476

Will do anything in cake and fondant to create the cake of your child's dreams — previous numbers include a ketchup bottle, 'My Little Pony's Castle' and Thomas the Tank Engine. Min £10. Prefers 2 weeks notice.

The Finishing Touch
667 0194

Will make cakes to any design (within reason) and have plenty of tins and pictures to give you ideas.

Mr Boni
229 5319

Award winning ice cream cakes in a variety of designs. Numbers, hearts, trains and a 'house' to serve up to 20. Placed 2nd in UK Championships. Remember to leave room in the freezer. Leaflet available.

Party Piece
445 2716

Will make any cake to order, from Mickey Mouse to a Care Bear. Special diets also catered for.

Silver and Gold
334 2533

Specialists in Christening cakes and will make most shapes and sizes.

CAKE TINS FOR HIRE

The Finishing Touch
134 Nicolson St, Newington 667 0914

£5 deposit, 70p-£1/night. Numbers, letters, boats, trains, dolls. Good instructions.

Partytime
63 Raeburn Pl, Stockbridge
332 2261

£5 deposit, 70p-£1/night. Numbers, letters, cars, boats, etc. Good instructions.

Studio One
71 Morningside Rd, Morningside
447 0452

£5 deposit, £1/night. Letters, numbers, hearts, squares.

The Wooden Spoon
46 St Stephen St, Stockbridge
226 5377

£5 deposit, £1/night. Animals, numbers, hearts.

ENTERTAINMENT

Most of the entertainers we contacted felt their acts weren't suitable for under 5s and stressed that there was nothing worse than granny giving a running commentary to tots. It is most important when looking for an act to tell them the age span of children and whether you have seen them before as many have several routines. The 2 below have been recommended and enjoyed by young children.

Mr Boom
229 8908

. . . and he comes from the moon! An entertaining one-man-band. Ideal for youngsters. Help bang the big bass drum. Audience participation is part of the show. Mr Boom writes his own songs but also includes nursery rhymes, favourite hits and Scottish children's folk songs.

Scott Lovat
331 1986

Many varied shows including magic, puppets, and balloon sculpture. Excellent theme of 'don't go with strangers' runs through the shows. Some audience participation (although he usually chooses an older child). Children get a picture to colour at the end of the show and when handed in at future shows receive a 'balloon sculpture' as does the child chosen to help with the magic. Real white rabbit!

The **Edinburgh Advertiser** has a **Junior Choice** column with party ideas. See 'Hiring' section for inflatables — bounce the afternoon away. If you have a video recorder you could hire a tape of your child's favourite character, most video shops have a selection of those on TV or Walt Disney. We also believe you can hire cartoon film shows but unfortunately we couldn't find a suitable source. It can be entertaining to dress up for the day. The 'Hiring' section has some contacts.

59

Mum and Dad can take the plunge too! But remember that some children can be quite terrified when a 'gorilla' strolls into the party and it often makes things worse when the head comes off to reveal . . . DAD! The most suitable fancy dress ideas for this age group don't cover the face. Libraries have books with ideas and some dressmaking books have patterns that can be adapted. We hope we've covered everything. Do remember that at the end of the day the whole idea is to have fun and younger children especially enjoy the simplest of ideas.

Photographers

Most commercial photographers are willing to photograph your child in their studio, your home, or, perhaps most commonly where toddlers are concerned, in your playgroup or toddler group with a percentage going to the group funds. Many will let you take a change of clothes and have a brother or sister included too. You may find some photographers call on houses hoping to find a mum willing to have her 'pride and joy' photographed and many children are happier in their own surroundings. It's always worth comparing prices before you go ahead (always check identification before allowing a stranger into your home). Children seem to find the equipment fascinating and tend to stare at it rather than smile. However the 2 photographers below

have been recommended by mothers who found that children felt at ease with them. Phone for their details or try one of the many in 'Yellow Pages'.

Raymond Lintern
23 Kilmaurs Rd
667 7224

Mainly does playgroups etc, but may consider a private sitting in the holidays.

Peter McKenzie
Jenners
225 2442

This studio is within Jenners department store. There are toys to distract the children. A variety of pictures are taken from which you choose the ones you would like enlarged.

The **Edinburgh Advertiser**, often has advertisements for companies who will take a video film of your baby's christening or children's party.

Pre-School Play & Education

'Education' in the formal sense is compulsory from the year in which a child turns 5; and whilst there is less formal provision for pre-school children, parents generally have more choice about the way their child is cared for and educated, as well as more opportunities to become involved with groups of children.

Progression could be from a parent and baby group which would take the child to the age of one, or until walking; then on to a toddler group until about 2½ or 3. At that stage you could be faced with a choice between a playgroup or nursery which is ultimately under the control of the Social Work Department whether it is run by parents or privately, or a nursery school or nursery class run by the Education Department or attached to an independent school. Some children in fact attend both, by going to a playgroup for a year and then to a nursery class for the final year before school, but others spend two years in a playgroup or nursery. Or you may be looking for full day care for your child from a few months old. In this and the following chapter we give information on the options available.

The Social Work Department keeps records of playgroups and private nurseries as well as of some parent and toddler groups, but not all of these register. We have compiled our lists from the SW lists, and also from the responses to questionnaires; and most of the information has been checked by phone calls. We hope the information given here will set you off on your search. In some cases it has been impossible to give contacts and phone numbers, because secretaries frequently change. The best plan might be to turn up at your chosen group on the day. As the Social Work Department organises its records according to areas, we have tried to follow them too. Thus to find the group most convenient for you, first identify the areas in which to look.

Area A includes: Balerno, Burdiehouse, Central, Churchhill, Colinton, Colinton Mains, Comiston-Buckstone, Craiglockhart, Craigmillar, Currie, Fairmilehead, Grange, Kaimes, Liberton, Longstone, Marchmont, Mayfield, Moredun, Morningside, Newington, Niddrie, Oxgangs, Pleasance, Stockbridge.

You could also contact:
Jean Donaldson, Shona Herald or Julie Brechin, Oxgangs Social Work Office, 4 Oxgangs Path, Edinburgh (445 4451).

Area B includes: Broughton, Canonmills, Comely Bank, Craigentinny, Goldenacre, Granton, Joppa, Leith, Lochend, Pilton, Portobello, Trinity, Wardie, Willowbrae.

You could also contact:
Anne Campbell or Linda Good, Lothian Regional Council Social Work Department, Leith Area Office, 9-11 Giles St, Edinburgh (553 2121).

Area C includes: Barnton, Blackhall, Broomhouse, Broomhall, Bruntsfield, Clermiston, Corstorphine, Craigmount, Cramond, Dalry, Davidsons Mains, East Craigs, Gorgie, Gyle, Juniper Green, Kirkliston, Muirhouse, Murrayfield, Polwarth,

Ratho, Saughtonhall, Sighthill, South Queensferry, Tollcross, Viewforth, Wester Hailes.

You could also contact: Phil Dummer, Mairi Nye or Anne Wilson, Wester Hailes Social Work Office, Wester Hailes, Edinburgh (442 4131).

There may be other groups in your area — check with your Health Visitor or Health Centre noticeboard. Some supermarkets, newsagents and toy shops also post information on noticeboards and in windows. Information might also be obtained from: The Scottish Pre-School Play Association (SPPA), 15 Smith's Pl, Edinburgh (553 2185), and from your local National Childbirth Trust representative (phone 225 9191, Mon-Fri 9.30-11.30, for name and address). Details of multi-lingual groups and of groups for children with special needs may also be obtained from SPPA. Groups are often held in church halls, so it may be worth checking there too (you do not have to be a member of the church). If possible, phone and check whether there are any vacancies before turning up at the groups; and it is also advisable to check the group personally for atmosphere and safety standards.

PARENT AND TODDLER GROUPS

Parent and toddler groups are generally set up by local parents and, as adults usually stay with the children, they are places where you can meet other adults and babies and toddlers (age range 0-3) for a few hours once or twice a week, normally during school terms. Although most children are taken by their mothers, childminders, nannies, grandmothers, fathers, aunts, etc are also welcome! Sometimes pre-walking babies meet in a separate room, so that they don't get knocked over. Facilities and standards vary, but most places have a selection of toys and puzzles, paints and some larger pieces of equipment (eg slides, climbing frames, large trucks). Prices range from nothing to approx £3/term, with small charges for tea and coffee. There is often a snacks rota, and parents usually help to set up and tidy away the toys. Where we know outdoor play is available, this has been mentioned. The following list follows the Social Work Dept areas mentioned above (although they do not keep lists of parent and toddler groups). If you cannot find a group listed near you, try the sources suggested above.

AREA A

BALERNO:

Balerno Parent and Toddler Group, St Mungo's Church Hall/Mon, Wed, Fri 10-11.30/Contact: Liz Keyden, 449 7134

CENTRAL:

Bristo Baptist Church, Queensferry Rd, Fri 9.45-11.30/Contact: Mrs Martin, 332 9234
St. Anne's Community Centre, South Gray's Close/Tues, Thurs 9.45-11.45/Contact: Mrs Parfeymon, 557 0469
University Day Nursery (Junior), See 'Playgroups and Nurseries Area A'

COLINTON:

Stableroom, Colinton Parish Church Hall/Spylaw Bank Rd/Wed 1-3, Thurs 9-11.30/Contact: Barbara Badger
St Cuthbert's Church Hall, Westgarth Ave/Mon 9.30-11.30, Tues 2-4/Contact: Lesley MacPherson

COMISTON-BUCKSTONE:

St Fillan's Church, Buckstone Drive/Thurs 2-3.30/Contact: Mrs Tilston, 445 3964

CRAIGMILLAR:

Craigmillar Park Church, Craigmillar Park/Wed 10-11.30/Contact: Mrs Patterson, 668 2319

FAIRMILEHEAD:

Fairmilehead Parish Church, Frogston Rd/Mon, Tues, Thurs 10-11.45; 2-4 (Over 1)/Tues 2-4 (Under 1)/Outdoor Play/Contact: Hilary Ross, 445 5195

LIBERTON:

Church Hall, Kirk Gate/Mon, Thurs, Fri 9-11.30/Contact: Morag Skinner, 664 5351

LONGSTONE:

Hearts Supporters Club, Inglis Green Rd/Mon 1.30-3, Wed 9.30-11.30/ Contact: Mrs Porteous, 443 3096

MARCHMONT:

Marchmont St Giles, Kilgraston Rd/Thurs 10-12/Contact: Frances Brown, 667 1404

MAYFIELD:

Mayfield Church, Upper Hall, Mayfield Rd/Tues, Fri 9.15-11.30/Contact: Margaret Barclay, 667 5299
Reid Memorial Church Hall, West Savile Ter/Tues 10-11.30 age under 2/Wed, Thurs 10-11.30 age 2-3/Contact: Lorraine Adam, 667 8097

MORNINGSIDE:

Baptist Church, Holy Corner, Morningside Rd/Tues, Thurs 10-11.45/Open all year/Contact: Mrs Duncan, 447 8198
Cluny Parish Church, Cluny Church Centre, Cluny Drive/Thurs 9.30-11.30/ Outdoor play/Contact: Helen Hughes, 447 3001
Greenbank, Greenbank Church, Braidburn Ter/Wed, Thurs 10-11.45/Contact: Mrs Buchanan, 447 4109
Morningside Baptist Church, Tues, Thurs 10-12/Contact: Sister Sandrock, 229 1030

NEWINGTON:
Duncan Street Baptist Church, Duncan St/Tues, Thurs 10.15-12, Fri 2.30-4.30/ Contact: Shirley Gibb, 667 4029
St Peter's Church Hall, Lutton Pl/Tues 2.30-4.30/Open most of year/Outdoor play/Contact: Lesley Nock, 667 5309

PLEASANCE:
Southside Community Centre, James Clark School, Pleasance/Tues, Thurs 10-12

STOCKBRIDGE:
St Bernard's International, St Bernard's Church Centre, Dean St/Mon, Fri 9.30-11.30, Wed 2-4/Contact Mon: Susan White, 556 1787/Wed: Debbie Albrow, 225 6611/Fri: Andrea Anderson, 343 1599
Stockbridge Health Centre, Tues 9.30-11.30, 1.30-3.30/Contact: Linda Bain, 552 3950

AREA B

CANONMILLS:
St Philip's, Logie Green Rd/Tues 10.30-12.30/Thurs 1.45-3.30/Open all year/ Contact: Mrs Lynch, 556 7773

COMELY BANK:
Comely Bank Toddlers' Club, St Stephen's Church/Thurs 9.30-11.30/Contact: Mrs Cormack, 332 5485
Dean Tots, Dean Parish Church Hall, Ravelston Ter/Tues, Thurs 9.30-12/ Outdoor play/Contact: Rona Stephen, 225 3899

JOPPA:
Brunstane Community Centre, Tues, Thurs 9.30-11.30/Contact: Mrs Campbell, 669 8760
St Philip's, Brunstane Rd Nth, Joppa Rd/Fri 10-11.15/Contact: Mrs Burns, 669 5277 or Mrs Sinclair, 669 1734

LEITH:
Bonnington Primary School, Bonnington Rd/Children over 18 mths/Wed 9.15-11.15/Contact: Jackie or Anne-Marie, 554 3040

PILTON:
Old Kirk, Pennywell Rd/Tues 9.30-11.30/Contact: Mrs Moir, 332 4354

PORTOBELLO:
Greengables, Contact: Mrs Scholes 669 9083
Portobello Toddlers' Playgroup, Beach Lane, Portobello/30 places/Mon-Fri 9.15-11.45/Contact: Mrs McGuire, 669 5530

TRINITY:
Trinity, Craighall Gdns/Mon-Fri 9.30-11.30, 2.30-4/Open all year/Contact: Mrs Innes, 552 8249
Victoria Park, Children's Centre, Newhaven Rd/Mon, Tues, Thurs, Fri 10-12/ Contact: Marion McNeil, 554 4077

WARDIE:
Wardie Parish Church, Thurs 10-12/Contact: Frances Kelly, 552 3561

AREA C

BLACKHALL:
St Columba's Church, Tues 10-12, 1.30-3.30/Contact: Mrs Graham, 332 5471

CORSTORPHINE:
Belgrave, Belgrave Halls, 34 Belgrave Rd/Mon 1.30-3/Contact: Susan Edmunson, 334 9998
Craigsbank Church, Craigsbank/Mon, Thurs 10-11.30/Contact: Mrs Neumann, 339 2968
Fox Covert, Fox Covert RC School, Clerwood Ter/Tues 1.30-3/Outdoor play/ Contact: Mrs Phillips, 334 4333
Jack and Jill Club, St Anne's Church Hall, Kaimes Rd/Wed 9.30-11.30/Open all year/Outdoor play/Contact: Kaitreen Panther, 334 2881
St Ninian's Church, St Ninian's Church Hall, St Ninian's Rd/Tues 10-12/ Contact: Ann Lyon, 334 3742

CRAIGMOUNT:
Craigmount School, Craigs Rd/Tues 10-11.30, Fri 10-11.30, 2-3.30/Contact: Mrs Tait 339 3504

DALRY:
St Bride's Community Centre, Orwell Ter/Fri am/Contact: Pam Harper, 337 5977
St Michael's Church Hall, We believe a group meets here, but have no information

EAST CRAIGS:
East Craigs Church Centre, Bughtlin Mkt/Thurs 10-11.30/Contact: Mrs Maison, 339 1906

GYLE:
St Thomas's Church, Glasgow Rd/Tues 10-11.30/Contact: Mrs Bunyan 334 6586

JUNIPER GREEN:
Community Hall, Mon-Fri 2-3.30/Outdoor play/Contact: Mrs Anderson, 453 4390

MURRAYFIELD:
Murrayfield Mother and Baby Group, Murrayfield Church Hall (upstairs)/ Babies up to 1 year/Mon 10-11.30/Contact: Nancy Thomas, 337 6529 or Ray Lynch, 337 4766

Murrayfield Parish Church, Ormidale Ter/Mon-Fri 10-11.30/Children 1-3 years/Contact: Eleanor Taylor, 346 1555 or Ginty Moffat, 337 5592

SAUGHTONHALL:
Saughtonhall Recreation Hall, Saughtonhall Ave/Mon 1.30-3.30, Thurs 10-11.30/Open all year/Contact: Helen McNeill, 337 6930

PLAYGROUPS AND PRIVATE NURSERIES

PLAYGROUPS

These are under the care of the Social Work Department and have access to the Community Co-ordinator for the Under 5's assigned to the area of the Playgroup. Contact the Social Work Department responsible for your area (see above) for further details. There are 3 types of playgroup:

Community Playgroups which receive a grant each year to cover wages, rent, insurance and fees. A small charge per session is set by the Social Work Department. Groups are run by a committee of parents elected each year and parents help regularly on a rota basis.

Private Playgroups. These do not have a Social Work Department grant, so fees are usually higher than community playgroups (ranging from approx £7.20-£75 per term). Some are run by a parents' committee, some ask for a rota of parent helpers, and some employ playleaders. The age range is usually 2½ (or 3) to 5. Most groups are run on a part-day basis, 2 or 3 times per week, normally during school terms.

Home Playgroups. These are small, private playgroups of between 6 and 20 children, usually run in the Leader's home. Costs vary.

There is often a waiting list for playgroups and it is advisable to put your child's name down as soon as possible. It is also advisable to check safety standards personally. Prices have been included where possible, and where we know that outdoor play is available, this has been mentioned.

PRIVATE NURSERIES

These are generally more expensive than playgroups, are often open 5 days per week and have extended hours to help working parents. Nurseries indicated with a ★ provide full day places. Some are open only during school terms, others practically all year. The age range is generally 2½ (or 3) to 5, although some take younger and/or older children. Parental help is not normally required. Costs vary and where possible these have been included below. Again, there is often a waiting list, so you should contact those in your area as soon as possible to put your child's name down. As with playgroups and parent and toddler groups, it is advisable to check safety standards personally.

A Montessori Nursery School, where the emphasis is on enabling children to develop at their own rate in a non-competitive environment, will be opening shortly.

Details from Jackie Ley, 41 Elliot Rd, Colinton, 441 2392.

The lists below are arranged in the same areas as the lists for parent and toddler groups above. Refer to the beginning of the chapter to find the appropriate area list.

AREA A

BALERNO:

Balerno Playgroup, Community Centre, Main St/24 places/Mon-Fri 9.30-12/Contact: 449 6451

Compass Playgroup, Dean Park Youth Wing, Marchbank Gdns/22 places/ Mon-Fri 9.30-12 and Mon, Thurs, Fri 1.15-3.15/Outdoor play/Contact: 449 4530

Dean Park Playgroup, Community Centre, Main St/25 places/Mon-Fri 9.15-12/Contact: Flora Skelly, 449 5573

BURDIEHOUSE:

Burdiehouse Playgroup, Burdiehouse Church Hall, Gracemount Drive/25 places/Mon-Fri 9-12

CENTRAL:

Dublin Street Playgroup, Baptist Church Hall, Dublin St/20 places/Mon, Tues, Thurs, Fri 9.15-11.45/Contact: Mrs Dunlop, 554 0797; Judy Chalk, 557 0972 or Jessica Pearson, 557 0825

Edinburgh University Department of Psychology Nursery, 7 George Sq/25 places/Mon-Fri 9-12/Contact: Mrs Slade, 667 1011 ext 4443/Free

★ **Elim Church Nursery,** 29 Candlemaker Row/30 places/Mon-Fri 8.30-5.30/ Contact: 225 3633

★ **Little Marco's Nursery,** 59 Grove St/228 2431/Mon-Fri 9-12; 1-5 or 9-5/am £20; pm £25; full time and lunch £50/Contact: 228 2141

Moray House Nursery, Moray House College of Education, Royal Mile/ Mon-Fri 9.30-11.30, 1.30-2.30/Outdoor play/Contact: Miss Cameron, 556 8455/Free

★ **New Town Nursery,** 12 Dean Ter, Stockbridge/Mon-Fri 8-1, 1-6/Age Walking-5/Open all year/Outdoor play/£45 per week all day, £22.50 half day/332 5920

★ **Royal Mile Nursery,** 1 Lyon's Close, 215 High St/22 places/Mon-Fri 8-1, 1-6/Open all year/Outdoor play/£45 per week all day, £22.50 half day/226 6574

★ **University Day Nursery (Junior),** 14 East Preston St/Mon-Fri 8.45-5/Age 6 wks-2 yrs/for children of university and college students and employees/ means tested (approx £55 full-time)

★ **University Day Nursery (Senior),** 79 Dalkeith Rd/Mon-Fri, 8.45-5/age 2-5 yrs/for children of university college students and employees/means tested (approx £55 full-time)

★ **University Playgroup/**Mon-Fri 9-5 with an hour for lunch/max 20 hours per week (flexible)/charged hourly/arranged through Students' Association

CHURCHHILL:

Holy Corner Community Group, Holy Corner Church Centre, Chamberlain Rd/24 places/Mon, Tues, Thurs, Fri 9.15-11.45

COLINTON:

Colinton Episcopal Playgroup, Episcopal Church, Westgarth Ave/28 places/Wed-Fri 8.45-12, 1.45-3

Colinton Nursery, St Cuthbert's Church Hall, Westgarth Ave/Tues, Wed, Thurs, Fri 9-12, Wed, Fri 12.45-2.45/Outdoor play/Contact: Mrs Wilson, 441 2891

Stableroom Playgroup, Colinton Parish Church, Spylaw Bank Rd/14 places/Mon, Wed, Fri 9.30-11.30/Outdoor play/Contact: Barbara Badger, 442 1843/£1.50 per session

COLINTON MAINS:

Colinton Mains Playgroup, Colinton Mains Community Centre, Firrhill Loan/24 places/Mon-Fri 9.15-11.45/Contact: 441 6597

COMISTON/BUCKSTONE:

Comiston Playgroup, Pentland Community Centre, Oxgangs Brae/30 places/Mon-Fri 9-11.25/Contact: 445 2871

Mrs Hunter (Home Playgroup): 15 Braid Mount/8 places/Mon-Fri 9-12/ Contact: 447 5951

St Fillan's Playgroup, St Fillan's Church, Buckstone Drive/32 places/Mon, Tues, Thurs, Fri 9.30-12/Contact: Mrs Landes, 445 1642

CRAIGLOCKHART:

Goosey Gander (Home Playgroup), 1 Elliot Park/12 places/Mon-Fri 9-12/ Contact: Mrs Thomson, 441 2405

CRAIGMILLAR:

Craigmillar Playgroup, Sandy's Boys' Club, Craigmillar Castle Ave/24 places/Mon-Fri 9-12/Contact: 661 4064

★ **Stewart House Nursery,** 2 Craigmillar Park/12 places/Mon-Fri 8.30-5.30/ Open most of year/Outdoor play/Contact: Norma Haig, 339 3794

CURRIE:

Currie Community Playgroup, Gibson Craig Hall, Lanark Rd West/80 places/Mon, Wed, Thurs 9.30-12

Currie Playgroup, Juniper Green Scout Premises, 45 Lanark Rd West/16 places/Mon-Thurs 9.30-11.45

Jubilee Playgroup, Youth Club, Lanark Rd West, Currie/12 places/Mon-Fri 9.15-12/Contact: 449 6224

Riccarton Playgroup, Riccarton School, Currie/16 places/Mon-Fri 9.15-11.45

FAIRMILEHEAD:

Fairmile Church Nursery, Frogston Rd/Mon-Fri 9-12/Open all year/Outdoor play

Fairmile Kindergarten (Home group), 2 Oxgangs Rd/16 places/Mon-Fri 8.45-12/Outdoor play/Contact: Mrs Kendall, 445 1566

GRANGE:

Grange Kindergarten (Home Playgroup), 5 St Thomas's Rd/8 places/Mon, Tues, Thurs, Fri 9.30-12/Contact: Mrs Sinclair, 667 4250/£65 per term

KAIMES:

Pentland Nursery, Pentland Sports Club, Frogston Rd East/24 places/Mon-Fri 9.15-12.15/Contact: 445 2561

LIBERTON:

Mrs Allan (Home Playgroup)/17 Mid Liberton/6 places/Mon-Fri 9.30-12/Contact: 666 0573

★ **Braid Hills Nursery,** Guthrie Court, 10 Lasswade Rd/24 places/Mon-Fri 8.45-12, 1-4. Packed lunch if required/Outdoor play/Contact: Miss Black, 664 3094/£25 per week

LONGSTONE:

Longstone Playgroup, Longstone School Annexe/20 places/Mon-Fri 9-12

Redhall Playgroup, 113 Redhall Drive/10 places/Mon-Fri 9-11.45

MARCHMONT:

Marchmont St Giles Playgroup, Marchmont St Giles Church Hall, 1 Kilgraston Rd/30 places/2½-4 yrs Tues, Wed, Thurs; over 4 Mon-Thurs/Outdoor play/Contact: Mrs Christie, 447 5016/Approx £50 per term

MAYFIELD:

Mayfield Playgroup, Mayfield Church House, 18 W Mayfield/24 places/Mon 9.30-11.45; Tues, Thurs, Fri 9-11.45/Outdoor play/Contact: Jill Currie, 667 5563

Playtime Nursery, Reid Memorial Church, West Savile Ter/16 places/Mon-Fri 9.30-12/Contact: Marilyn Morris, 664 8308/£2.50 per day/£11.25 per week

MOREDUN:

Moredun Primary Playgroup, Moredun Primary School, Moredunvale Pl/20 places/Mon-Fri 9.15-11.45; Mon-Thurs 1-3

MORNINGSIDE:

Cluny Church Playgroup, Cluny Church Centre, Cluny Drive/12 places/ Mon-Fri 9.30-12/Contact: 447 9615

Mrs Coutts (Home Playgroup), 17 Cluny Ave/8 places/Mon, Tues, Thurs, Fri 9.30-12/Contact: 447 5639/£60 per term

Cranley Playgroup, Thistle Tennis Club, 177 Colinton Rd/20 places/Mon-Fri 9-12.30

Greenbank Playgroup, Greenbank Church Hall, Braidburn Ter/30 places/ Mon-Fri 9.15-11.45/Outdoor play/Contact: Mrs Robertson, 445 1000/£45 per term

Hermitage Playgroup, Cluny Church, Cluny Gdns/20 places/Mon-Fri 9-12/ Contact: Mrs Paul, 667 5213/£65 per term

Morningside Parish Church Playgroup, Morningside Parish Church Hall, 2 Newbattle Ter/40 places/Mon-Fri 9.15-11.45

Nile Grove Community Playgroup, Braid Church Hall, Nile Grove/24 places/Mon-Fri 9.15-11.45/Outdoor play/Contact: Jane Bradley, 447 0145

Mrs Simpson (Home Playgroup), 118 Braid Rd/12 places/Mon, Tues, Thurs, Fri 9.30-12/Outdoor play/Contact: 447 5059

NEWINGTON:

Duncan St Playgroup, Baptist Church Hall, Duncan St/20 places/Mon-Thurs 9.30-12, Fri 9.30-11.45/Contact: June Ewing, 667 5966

Cameron House Nursery, 10 places/Mon-Fri am and pm/Contact: Mrs Stewart, 667 5117/15p per week

Mentone Nursery (Home group), 7 Mentone Ter/10 places/Tues, Thurs, Fri 9.30-2/Outdoor play/Contact: Anne-Marie Rodnes 667 2682/£2.25, 1 day; £4, 2 days; £5, 3 days

NIDDRIE:

Niddrie Playgroup, 65 Niddrie Mains Ter/14 places/Mon-Fri 9-12, 12.15-3.15/Contact: 661 5877

OXGANGS:

Dreghorn Playgroup, 5 Dreghorn Gdns/16 places/Mon-Fri 9.30-12 and 1.30-3.30

St John's Playgroup, St John's Church Hall, Oxgangs Rd Nth/30 places/ Mon-Fri 9.15-11.45

PLEASANCE:

Pleasance Playgroup, Pentland Room, 60 The Pleasance/Mon-Fri 9-1, 2-6/Contact: 557 1148

STOCKBRIDGE:

Doune Terrace (Home Playgroup), 8 Doune Ter/20 places/Mon-Fri 9-12/ Contact: M. E. Graham, 226 2722/£135 per term

International Playgroup, St Bernard's Church Hall, Dean St, Stockbridge/ 24 places/Tues-Thurs 9.15-11.45/Contact: Elizabeth Hargreaves, 556 8611/ ±£17 per term

AREA B

BROUGHTON:

★ **Annandale Nursery,** 3A Annandale St/8 places (takes children from 1 yr old)/Mon-Fri 8-6/Contact: 556 3260
★ **Bellevue Nursery,** Bellevue Baptist Church, East London St/15 places/Mon-Fri 8.30-5.30
Broughton Playgroup, Drummond High School, Cochran Ter/20 places/Mon-Fri 9.15-11.45/Contact: Mrs Ireland, 556 8291
Drummond High School, Tues, Thurs, Fri 9.30-12.30/Contact: Hilary Patrick, 556 3621

COMELY BANK:

Buckingham Playgroup (Home group), 21 Buckingham Ter/24 places/Mon-Fri 8.45-12.15/Contact: Mrs Hunter-Blair, 332 5787
Stockbridge Playgroup, Carrington Youth Wing, Broughton High School/20 places/Mon, Wed, Thurs, Fri 9.15-11.45/Outdoor play/Contact Mrs Watt, 332 6316/Approx £14 per term

CRAIGENTINNY:

Craigentinny/Lochend Playgroup, Loaning Rd/24 places/Mon-Fri 9-11.30
Mrs McInally (Home Playgroup), 44 Christiemiller Ave/10 places/Mon-Fri 9-12/Outdoor play/Contact: 669 2658

GOLDENACRE:

Bangholm Playgroup, Holy Cross Church Hall, Ferry Rd/30 places/Mon-Fri 9.15-11.45/Contact: Mrs Lonie, 554 7685
Edzell Lodge Nursery, St James's Church Hall, Goldenacre/24 places/Mon-Fri 8.45-12/Outdoor play/Contact: Mrs Anderson, 343 1277/£60 per term
Summerside Playgroup, St Serf's Church Hall, Clark Rd/25 places/Mon-Fri 9-11.45/Outdoor play/Contact: Mrs Livingstone, 552 1722/Approx £12 per term

GRANTON:

Granton Toddlers' Play Centre, Granton Parish Church, Boswall Parkway/24 places/Mon-Fri 9.45-11.45/Contact: 552 8629

LEITH:

Dalmeny Street Playgroup, Dalmeny Church Hall, 40 Buchanan St/24 places/Mon-Fri 9-12/Contact: Mrs Somerville, 669 1891
St Margaret's Playgroup, St Margaret's Church Hall, Easter Rd/24 places/Mon-Fri 9.15-11.45/Contact: 661 7065
Victoria Park Children's Centre, Newhaven Rd/a group open to all, but particularly Asian women with children under 5/Tues 1-3.30/Contact: Ghazalla Farooq, 556 0441 or Anne Cairns, 554 4077 or Parveen Ahmed, 553 6809

LOCHEND:

Lochend Toddlers' Play Centre, Lochend Parish Church, Restalrig Rd Sth/24 places/Mon-Fri 9.30-11.30/Contact: Mrs Hendrie, 554 0938

PILTON:

Royston/Wardieburn Playgroup, Community Centre, Pilton Drive/24 places/Mon-Fri 9-11.30/Contact: 552 5700

★ **Telford 3-5s Club,** Fet-Lor Boys' Club, Crewe Rd/24 places/Mon-Fri 8.30-4/ Contact: Mrs Sinclair, 332 4506

West Pilton Playgroup, Community Centre, West Pilton Grove/16 places/ Mon-Fri 9.15-11.45/Contact: 552 7809

PORTOBELLO:

Abercorn Playgroup, 1 Abercorn Ter, Portobello/Mon-Fri 9.10-11.50/ Outdoor play/Contact: Mrs Wotherspoon, 669 5312

St James's Playgroup, Parish Church Hall, Rosefield Pl, Portobello/Mon, Tues, Thurs, Fri 9-12/Contact Mrs Peden, 669 6277/Approx £24 per term

St Mark's Playgroup, High St, Portobello/24 places/Mon-Fri 9-11.45/ Outdoor play/Contact: Mrs Gibb, 669 4871

Tower Bank Nursery, Bath St, Portobello/Mon-Fri 9-12, 1-3/Outdoor play

WARDIE:

Wardie Residents' Playgroup, Wardie Residents' Club, Granton Rd/30 places/Mon-Fri 9-11.45/Outdoor play/Contact: Mrs Dunlop, 552 3301

WILLOWBRAE:

Willowbrae Play Centre, Willowbrae House, Willowbrae Rd/36 places/ Mon-Fri 9.15-11.45; Mon, Wed, Fri 12.45-3.15/Contact: Mrs Isaacson, 661 3550

New Restalrig Playgroup, New Restalrig Parish Church, Willowbrae Rd/24 places/Mon-Fri 9.15-11.45/Contact: Mrs Gilhooley, 661 1622

Northfield Playgroup, Northfield/Willowbrae Comm. Centre, Northfield Rd/ 36 places/Mon-Fri 9.15-11.45, 12.45-2.45/Contact: Mrs Barclay, 669 3168

AREA C

BARNTON:

St Margaret's Kindergarten (Home Playgroup), 42 Barnton Park Gdns/12 places/Outdoor play/Mon-Fri 9-12/Contact: Mrs Scott, 336 4532

BLACKHALL:

Blackhall Playgroup, St Columba's Church, Hillhouse Rd/20 places/Mon, Tues, Wed, Thurs 9.30-12; 1-3.30/Contact: Mrs Thomson, 336 3162

BROOMHOUSE:

Broomhouse Playgroup, St David's Church Hall, Broomhouse Cres/20 places/Mon-Fri 9.15-11.30/Contact: Mrs Vincenti, 336 3734

BROOMHALL:

Broomhall Playgroup, Broomhall Scout Hut/24 places/Mon-Fri 9.30-11.30; 1.30-3.30/Contact: Mrs Milsom, 334 6507

BRUNTSFIELD:

Barclay Church Playgroup, Bruntsfield Place/20 places/Mon-Fri 8.35-12/ Contact: Marion Reid, 229 8133/Approx £75 per term
Bruntsfield Playgroup, Bruntsfield Primary School, Montpelier/20 places/ Mon-Fri 9.15-11.45/Contact: Mrs Brodie, 228 1197

CLERMISTON:

Clermiston Playgroup, Child Health Centre, Rannoch Ter/24 places/Mon-Fri 9.15-11.45/Contact: Mrs Pryde, 334 7390
Fox Covert Playgroup, Fox Covert RC School, Clerwood Ter/24 places/ Mon-Fri 9.15-11.45/Outdoor play/Contact: Mrs Phillips, 334 4333

CORSTORPHINE:

Belgrave Playgroup, Belgrave Halls, 34 Belgrave Rd/24 places/Mon-Fri 9.30-12/Outdoor play/Contact: Mrs Hunt, 334 6416
Kirk Loan Nursery, Old Parish Church Hall, 70 Corstorphine Bank Drive/36 places/Mon, Tues, Thurs, Fri 9.15-11.45/Outdoor play/Contact: Mrs Banks, 334 9018
St Thomas's Playgroup, Church Hall, Glasgow Rd/24 places/Mon-Fri 9.30-12/Outdoor play/Contact: Mrs Nicoll, 334 1407

CRAIGMOUNT:

Craigmount Playgroup, Community Wing, Craigmount High School, Craigs Rd/24 places/Mon, Thurs, Fri 9.15-11.45/Contact: Mrs Lightfoot, 339 1457

CRAMOND:

Cramond House Playgroup, Cramond Glebe Rd/60 places/Mon-Fri 9-12/ Outdoor play/Contact: Mrs Stocks, 336 3212

DALRY:

St Martin's Playgroup, St Martin's Church, Muireston Cres/24 places/Tues, Wed, Thurs, Fri 9.15-11.45/Contact: Mrs Hadden, 346 2113

DAVIDSON'S MAINS:

Jack & Jill Playgroup, Scout Hall/20 places/Mon-Fri 9.15-12.15/Contact: Mrs Burton, 336 8350
Panda Playgroup, Davidson's Mains Church Hall/16 places/Tues-Fri 9.15-12/Contact: Mrs Burt 382 2071

EAST CRAIGS:

Craigsbank Playgroup, Craigsbank Church Centre, Bughtlin Mkt/24 places/ Mon-Fri 9.15-11.45/Contact: Mrs Hay, 339 5937/£36 per term

GYLE:

Gylemuir Playgroup, Gylemuir School, Wester Broom Pl/24 places/Mon, Wed, Fri 9.15-11.45/Outdoor play/Contact: Mrs Green, 334 4840

JUNIPER GREEN:

Juniper Green Nursery, Juniper Park Rd/30 places/Mon-Fri 9.15-12; Wed, Thurs 1-3.30/Outdoor play

KIRKLISTON:

Kirkliston Playgroup, Kirkliston Health Centre, The Glebe, Kirkliston/20 places/Tues, Thurs, Fri 9-11.30/Mon, Tues, Thurs 1.15-3.15/Contact: Mrs Sands, 333 1131

MUIRHOUSE:

Craigroyston Playgroup, Community Centre, Pennywell Rd/24 places/Mon-Fri 9.15-11.30/Contact: Mrs Stirling, 332 7360
Inchmickery Playgroup, Inchmickery Court, Muirhouse Grove/24 places/ Mon-Fri 9.15-11.45; 1-4/Contact: Mrs Robertson, 552 6447
St Paul's Playgroup, St Paul's Church, Pennywell Rd/Mon-Fri 9.15-11.45, 1-3.30/Contact: Mrs Howlet, 552 6614

POLWARTH:

Harrison Playgroup, Phoenix Club, Harrison Pl/24 places/Mon-Fri 9.30-11.30/Contact: Mrs Montgomery, 337 6438
North Merchiston Playgroup, 48 Watson Cres/20 places/Mon-Fri 9.15-12.15/Contact: Mrs Moyes, 337 6973
Polwarth Parish Church Playgroup, Polwarth Ter/20 places/Tues, Wed, Thurs 9.30-12/Contact: Mrs Paget-Tomlinson, 19a Royal Cres

RATHO:

Newbridge/Ratho Playgroup, Community Centre, Station Rd/20 places/ Tues, Wed, Thurs, Fri 9.30-12/Contact: Mrs Merritees, 333 4646
Ratho Church Hall Playgroup, St Mary's Church Hall, Baird Rd/20 places/ Tues, Wed, Thurs 9.15-11.45/Contact: Mrs Robertson, 333 1281
Ratho Community Centre Playgroup, 25 places/Mon, Tues or Thurs 9.15-11.45; 1.15-2.45/Contact: Mrs Hamblet, 333 4007/Approx £14 per term

SIGHTHILL:

Calder's Playgroup, Sighthill Primary School, 1 Calder Park/24 places/Mon-Fri 9.30-11.30/Contact: Wyn Wright, 1/1 Medwin House, 20 Calder Park
Sighthill Health Centre Playgroup, Calder Rd/24 places/Mon-Fri 9.30-11.30/Contact: Mrs Robertson, 443 6625

Sighthill Playgroup, Sighthill Community Centre, Sighthill Wynd/30 places/ Mon-Fri 9.15-11.45/Contact: Mrs Baillie, 443 4289

SOUTH QUEENSFERRY:

Dalmeny Village Playgroup, Dalmeny Church Hall/20 places/Mon, Wed, Thurs, Fri 9.30-12/Contact: Mrs McCarry, 331 2328
Milton Cottage Playgroup, Milton Cottage/18 places/Tues, Wed, Thurs 9.30-12/Contact: Mrs Graham-Brown, 331 1124
Roseberry Hall Playgroup/34 places/Mon-Fri 9-12/Contact: Mrs Bain, 331 1558
South Queensferry Community Centre Playgroup/21 places/Mon-Fri 9-12/ Contact: Mrs Lawson, 331 2754

TOLLCROSS:

Gaelic Medium Playgroup, Tollcross Primary School, Fountainbridge/20 places/Tues, Wed, Thurs 9.45-11.45/Contact: Sandra Hutchison, 339 7488/ £7.20 per term

VIEWFORTH:
★ **Rainbow Kindergarten,** 72 Gilmore Pl/24 places/Mon-Fri 8.30-5.30/Open all year/Outdoor play/Contact: 228 1668/£40 per week
Viewforth Church Playgroup, Viewforth/30 places/Mon-Fri 9.15-11.45/ Contact: Mrs Roberts, 229 8685

WESTER HAILES:

Hailes Playgroup, Hailesland Community Centre, Hailesland Pl/24 places/ Mon-Fri 9.30-12/Contact: Mrs Whitehead, 442 3652
Murrayburn Playgroup, 1 The Greenway, Wester Hailes/20 places/Mon-Fri 9.30-11.30/Contact: Mrs Quinn, 453 1897
Wester Hailes Playgroup, 4/51 Hailesland Park/20 places/Mon-Fri 9-11.30; 1-3.30/Contact: Mrs Stewart, 453 2619

NURSERY SCHOOLS AND NURSERY CLASSES IN PRIMARY SCHOOLS

These are run by the Lothian Regional Council Department of Education for children from age 3 to 5 and are normally operated on a part-day basis (either am or pm) 5 days a week during school terms. There is no parental rota.

There is often a long waiting list and you should put your child's name down as soon as possible after his or her 2nd birthday. At some schools you may be more likely to get a place if you request an afternoon session — check with the Head Teacher when you fill in the application form. Below is a list of Nursery Schools and Primary Schools with Nursery Provision in Edinburgh. Copies of the complete list containing all the schools below and all others in the Lothian area may be obtained from Mrs D. Combe, Lothian Regional Council, Education Department, 40 Torphicen St EH3 8JT (229 9166 ext 2177).

NURSERY SCHOOLS

Albany School, 30 Madeira St EH6 4AI/554 3683
Balgreen School, 175 Balgreen Rd EH11 3AT/337 1454
Calderglen School, Wester Hailes Rd EH11 4NG/453 5754
Cameron House, Cameron House Ave EH16 5LR/667 5117
Children's House, Wauchope Ter EH16 4NU/661 1401
Cowgate, 144 Cowgate EH1 1RP/225 7251
Grassmarket, 11/15 The Vennel EH1 2HU/229 6540
Greengables, 8a Niddrie House Gdns EH16 4UR/669 9083
High School Yards, High School Yards EH1 1LZ/556 6536
Hope Cottage, Cowan's Close, East Crosscauseway EH8 9HF/667 5795
Liberton, Mount Vernon Rd EH16 6JQ/664 3155
Lochrin, West Tollcross EH3 9QN/229 7743
Princess Elizabeth, Clearburn Cres EH16 5ER/667 0946
St Leonard's, North Richmond St EH8 9SY/667 4674
Stanwell, Junction Place EH6 5JA/554 1309
The Spinney Lane, 13a The Spinney EH17 7LD
Tynecastle, McLeod St EH11 2NL/337 5461
Westfield Court, Westfield Court EH11 2RJ/337 4914

NURSERY CLASSES IN PRIMARY SCHOOLS

Abbeyhill, Abbey St EH7 5SJ/661 3054
Bonaly, Bonaly Grove EH13 0QD/441 7211
Bonnington, Bonnington Rd EH19 3HR/554 1370
Broomhouse, Saughton Rd EH11 3RQ/443 3783
Broughton, Broughton Rd EH7 4LD/556 7028
Brunstane, Magdalene Dr EH15 3BE/669 4498
Burdiehouse, Burdiehouse Cres EH17 8EX/664 2351
Carrick Knowe, Lampacre Rd EH12 7HU/334 4505
Clermiston, Parkgrove Pl EH4 7NP/336 3361
Clovenstone, 54 Clovenstone Park EH14 3EY/453 4242
Corstorphine, Corstorphine High St EH12 7SY/334 3865
Craigmillar, Harewood Rd EH16 4NT/661 3481
Craigmuir, West Pilton Park EH4 4ET/332 6666
Dalry, Dalry Rd EH11 2JB/337 6086
Drumbrae, Ardshiel Ave EH4 7HP/339 5071
Duddingston, Duddingston Rd EH15 1SW/669 5092
Dumbryden, Dumbryden Gdns EH14 2NZ/453 5686
East Craigs, 79 Craigmount Brae EH12 8XF/339 7115
Fernieside, Moredun Park Rd EH17 7HL/664 2154
Ferryhill, Groathill Rd North EH4 2SQ/332 4244
Flora Stevenson, Comely Bank EH4 1BG/332 1604
Fort, North Fort St EH6 4HF/554 7101
Gracemount, Lasswade Rd EH16 6UA/664 2331
Granton, Boswall Parkway EH5 2DA/552 3987
Gylemuir, Wester Broom Pl EH12 7RT/334 7138
Hailesland, Hailesland Pl EH14 2SL/442 3894

Hermitage Park, Hermitage Park EH6 8HD/554 2952
Hunter's Tryst, Oxgangs Green EH13 9JE/445 1510
Inchview, West Pilton Ave EH4 4BX/332 8186
James Gillespie's, Whitehouse Loan EH9 1AT/447 1014
Juniper Green, 20 Baberton Mains Wynd EH14 3EE/442 2121
Leith Walk, Brunswick Rd EH7 5NG/556 3873
Liberton, 299 Gilmerton Rd EH16 5UD/664 2337
Lismore, Bingham Ave EH15 3HZ/669 4588
London Street, East London St EH7 4BW/556 4008
Longstone, Redhall Grove EH14 2DU/443 4743
Muirhouse, Muirhouse Pl West EH4 4PX/332 2793
Murrayburn, Sighthill Loan EH11 4NP/453 5339
Niddrie, Niddrie Mains Rd EH15 3HG/669 1658
Orwell, Orwell Pl EH11 2AD
Oxgangs, Colinton Mains Drive EH13 9AE/441 3649
Peffermill, Craigmillar Castle Ave EH16 4DH/661 3456
Prestonfield, Peffermill EH16 5LJ/667 1336
Roseburn, Roseburn St EH12 5PL/337 6096
Royal Mile, Canongate EH8 8BZ/556 3347
At this school there is a Special Class for children with learning difficulties
Royston, Boswall Parkway EH5 2JH/552 4534
St David's RC, West Pilton Pl EH4 4DF/332 3500
St Francis's RC, Niddrie Mains Rd EH16 4DS/661 3053
St John's RC, Hamilton Ter EH15 1NB/669 1363
St John Viarney RC, Ivanhoe Cres EH16 6AU/664 1742
St Joseph's RC, Broomhouse Cres EH11 3TD/443 4591
St Mark's RC, 63 Firhill Cres EH13 9EE/441 2948
St Mary's RC, Links Gdns EH6 7JG/554 7291
St Peter's RC, 25 Falcon Gdns EH10 4AP/447 5742
Silverknowes, Muirhouse Gdns EH4 4SX/336 1508
Stenhouse, Stevenson Dr EH11 3HL/443 1255
Stockbridge, Hamilton Pl EH3 5BA/332 6109
Towerbank, Figgate Bank EH15 1HX/669 1551
Westburn, 55 Sighthill Rd EH11 4PB/442 2997

INDEPENDENT SCHOOLS

Some of the independent schools in Edinburgh have nursery departments. These are listed below, with fees for 1986/87. Unless otherwise stated, 3 is the minimum age. The Scottish Independent Schools Information Service at 18 Hanover St (225 7202) will send you a free booklet containing basic information about all the Independent Schools in Scotland.

Cargilfield School, 37 Barnton Ave West EH4 6HU/336 2207/£200 per term/ Co-educational
Edinburgh Academy Preparatory School, Arboretum Rd EH3 5PL/552 3690/ £180 per term/Co-educational nursery class at Denham Green, Clark Rd

George Heriot's School, Lauriston Pl EH3 9EQ/229 7263/£110-£165 per term/Co-educational

George Watson's College, Colinton Rd EH10 5EG/447 7931/£179 per term/Co-educational

The Mary Erskine School/Daniel Stewart's and Melville College Combined Junior School, Queensferry Rd EH4 3EZ/332 7925/£179 per term/Co-educational

Rudolph Steiner, 38 Colinton Rd EH10 5BT/337 3410/£185 per term/Co-educational day school from kindergarten to university entrance with space for 350 pupils. The kindergarten is an integral part of the school and has four groups with space for a total of 50 children aged 4-6. The central aim of the education is to develop and unite in a harmonious way the child's thoughts, feelings and actions. Financial contributions are arranged by interview with the administrator.

St Denis and Cranley School Ltd, 3 Ettrick Rd EH10 5BJ/229 1500/£150 per term

St Margaret's School Ltd, East Suffolk Rd EH16 5PJ/668 1986/£150 per term/Co-educational nursery

---

LOOKING FORWARD TO STARTING SCHOOL

There is only one entry date to primary school in Scotland, and that is in August. A child whose 5th Birthday falls between 1 Mar and 28 Feb the following year may start school in August. Some children will be entering school 6 months after their 5th birthday, while others will be starting school 6 months before their 5th birthday. For these younger children, it is not compulsory to start in August. If you want advice about the best starting date for your child, get in touch with your local school or the Divisional Education Officer. They will also be able to advise if you have just arrived from England or Wales, where the admission ages differ.

To enrol your child at the school in your catchment area, telephone the Head Teacher and arrange an appointment. This can be done any time during the 12 months prior to your child's admission to school.

If you wish to send your child to a school which is outside your catchment area, your request will be considered provided there is a place available. For details of all local primary schools contact the Divisional Education Officer (Edinburgh Division), Lothian Region Education Department, 40 Torphicen St EH3 8JT (229 9166). A prospectus for the school should also be available from the Head Teacher.

SPECIAL SCHOOLS

If you feel that your child may benefit from attending a special school, for whatever reason, contact the Special Schools Services, Child Guidance Centre, Torphichen St, Edinburgh 3 (229 2212)

LOCAL PLAY ORGANIZATIONS

Scottish Pre-School Play Association
15 Smith's Pl, Leith
553 2185

Mon-Fri 10-3 (closed during school holidays)

Provides information about parent and toddler groups and playgroups, including how to set them up. Also sells play materials, eg paint, clay, pens, etc, in bulk at reduced prices. Conferences and Annual Meetings, at which crèches for under 5s are provided.

Moray House Play Resource Unit
Moray House College of Education, Holyrood Rd
556 8455 (Elizabeth Allen)
Mon-Fri 9-5

The Play Resource Unit is a Community Programme Project sponsored by the School of Community Studies, Moray House College of Education, and is funded by the Manpower Services Commission. The Unit can be used by anyone involved in play, including individuals. There is an Information Bank with ideas on adventure playgrounds, children with special needs, play ideas, pre-school play, hospital play, toys, play equipment and much more. There is an opportunity to make contact with others involved in play — and advice is given on setting up playgroups and mother and toddler groups. The Unit can also provide a list of organizations directly involved in play.

Mobile Projects Association (Scotland)
12 Picardy Pl EH1 3JT
556 7580 (Marianne MacLennan)

Services existing mobile play projects, giving advice on legal, technical, health and safety aspects.

Playbus
Mobile play centres which visit areas and give parents a chance to meet staff who will advise on local playgroups, etc. Play area for children. Run by Social Work Department. For further details contact Alice Leach, Shrubhill House, Shrub Place 554 4301, and look in papers for visits to your area.

Childcare

If you want to, or have to return to work or to study, are ill, or for some other reason are unable to look after your child, you will have to make arrangements for someone else to do so. If circumstances are particularly difficult the Social Work Department (Lothian Regional Council) may be able to assist. Otherwise there are 'workplace' nurseries at several colleges of further education, Edinburgh University and at the Royal Hospital for Sick Children, and the Scottish Office is considering a summer holiday playscheme for the children of civil servants employed in the Edinburgh area. There are also several private nurseries that provide full day care. (These are marked by a ★ in 'Pre-School Play and Education'.) Alternatively you may send your child to be looked after by a childminder in her own home. Choosing someone else to care for your child can be extremely stressful. Most of us hope at the outset that whatever arrangement we make will be permanent, but this is not always possible. Children's needs do change however, and forced changes in care arrangements, whilst unwelcome for their disruption at the time, can also bring with them new opportunities. Remember too, childcare expenses are not tax deductible! This section provides some guidance on how to go about finding someone; it should also be of interest to anyone considering looking after children other than her own.

Useful books are 'The Working Mother's Handbook' from Clapham NCT Working Mothers' Group, 167 Fentiman Rd, London SW8 1JY; and 'Looking After Children: Information for Childminders' from Dept of Social Work, LRC. (See 'Pre-School Play and Education' for address.)

CHILDMINDERS

Childminders care for children in their own homes. By law, they must be registered with the Social Work Department, if they care for a child to whom they are not closely related for more than two hours a day for reward. Registration involves health, police and home safety checks and is reviewed 3-yearly. People who live in tenements or high-rise flats might not be registered due to fire regulations. Childminders are approved to care for not more than 3 children under 5, including their own. In practice, many childminders are not registered.

How to Find a Childminder

A list of all registered childminders is available from Social Work Area Teams in Lothian, see 'Pre-School Play and Education'. Health Visitors may also have copies of this list, and may know local childminders. Other working parents are also worth approaching since they may have been through this themselves and know of a childminder who might be suitable.

How Much Will it Cost?

The National Childminding Association recommends a standard rate which increases each autumn. Rates in Edinburgh are currently £35 per week (double for 2 children). Childminders are responsible for their own Tax and National Insurance payments and should have their own Public Liability and Accident Insurance cover. Registered childminders can arrange this through the Lothian Childcarers' Association, c/o 15 Smith's Pl EH6 8HT, 553 2185.

Choosing a Childminder

Working from the list you will need to phone round to find out who has vacancies and arrange to go to see them.

Discuss the details of the contract eg cost; min and max hours and flexibility of these; what is included in the cost (food, nappies and outings are often excluded); what holidays the childminder takes, and whether you will have to pay a holiday retainer; any particular exclusions (eg not school holidays).

Try to find out the type of care being offered eg activities, other children currently with minder, diet, attitudes to discipline. There may be other things important to you which you will want to ask about (eg smoking, sexism).

Discussion and negotiation early on can help to make things easier for both you and your childminder.

In the end, you will probably choose the person you feel most comfortable with. It is worth following your feelings about whom your child will be most settled with — and a good childminder will usually ask you a lot of the above questions.

CHILDCARE IN YOUR OWN HOME

If you can afford to do so, it may be easier to employ someone to look after your child or children in your own home, either by coming in each day, or living in with you. Choosing between these options will be a personal matter, but perhaps also financial, since it does cost much more to employ live-in help. If you want to arrange come-in or live-in care, this is how you might try to find the right person.

Local contacts or friends etc might suggest someone tried and tested. Advertising — in 'The Scotsman' or 'Evening News' (Fri) — usually elicits many responses; a one-day advert should be sufficient. It is worth thinking beforehand about the sort of person you are looking for and to specify this, eg trained or untrained, older or younger. This can reduce the responses to a more manageable size. If you want an NNEB-trained person (nursery nurse) and wish to employ someone newly qualified, contact the local colleges of further education offering this training (Queen Margaret College 339 8111, Esk Valley College 663 1951, Stevenson College 453 6161, West Lothian College, Bathgate 634300).

Conditions of Service

You should decide beforehand what you are offering in terms of hours, holidays, extra duties (eg babysitting, housework, making meals, taking child to playgroup, swimming etc). Pay rates vary widely, both for come-in and live-in care. (Come-in care pays around £45.70/wk at present.) Take into account training, experience, and number of children as well as extra duties.

Make sure you take into account the additional cost to you of National Insurance and Tax payments. These can amount to at least a third more than the person's take-home pay.

Interviews

Selecting the right person will again be based on your intuition as well as what you know about the person. Get references from previous employers wherever possible.

Contract

It is important to have mutual expectations clear at the outset. A written contract, stating all the agreed conditions of service is very helpful in preventing problems later on, or at least making them easier to sort out.

CHILDREN'S CENTRES AND DAY CARE

Lothian Regional Social Work Department run 15 children's centres to help care for young children who, for social or health reasons, would benefit from this care. This service is free and may be offered Mon-Fri 8-6. For further information contact Lothian Regional Council Department of Social Work, Shrubhill House, Shrub Place 554 4301.

Day Care

This may be offered as an alternative to children's centres. Day carers are registered by the Social Work Department to care for children in the carer's own home. This service is free. Application for places is through the Children's Centre and, as with the Centre applications, this offers a service to parents who have social, financial or health problems.

ORGANISATIONS INVOLVED IN CHILDCARE

Lothian Child Carers' Association
15 Smith's Pl EH6 8HT
553 2185
9-1

Information and help with any aspect of childminding or day-caring. Also organises informal meetings and coffee-mornings for childcarers and the children they are looking after.

National Childminding Association
204-206 High St, Bromley, Kent BR1 1PP
01-464 6164

National co-ordinating organisation, which aims to improve conditions for childminders, parents and children, and produces a handbook for childminders, a guide for parents and various leaflets and reports in several languages.

Social Work Area Offices
See 'Pre-School Play and Education'

AGENCIES THAT PROVIDE HELP IN THE HOME

The following agencies will provide help in the home:

Bruntsfield Helping Hands
228 1382

Home helps, trained nannies and mothers' helps. Min 3 hrs/week.

J B Nursing and Staff Agency
447 9878

Home helps, live-in nannies, mothers' helps and babysitters. Min 3 hrs/week, £3.25/hr, plus introduction fee.

Mackays Agency
225 8389

Foreign Au-Pairs

The Homecarers
Mon-Fri 557 2222; pm and Sat, Sun 661 4044

Mothers' helps, school escorts, day and evening childcare, sleep-in duty.

BABYSITTING CIRCLES
These are groups of parents who get together to provide a baby-sitting service on a 'token' rather than payment basis. You are given a number of tokens and a list of local babysitters (often within walking distance). Tokens are normally for ½ hr or 1 hr each, and you are issued with up to 20, depending on your circle. You can call on baby-sitters as long as you have enough tokens to pay them, and more tokens can be earned when you go out to babysit for someone else. Some circles also operate overnight and daytime services, in addition to the normal evening service. To find out about circles in your area ask neighbours, local parents, your Health Visitor, local NCT or look on noticeboards.

The Scottish Council for Single Parents has recently set up a register for single parents, access to which is free of charge. Information maybe obtained from the council at 13 Gayfield Sq 556 3899.

All these circles are organised on a purely informal basis and it's up to you to decide if you are happy with the way the circle is run.

LIBRARIES

There is a complete list of public libraries in the telephone directory, listed under Edinburgh on the page devoted to the City of Edinburgh District Council, subsection Recreation Dept. To obtain tickets for children of any age go to your local library. You will be issued with 3 tickets per child. You are responsible for your offspring's borrowed books and for handing them back in reasonable condition and on time, although there are no fines on books overdue on children's tickets.

For information about activities such as storytelling, look out for notices in the library, particularly during the school holidays when there are more likely to be organised attractions. The noticeboards can also be a mine of useful information both of local and more general interest, and are well worth keeping an eye on. Libraries maintain a diary of forthcoming local events, as well as lists and books of local information. See 'Sources of Information'. For more information on general policy contact the Librarian in charge of Youth Services at Edinburgh Central Library 225 5584.

All the libraries have a kinderbox and small chairs with a basic stock of board books and other books for babies and toddlers. It is planned to put toys to be used by children visiting the library into those libraries which have enough space, and a few already have these. At present the extra facilities for children fall into 3 groups:

1) Those which have drawing facilities for pre-school children, eg a table with small chairs, crayons and paper:
Dundee St, Colinton, Kirkliston, and Newington.
2) Those which have (in addition to 1 above) toys, eg beakers, jigsaws, a playhouse:
Gilmerton, McDonald Rd, Leith, Muirhouse and Craigmillar.
3) Those which have (in addition to 1 and 2 above) games for primary school-age children, eg chess, draughts:
Blackhall, Sighthill, Moredun and Portobello.

Records and tapes are available in very few libraries at present:
Newington has both, Craigmillar has records, Muirhouse has tapes.

Standards of access and provision vary a great deal, mostly because of the limitations of the buildings. New purpose-built libraries usually have excellent all-round facilities. Portobello Library has good facilities but has recently moved its children's section upstairs — not ideal for parents with toddlers and pushchairs.

Opening hours can vary locally; some small libraries are only open part-time. Hours are displayed on a board outside the library.

Two libraries are outstanding:

🚶 **Newington Library** on the south side of the city has excellent access and public toilets (it won an award for its access for the disabled). The library is spacious and attractive and as well as providing kinderboxes, tables with paper and crayons, and chairs for young children it has a small selection of children's records and tapes.

🚶 **Blackhall Library** in the north of the city, also has good access with a ramp for pushchairs, as well as public toilets. The children's section is large and attractive with a large book stock, a kinderbox, chairs for the tinies and tables equipped with paper and crayons.

Apart from these two, libraries usually only have a staff toilet but you are unlikely to be turned away with a desperate toddler.

Edinburgh Central Library
George IV Bridge
225 5584
Mon-Fri 9-8.30; Sat 9-1

This library houses comprehensive public reference and information services, major collections of local history material, a reasonable adult fiction lending stock and a large non-fiction lending section; as well as the largest collection of books about children (eg play, education, problems etc). There are also extensive Music and Fine Art collections (Mon-Fri 9-9; Sat 9-1). The Children's Library, next door to the Central Library is open Mon-Fri 1-8.30; Sat 9-1. This is a very small library, with very little floor space, not really a Central library in the sense that the main library is. Public toilets are in the basement of the main building.

The Mobile Library Service visits more than 60 locations in the Edinburgh area, ranging from small villages such as Dalmeny, to large urban locations such as Wester Hailes. A wide variety of books are available, including a varied and changing children's selection. For details phone the Central Library 225 5584.

Toy Libraries

Toy libraries are, as their name suggests, centres for lending toys and are primarily geared to under 5's and handicapped children. They are also drop-in centres and all have coffee (except the St Bernard's Resource Centre). Guidance can be given on toys best suited to your child.

Toy libraries are open to anyone and are cheap (eg 20p for large toy, 10p for small toy for 3 weeks). There is sometimes an initial registration fee. The range of toys available for hire depends on the storage space of the premises; some even stock climbing frames.

The Women's Royal Voluntary Service (44 Albany St EH1 3QR, 556 4284) run most of the toy libraries in Edinburgh and these (marked with ★), and others, are listed below. Opening times are mainly during school terms.

★ **Children's Centre**
Craigmillar Castle Gdns
Mon 9.15-11.30
Organisers: Mrs Moira Heywood 667 4238 and Kate O'Brien 667 8338

★ **Craigroyston High School Music Block**
332 7801
Wed 10-12
Organiser: Mrs Pat Brown 343 3406

Drummond Community High School
Cochran Ter
556 2651
Wed, Thurs 2-4; Fri 10-12
Organiser: Mrs Caroline Reid 332 9240

★ **Gilmerton Day Nursery**
Gilmerton Dykes St
Thurs 10-11.45
Organiser: Mrs Jean Llewellyn 667 8389

Gogarburn Hospital
175-9 Glasgow Rd, Corstorphine
Every day 10-4 (phone to check)
Open to all Gogarburn staff and patients and to the local community.
Organiser: Miss Chris Adamson 339 4242

★ **Hailesland Children's Centre**
6 Hailesland Pl, Wester Hailes
Thurs 9-11.30
Organisers: Mrs Christine Strachan 332 2812 and Mrs Jean Sim 449 5023

★ **Leith Community Centre**
New Kirkgate
554 4750
Wed 9.30-11.15
Organiser: Mrs Hilary Wyllie 669 3440

★ **Lismore Primary School**
Bingham Ave
669 4588
Wed 9-11.30
Organiser: Mrs June Bradley 669 1255

★ **North Merchiston Primary School**
Tay St
337 1434

Wed 10-11.30
Organiser: Mrs Fiona Wellburn 445 4539

★ **Pentlands Community Centre**
Oxgangs Brae
Thurs 9.30-11
Organiser: Mrs Mary Cant 441 3512

Prestonfield Toy Library
Cameron House Community Centre, Cameron House Ave
Mon 9-12

Ravelrig (Barnardo's)
527 Lanark Rd West
2nd Wed in every month
Organiser: Miss Beryl Packer 449 7161

★ **St Ann's Centre**
Cowgate
Thurs 10-11.30
Organiser: Mrs Doris Stanley 669 1871

★ **St Bernard's Education Centre**
Dean Park St, Stockbridge
Thurs 1.45-3.45
Organiser: Mrs Helen Dickinson 663 9338

This toy library is open to individuals as well as groups. It stocks large toys which may be borrowed for a term, eg slides, climbing frames. It is not a 'drop-in' centre.

★ **Stenhouse Children's Centre**
Ford's Rd (off Gorgie Rd)
Tues 10-11.30
Organiser: Mrs Fiona Wellburn 445 4539

★ **The Hut**
Greendykes Primary School, Greendykes Rd
669 7373
Tues 9.30-11.30
Organisers: Mrs Maureen Quinn and Miss Kate Frame 669 7373

Ăctivities for Children

For Playgroups, Toddler Groups and Nurseries, see 'Pre-School Play and Education'.

DANCE

Classes for younger children (ie 2½-4½ yr olds) usually teach music and movement. This may include nursery rhymes and simple dancing (hopping, skipping, toe-pointing, mime and moving in time to music.) Socialising (learning to wait your turn etc) is a key element in all dancing classes. A fair number of boys attend these early classes. Footwear is usually gym shoes, available from Mothercare and local shoe shops. There are many local dance classes, some of which are listed here. Others may be found through friends' recommendation, adverts in local libraries, community centres, shop windows and 'The Edinburgh Advertiser'.

The Scottish Council for Dance offers advice on choosing a teacher in their free leaflet 'So You Want to Dance' (available from the Honorary Secretary, Scottish Council for Dance, PO Box 410, WDO, EH12 6AR). It recommends doing some investigation into a teacher's qualifications, class content, and studio facilities before making a choice. It can be difficult to compare qualifications awarded by different bodies so apply to the Council if in need of clarification.

The Royal Academy of Dancing has introduced a registration system for teachers they recommend. The following list begins with local teachers registered with them.

RAD REGISTERED TEACHERS

Academy of Ballet
Joan Tucker (Dir)
Corstorphine New Church Hall, Kirk Loan, Corstorphine
664 6589

Classes for 2½-8 yr olds. Youngest children do music and movement with basic dance steps. From about age 4 classes are geared more towards ballet. Cost: £12.60 (age 2½-4), £14.15 (4-5 yrs) for 10 lessons.

Anne Bangham
Village Hall, Juniper Green
334 7642

Age 4+. Ballet. Sat 10-10.45.

Anne Frater School of Ballet
St Catherine's Hall, Grange Rd, Grange
229 3389

Class for 3-5 yr olds, Tues 3.30-4.15. £10 for course of 10 lessons. Simple ballet, toe pointing, mime etc. Concert in June each year.

Alwyn Tate
Christian Aid Hall, George IV Bridge
664 9844

Age 2½ upwards. ½ hour ballet, ½ hour tap, Wed 4-5 pm. 60p/class paid each week.

Jane Goulding
441 5607
St Fillan's Church Hall, Buckstone Dr, Wed 2.30 and 3.15; Fairmilehead Church Hall, Frogston Rd, Mon 2.30 and 3.15; Community Centre, Pedestrian Precinct, Balerno, Thurs 3 and Fri 2.45 and 3.30

Age 3+, ballet £14 for 10 lessons. 1st week is 'taster' class; you pay at the 2nd class.

Joyce Paterson School of Dancing
445 1159

Wester Hailes Education Centre, 5 Murrayburn Dr, Wester Hailes; St Salvador's Church Hall, Howe St West, Stenhouse; St Margaret's Church Hall, Easter Rd; Sighthill Community Centre, Sighthill Wynd.

Tap and ballet (age 3½ up); Highland (age 3 up) and modern dance (some 4 yr olds, mainly older). 80p/class paid weekly.

Lis Mackie Dance
332 0426 after 8 pm
Classes in Stockbridge, Murrayfield and Viewforth

Stockbridge and Murrayfield classes cover music and movement for 2½-4 yr olds. From age 4 the orientation is more towards ballet. Viewforth classes are for 4-6 yr olds and older, and cover tap and dance/drama.

Manor Ballet School
Mrs Neil Proudfoot (Dir)
225 6456
Studios at 4 Manor Pl, West End. Also classes at Marchmont St Giles Church, Kilgraston Rd, Marchmont.

The school offers music and movement classes for 2½-4 yr olds, and ballet classes for children of 4½ up. Each class lasts ¾ hour. £14.65 for a 10 week course.

Morag Alexander School of Dancing
Dalrymple Loan, Musselburgh
(49) 52722

Ballet classes for 3 yr olds up, Mon 3.15, Tues 2.30 and 3.30. Classes last ¾ hour. £14.50 for 10 weeks. 3 week trial period. Annual show in Brunton Theatre.

The Theatre School
106 St Stephen St, Stockbridge
226 5533

The nursery classes cover basic ballet, singing and mime. Children are grouped by age: 2½-3½ yrs, Tues 3.30; 3½-4½ yrs, Thurs 3.30 and Sat 9 am; 4½-5½ yrs (mostly ballet), Mon 3.30 and Sat 10.30. Cost between £17 and £21/10 week term.

DANCE TEACHERS NOT REGISTERED WITH RAD

Adell Dance Studios
Contact: 661 3447 (studios) or 556 5140 (teacher, Sue Morrow MUKA)
Northfield Venture Scout Hall, Northfield Rd. Sat 10.30-12 noon.

Age 3½ up. Ballroom dancing, disco and rock n' roll. £1/session.

Buckstone Dance Club
Contact: Mrs Aksel 228 3997 or Carol Caldwell 445 2821
Buckstone Primary School, 60a Buckstone Loan. Tues 5.15

Age 3 up. Modern, ballet and tap. Children can sit British Theatre Dance Association exams. 70p/class. (Part of youth club so non-profit-making.)

Dawn-Petrovna 3 Arts Dance Academy
Contact: 336 8585 Dawn-Petrovna Laing MBBO, FUKA, FBATD
Broughton High School, Carrington Rd, Comely Bank. Mon 4-5, Sat 10-11.

Age 3 up (sometimes 2½ yr olds taken). Children learn tap, simple ballet, mime and some percussion.

Older children learn ballet, tap or Highland. 75p/class.

Moira Drysdale Dip PE
4 Kilmaurs Rd, Newington 667 2638
Wed 2-3

Age 3 up. Music and movement with basic ballet steps, singing and some percussion. £15 for 10-week term.

Pamela Allam AISTD, BTDA
(02594) 2850 or 2973
St Cuthbert's Church Hall, Westgarth Ave, Colinton, Mon; St Columba's Church, Queensferry Rd, Blackhall, Thurs.

2½ to 4½ yr olds are taught music and movement and the beginnings of ballet. Older children do ballet. Classes last ¾ hr and cost £22 for 10-week term.

Rebecca Walker Dance Studios
Rebecca Walker (Dir) MBBO (Adv), ODTS, UKAPTD, 14 Orwell Ter, Dalry
337 0748

2½ to 4 yr olds have informal classes of ½ hr ballet and ½ hr tap with nursery rhymes etc. Classes on Mon, Tues, Thurs and Fri 3-4 pm. 4 to 6 yr olds have more formal classes also in ballet and tap, on the same days from 4 to 5 pm. The older age-group can also do discodancing. £14.85 for 10 lessons, taken over a 12-week period to allow for occasional non-attendance.

Sighthill Community Centre
Sighthill Wynd, Sighthill
453 6078

Majorettes 'Baby' team. Basic majorettes routines, marching etc for children aged 3-5 yrs. Mon 6.30-7.30. 50p/session, plus centre membership.

GYMNASTICS

McLeod St Sports Centre
22 McLeod St, Dalry
337 3252

'Gym Joey' for children aged from 3-6 yrs. Beginners' gymnastics to music. Sun 12.15-1, Mon 3.15-4. Costs 75p (60p to centre members; membership costs £1.50).

Tumbletots
Pentland Community Centre, Oxgangs Brae, Oxgangs, Mon; St Kentigern's RC Church Hall, Parkgrove Ave, Barnton, Fri.
Contact: Lesley Malone (5) 845764.

Specially designed programme of gymnastic activities to help children develop coordination, balance, climbing skills and agility. All with appropriate equipment. Supervision is by specially trained staff. Children can start once they are walking. Mums stay if children are under 3. Membership and insurance £5.75/yr (includes T-shirt, badge, comic and parents' information sheet.) Each session lasts ¾ hr and costs £1.40 — you pay each 5-week block in advance.

MUSIC

Most of the music classes mentioned below teach listening skills and moving in time to music. The reason most music classes for under 5s do not involve specialising in a particular instrument is simply that the children physically cannot cope with it — their hands are not big enough, they don't have the lung power etc. The exception to this is the violin which can be successfully reduced in size without sacrificing its normal tone.

It is advisable to book in advance for all these classes.

Mrs Lundy
18 Dalrymple Cres, Grange
667 5360

Half-hour sessions for 3-4 yr olds, Thurs 2.30. Children listen, play bells, drums, tambourine, Chinese blocks etc, and move in time to music. 4-6 yr olds have ¾ hr classes starting at 3.15. In addition to the above they cover action songs and conducting and playing in their own band. 10 lessons/term, year starts mid-Sept. A waiting-room is provided for Mums.

Morningside Junior Music Workshop
Cluny Church Centre, Cluny Dr/Braid Rd, Morningside
Contact: Mrs B Jenkins 447 6858 or Mrs M Paterson 447 4148

A non-profit-making class for children aged 3-5. ½-hr sessions are held on Mon and Wed at 2 pm. Music through play with percussion instruments, plus singing and miming games. £1.50 enrolment fee, then £10 for a 10-week term. 3 terms 1 yr starting end Sept.

St Mary's Music School
Old Coates House, Manor Place
225 1831 Mrs Richardson, Mon-Fri 9.30-1

Hour-long classes for children aged 4 up are held on Sat between 10 and 1 pm. Classes include musical games, singing, listening and using percussion instruments. Cost: £12.50 for 10- or 11-week term.

VIOLIN

Julia Fowler
2 Birch Court, Barnton
339 7463

Teaching is by the Suzuki method. Stress is laid on learning to listen as children learn to play by ear. Tuition can be individual or in small groups. Individual cost: £4 per ½ hr lesson. If child is part of a small group cost is £20 to £30 for 10 lessons. Best time to book: June/July for autumn session. Ms Fowler also teaches 3-5 yr olds attending the New Town Nursery on Wed am.

PLAY CENTRES

Jack Kane Centre
208 Niddrie Mains Rd, Niddrie
669 0404

Mon, Thurs 4-5, after-school play session for under 10s with 'Marvin the Monkey' inflatable, plus hoppers and swing balls. Cost 10p. Due to the presence of older children this is probably best suited to the over 4s. During the school holidays play sessions take place Mon-Fri 10-12, 2-4. See 'Activities for Parents, Sports Centres' for more information.

Little Marco's
Marco's Leisure Centre,
51-95 Grove St, Haymarket
228 2141
Mon-Fri, Sun 9.30-8; Sat 9.30-9

Members' children £1 for 1½ hr, non-members' children £1.50. Except Sat and Sun 1-5 (peak-time) when charge goes up to £1.50/£2; and Mon-Fri 9.30-4, 50p/75p when parent using other Marco's facility. See 'Activities for Parents. Specific Sports Activities, Keep Fit/Aerobics'.

Children's indoor adventure playground with lots of large play apparatus — slides, tunnels to crawl through, soft play area, large ball pool — as well as slot rides, mini space-invaders, a non-stop cartoon theatre and a roller derby. Best suited to children aged 2 up. With under 4s pick a quiet time as over 5s can be over-powering. In one corner is a small sitting area for Mums and Dads — perhaps the best place for quiet breastfeeding. Nappy change surface in ladies' toilets.

Supervision is probably best done by parents, although there are normally 4 staff on duty, and this goes up to 10 or more on Sat and Sun afternoons. Little Marco's can be used also by toddler groups and playgroups as a treat at a cost of £1.50/child for 2 hrs play plus still-orange drink for kids. Contact Caroline Rumney 228 2141 ext 44/46 to book. Free supervision can be arranged if parents want to use Marco's — book in advance.

Parties hosted in the snack-bar next to the play area in Little Marco's. See 'Birthdays and Celebrations'. See also 'Creches while Shopping' and 'Pre-school Play and Education' for more information on Little Marco's.

Bar/Cafe (downstairs)
Mon-Sat 9 am-m'night
£, Breastfeeding permitted, bottles heated, children's portions, feeder beakers.

Self-service bar/cafe with large comfy seating area. Food served includes burgers, quiche, salads, soups etc.

Meadowbank Sports Centre
139 London Rd, Meadowbank
661 5351

Soft play equipment available to 2½-10 yr olds, and disabled people of any age. Mon, Fri 10-5; Tues, Wed 10-12; Thurs 10-4, 60p/child. Equipment includes giant building blocks, balls cylinders, a slide and a maze, all made of plastic-covered foam, so that there are no hard surfaces or sharp edges. Children have fun while developing movement skills. Can be booked by groups at £3/hr, free for disabled people. Book at least 14 days in advance. See 'Activities for Parents, Sports Centres'.

RIDING

All the stables mentioned below recommend wearing warm clothes: gloves, scarves, jackets, etc. Opinions vary as to footwear with some favouring wellies for leg protection, while others prefer footwear with a small heel. Stretchy trousers are better than jeans as a stiff fabric can rub the skin. Stables stress that children should not be pushed into riding against their will.

Silverknowes Riding Centre
Muirhouse Parkway, Silverknowes
332 7777

Age 3 up. Lessons on Fri 3.30 or afternoons by arrangement. £3 for ½ hr. Wellies recommended.

Tower Farm Riding Stables
85 Liberton Dr, Liberton
664 3375

Age 4 up. Beginners' classes Sat, Sun 12 noon; Tues, Fri 4.15 for 1 hour. £5/class for under 10s. Flat shoes with small heel recommended.

Weftmuir Riding Centre

Totley Wells Grange, Nr South Queensferry
331 2990

Age 3 up, £2.50 for ½ hr class. Under 3s can.have a brief shot on a pony for no charge.

SKATING

Murrayfield Ice Rink

Riversdale Cres, Murrayfield
337 6933

Beginners are advised to start with group tuition available to all ages (parents at same time as children) from a professional skater on Sun 10-11.30; Wed 5.15-7.15. £1 admission plus 30p skate hire. Skates available from children's size 8. Beginners' sessions without tuition also available, 70p plus skate hire.

SKI-ING

Hillend Ski Centre

Biggar Rd, Hillend
445 4433

Open year-round 9.30-9. Largest artificial slope in Europe with chairlift. Cafe and toilets. Min age for instruction is 6 yrs. Under 5s with parental supervision are admitted only by special permission of the management. Equipment for hire is not suitable for under 5s. Chairlift can be used by sightseers.

SWIMMING

Most babies love moving in water once the initial fear of being uncovered has gone. Swimming is an excellent way of exercising the body and more and more parents are introducing their children to the pleasures of water early in life. Safety is another motivating factor.

Opinions vary as to when to start your child off (3 mths is probably the average), but whenever you start, here are a few things to remember:

Have a healthy respect for the dangers of water. Always stay near to your child when she is in or near water.

Allow at least 1 hour after a feed before entering the water. Respect your child's wishes. Do not force her into the water if she dislikes it. Wait and try again in a week or so. Babies get chilled easily. Take them out at the first signs of cold

What to wear. Most local parents dress babies in towelling pants, while toddlers often wear miniature bathing suits. Nappies are far too cumbersome when wet.

Buoyancy Aids. Small arm bands are available. The type with 2 (or more) air chambers and non-returnable valves are safest. The triangular type with a flat section next to the body will stop your child wobbling too much. (Available from the Early Learning Centre, sports shops etc.) Remember: arm bands are not life savers.

Classes for Under 5s. Of the pools in Edinburgh the Commonwealth, Portobello, Dalry and Dunfermline College currently run classes for babies and young children. All must be booked in advance. (When Warrender Baths reopen in April 1987 it too will run children's classes.)

These early classes are intended to develop your child's confidence and

92

pleasure in the water. They teach some of the basic skills, leading towards learning to swim, and show parents how they can help their children.

As regards a proper stroke, experts say that it is better to let under 5s develop their own way of swimming, through playing regularly in water. Perfecting a stroke can come later. In fact the longer you leave it, the quicker they learn. The Amateur Swimming Association publishes a useful booklet called 'Babes in the Water' (£4+P&P), available from the ASA, Derby Square, Loughborough.

POOLS GUIDE

General Notes (Please read these first)

1) Closing times given in this section refer to the time you are required to leave the water — pools close 20 mins later. Last tickets are usually sold 20 mins before the water exit time; eg if the time given is 3.40, you must arrive at the pool by 3.20 at the latest to gain entry.

2) Water temperature is 83-84°, unless otherwise stated.

3) All pools have showers and hairdryers. Hairdryers all take 5p coins.

4) At most pools it is possible to hire towels. In an emergency, costumes may also be available. At Portobello the charge is £2 (deposit) plus 40p.

5) In general the admission charge entitles you to unlimited swimming time. However, when pools are busy eg during school holidays, they may run sessions of limited duration — usually 40 mins.

6) During holidays opening times may vary. Many pools have special activities at certain times of year (eg galas, inflatables in the pool) so it's always best to check in advance.

7) All pools without cafeterias have hot drinks machines.

Dalry Baths
Caledonian Cres, Dalry nr Haymarket
667 7211 — ask for Dalry Baths
Mon-Fri 12-1.20; Tues, Thurs, Fri 5.30-6.40, 7-7.40; Sat 9-3.40; Sun 9-11.40 (Sat, Sun 40 min sessions in operation starting on the hour)
Adults 35p, children 3-16 yrs 20p, OAPs free.

Victorian baths with changing cubicles round the pool, where you can leave both clothes and pushchairs. Extra changing area for ladies at one end. Playpen on poolside. Classes. 'Mums and Tots' session on Tues 1.30-2 with a teacher in attendance. Book in advance — £4.40 for 8 lessons. Babies and pre-school children together.

Dunfermline College of Physical Education
Cramond Rd Nth, Edinburgh EH4 6JD
336 6506

The college runs classes for 'Parents and Babies' (3 mths-2 yrs) and 'Parents and Toddlers' (2½-5 yrs) during the school year. Book in advance for a course of 5 or 6 ½ hr lessons, costing £4.60 and £5.50 respectively. (There is a booking form at the end of their activities leaflet. When writing for a leaflet enclose a large SAE.)

The college is modern and almost entirely on 1 level. There are no playpens in the changing area but you can take pushchairs in. There are sockets so you can use your own hairdryer; no hairdryers are provided. There are no lockers (you leave your clothes in the cubicles) so it's best to leave valuables at home.

During the summer the pool is open to the public: Sat 3-6; Sun 4.30-6. Adults 55p children 45p.

The college cafeteria which serves snack meals at reasonable prices is open to college users. No highchairs but pushchairs are allowed in. See 'Annual Events' for school holiday activities, and 'Activities for Parents, Sports Centres' for adult classes with creche.

Glenogle Baths

Glenogle Rd, Stockbridge
667 7211 — ask for Glenogle Baths
Mon, Wed, Fri 12-7.40; Tues, Thurs 12-3.30, 5.30-6.40, 7-7.40; Sat 10-3.40 (sessions starting on the hour); Sun 9-11.40. During the summer, sessions in operation starting on the hour.
Adults 35p, children 3-16 yrs 20p, OAPs free.

Victorian baths with cubicles round the pool — you can leave clothes and pushchairs. Lots of stairs up to cash desk and pool, but help available on request (staff very obliging). Playpen on poolside. Temperature 80°.

Infirmary St Baths

Infirmary St, nr South Bridge
667 7211 — ask for Infirmary St Baths
Mon-Fri 8-7.40; Sat 9-3.40
Adults 35p, children 20p, OAPs free.

Airy Victorian baths with changing cubicles round the pool. Pool is upstairs, but staff very helpful. Ask at cash-desk for help with pushchair. Regulars say water is warmer here! Playpen on poolside.

Portobello Baths

Bellfield St, Portobello (entrance on Promenade)
667 7211 — ask for Portobello Baths
Mon-Fri 9-7.40; Sat, Sun 9-3.40. Sessions only if busy
Adults 35p, children 3-16 yrs 20p, OAPs free, spectators 20p.

Victorian baths with lots of amenities: large pool, small pool, health and fitness room with exercise and weights machines, Turkish baths, aerotone (an older form of jacuzzi), and cafeteria. Smaller pool has been imaginatively retiled and decorated and is used by children. 2 playpens on poolside. Changing areas: Gents on ground floor; Ladies' area, upstairs, has a playpen, changing table and large bin. Doors lock automatically — you memorise the number. Pushchairs must be left in the attendants' room at the entrance. Prams can be brought in by special request via a side entrance, and must be parked at the foot of the stair.

Classes: On Mon and Wed 2.40-3.10 there are informal 'Under 5s Fun' sessions with a teacher in attendance. Lessons are available on Tues and Thurs afternoons, cost 55p/lesson.

Refreshment Room

657 2210
Mon-Fri 9.45-7; Sat, Sun 9.45-3.15
£, High chairs (2), breastfeeding permitted, bottles heated, feeder beakers, parties hosted.

Small self-service cafeteria run by a co-operative of local Mums. Snacks and light meals are served: soups, salads, pizza, home-baking etc. Vegetarian choices always on the menu. Wide range of drinks including herbal teas. Kiddies' corner with toys and books. See also 'Birthdays and Celebrations'.

♒ Royal Commonwealth Pool
Dalkeith Rd, Newington
667 7211
Mon-Fri 9-8.40; Sat, Sun 10-3.40
Adults 65p, children 3-16 yrs 45p, OAPs 10p, spectators 20p. Children under 3 are free; accompanying adults pay 65p (10p of this charge is the key deposit, refunded when you leave).

A modern centre with the following amenities: large competition-sized pool, shallow teaching pool, diving pool with 2 boards, health and fitness room equipped with exercise and weights machines, solarium, sauna, large cafeteria and creche (at certain times). See 'Activities for Parents' for classes with creche. For reasons of hygiene pushchairs must be left in the foyer. Padlocks and chains are provided — keys obtained from the pay desk. The changing rooms are down a steep flight of stairs. The ladies' area has high-chairs (you can take these into your cubicle), playpens, nappy bins and a nappy-change table in row A. Hand driers are available in an attractive mirrored area, in addition to the wall mounted driers. Lockers must be locked with your key. Dads can have high chairs transferred to their area on request. Buggies are available downstairs for sleeping babies. The teaching pool is usually occupied by young children, and many parents change their babies' clothes on the wide shelf surrounding the pool, so they stay uncovered for the minimum time. The teaching pool temperature is 85°-86°, and even higher when babies' classes are scheduled. Playpen on poolside; chairs for spectators.

Classes for under 5s are available during term time and must be booked and paid for in advance. £4.40 for a course of 8 25 min lessons. Children are grouped in classes by age. Toilets are available upstairs and down.

Cafeteria
Mon-Fri 9-9 (main meals served 11.30-6.30); Sat, Sun 10-4.
£, High chairs (8), bottles heated, feeder beakers, parties hosted.

Spacious self-service cafeteria selling snacks and hot food at reasonable cost. Hot rolls available all day. After 6.30 pm pies, sausage rolls etc are available. Mothers wishing to breastfeed are usually directed to a nearby toilet. See also 'Birthdays and Celebrations'.

Victoria Baths
Junction Pl, Leith
667 7211 — ask for Leith Baths
Mon-Fri 9-7.40 (from 3-7 pm, sessions starting on the hour); Sat 9-3.40. During summer sessions in operation starting on the hour
Adults 35p, children 3-16 yrs 20p, OAPs free till 5 pm, spectators 20p.

Victorian baths with cubicles around the pool, plus ladies' locker room at the shallow end. (Lockers lock automatically, on closing — you memorise number,) Locker-room has table for changing babies. Playpen on poolside. Prams must be left at entrance but pushchairs are allowed on poolside.

Warrender Baths
Thirlestane Rd, Marchmont
667 7211 — ask for Warrender Baths

Closed for extensive renovations at the time of going to print. When reopened in April 1987 it will run ladies' sessions and children's classes.

Wester Hailes Education Centre Pool

5 Murrayburn Dr, Wester Hailes
442 4217

Mon, Tues, Thurs, Fri 9.30-9.10; Wed 9.30-8.10; Sat 10.30-4.30; Sun 9.30-4.30. These closing times are all 'water exit' times. Last admissions are 40 mins before this. Hour long sessions starting at 10 to, 10 past, and ½ past the hour. The colour of your band indicates the session you belong to. When the light goes on behind your colour on the indicator board, you must leave the water. In summer the pool is open longer.

Adults 60p, children 3-16 yrs 32p, OAPs 32p (5p is the key deposit refunded as you leave).

A modern pool operated by Lothian Region. Amenities include a large pool, a children's pool, a diving pool with 2 boards, and a cafeteria. The children's pool is graded in depth so small children can touch the bottom at one end. There are large plastic animals in and around the pool, also a mushroom house with slide into water. (Children under 4 must be supervised on the slide.) Changing areas: Ladies' area has playpens. These are taken to the poolside or into the gents' area on request. Lockers lock automatically on closure, so beware of locking the key inside. The ladies has a large mirrored area with power points, so you can use your own hairdryer. Pushchairs can be taken into the changing area and left with the attendants. See 'Activities for Parents' for adult activities with creche.

Cafeteria
Mon-Fri 9-9; Sat, Sun 9.30-4
£, High chairs (2), breastfeeding permitted, bottles heated, parties hosted.

Small self-service cafeteria offering a basic and inexpensive range of snacks and meals: egg, chips, salads etc. Toilets in cafeteria. See also 'Birthdays and Celebrations'.

FAMILY SWIMMING
During the summer holidays Wester Hailes runs family sessions. During the year Trinity Academy, Craigroyston Community High, Portobello High and Drummond High Schools all offer evening swimming sessions to families as part of the Community Education programme. Tel 229 9166 ext 2124 for up-to-date information. Dunfermline College can be booked by playgroups etc at weekends for family sessions.

SWIMMING IN THE SEA
The Edinburgh beaches from Cramond to Portobello are generally reasonably clean, but are unlikely to be consistently clear of sewage debris until about 1990. (They do not meet current EEC standards on the quality required of bathing waters). The area from Fisherrow to Port Seton is badly contaminated. On the Lothian coast the cleanest places to swim are Gosford Sands, Gullane Sands, Gullane Bay, Broad Sands, Peffer Sands and Ravensheugh Sands. It's OK to paddle at Dunbar and North Berwick but swimming may take you into fouler waters.

TRAMPOLINING

Windsor Leisure Centre
7a Windsor Pl, Portobello
669 1075
Tues-Fri 10-12, 2-6; Sat 10-6, Sun 12-6

An indoor centre housing floor-level trampolines, one bounceabout and a ball pool. Also snack-bar and toilets. Cost: £1 for ½ hr on 1 trampoline. (max of 2 children/trampoline.) It is always best to book in advance. For children aged 2-12. Children usually bounce bare-foot or in socks. The ball-pool is available for use before and after sessions.

Mother and Toddler session on Thurs 10.30-11.30. Cost: 50p/toddler. Saturday Club on Sat 10-12. £1 for 2 hrs use of centre, including cartoon show at 11 am.

Snack-bar
£, High chair, breastfeeding permitted, parties hosted.

Informal snack-bar selling crisps, biscuits, juice and hot drinks only. See also 'Birthdays and Celebrations'.

Activities for Parents

You could write a whole book on this subject alone! Clearly we do not have enough space here to include everything, so we have selected those activities which provide creche facilities. As a result we cover mostly daytime classes. However a wide variety of evening classes is provided in Edinburgh by many institutions. You will find some of these listed below under 'Further Sources of Information on Adult Classes'.

The advent of Women's Committees in the Councils of Edinburgh District and Lothian Region has brought the problems of women, and therefore also of parents, into sharper focus. This has led to a welcome increase in the provision of creche facilities, especially for women. Provision specifically for Dads is thin on the ground, but they can often use the creches supplied for women. Fund-ing for creches tends to require renewal each year, especially those funded by Urban Aid and the Man-power Services Commission, so there is no guarantee that creches funded this year will be funded next. On the other hand perhaps the Councils' provision will increase. One can but hope.

Due to such inevitable changes this list cannot hope to be accurate, so please check on a particular activity in advance. Equally this list does not claim to be complete, so it would be worthwhile approaching your local school, community centre or further education college to ask what they have to offer. Community centres are also very pleased to receive requests for activities, and do their best to respond where there is sufficient demand. For other courses with childcare provision, see 'Child-care'.

CENTRES OFFERING A VARIETY OF ACTIVITIES

Balerno High School
5 Bridge Rd, Balerno
449 5833

The Community Education Department runs many daytime classes during termtime: swimming, keep-fit, yoga, disco-dancing, language and technical courses, drama, Open University short courses etc. Days and times vary as they depend on the availability of spare accommodation in the school. Creche available for most classes, 30p/child. Some activities also available during school holidays.

Craigroyston Community High School
Pennywell Rd, Craigroyston
332 7801 George Rubienski

Wide variety of daytime classes available, including typing, languages, pottery, dress-making, English, music etc. In all classes adults are taught with school pupils. Community lounge provided for adults to chat or study in. School has an Under 5s Centre available for the care of local children only. Parents are encouraged to settle their children into the Centre by a series of visits before starting their chosen classes.

Drumbrae Primary School
Ardshiel Ave, Drumbrae
Contact the Rannoch Centre 339 5351

The Parents' Association runs informal classes in crafts, dress-making, yoga, art and English. No separate creche, but children play in same room as adults.

Drummond High School
Cochran Ter, Canonmills
556 2651

All kinds of day and evening classes: languages, computing, dress-making, exercise, typing, painting, car mechanics, maths, physics etc. Creche during school hours, 30p/session.

Leith Community Education Resource Centre
4 Duncan Pl, Leith
554 1509 (9.30-1.30)

A variety of classes, mostly run in the morning: yoga, keep-fit, woodwork, dress-making, soft furnishing. Well-supervised creche, which takes children from a few mths old up to 4 yrs. Classes cost £5 for 10 week term.

Pentland Community Centre
Oxgangs Brae, Oxgangs
445 2871

Variety of classes. Those with creche are as follows: slimming, fitness, aerobics, and art. Free creche on Tues, Wed and Fri mornings.

St Brides Community Centre
Orwell Ter, Dalry
346 1405

Classes in art, photography, computers, yoga, country dancing etc. Also Well Woman Centre and Parents' Centre, described more fully under 'Women's Support Groups' and 'Parenting Classes and Discussion Groups' below. Creche every morning Mon-Fri. Some classes are free.

Stevenson College of Further Education
Bankhead Ave, Sighthill
453 6161

Huge variety of courses in science,

art, technology, trade skills, SCE subjects etc. Creche for children of students enrolled on full- or part-time courses. Takes children aged 1-5 yrs. See subheadings 'Fresh Start etc' and 'Women's Support Groups' below for additional information.

Telford College of Further Education
Crewe Toll
332 2491

Huge variety of courses: new technologies, trade skills, SCE subjects, recreation subjects etc. Considerable flexibility of method of study available: full-time, part-time, day release, block release, as well as 'flexistudy' and Open Learning which permit you to study at home or in college at times that suit you, and allow you to study at your own pace. The college creche takes 3-5 yr olds. Cost to students is 50p/morning or afternoon session. See also subheading 'Women's Support Groups' below.

Tollcross Community Centre
Tollcross Primary School, Fountainbridge
229 8448

Activities include judo, dressmaking, tapestry weaving, painting, badminton, computers, etc. Creche available for most daytime classes, 25p/session.

Wester Hailes Education Centre
5 Murrayburn Dr, Wester Hailes
442 2201

Modern school/community centre providing opportunities for all ages to study or play. Amenities include a library, art, drama and music studios, technical workshops, swimming pools, games hall, gymnasium, racquet sport courts, and cafeteria. Classes on offer include yoga, table tennis, judo, dance, typing, theatre arts, computing, chemistry, languages and home economics etc. In 'O' and 'H' grade courses adults are usually integrated with older school pupils. Recreational classes have adults only. Creche available throughout school hrs for children of adults on courses, 10p for 1¼ hrs. Age range: baby to 5 yrs. Book your class then check if creche space available. A user's card is necessary if you want to book facilities or hire equipment. See 'Activities for Children, Swimming' for information on the pools and cafeteria.

ARTS AND CRAFTS CLASSES

＊ Gorgie City Farm
51 Gorgie Rd, Gorgie
337 4202

Daytime and evening classes in arts, crafts and handiwork eg tapestry, clay-modelling etc. Inexpensive. Free creche for daytime classes with qualified supervision.

A. Oram
60 The Pleasance
337 8841

Daytime classes with creche, Mon-Fri 10-3. Life drawing, painting, still-life etc. All levels. Nine week course, ½-day £34, full-day £66. Discounts for students, OAPs and UB40s. Also evening classes available.

Triangle Arts Centre
West Pilton Bank, Pilton
332 0877 Candice

Variety of workshops: photography, ceramics, pottery, video, drama, Tai

Chi (a non-combat martial art) etc. Centre offers creche for at least 1 course, sometimes more. The Triangle also acts as a social centre for many age groups who are welcome to use facilities and organise informal activities for themselves.

Cafeteria
Mon-Fri 9.30-2
£, Bottles heated, breastfeeding permitted

Self-service cafe selling chips, hamburgers, soup, stovies etc. Also wholefood quiches, pizza, and scones from the Breadwinner Bakery. Toilets in cafe. Lots of schoolchildren at lunchtime.

Wilkie House
Guthrie St
225 2079

Beginners' classes in drama, art and dance; drawing and painting workshop for the unemployed; theatre group open to the mentally-handicapped. All free. Free creche Mon-Fri 9.30-4.30.

ENGLISH CLASSES

Neighbourhood English Teaching (NET)
Leith Adult Education Centre, 4 Duncan Pl, Leith
554 7144 Flick Thorpe

NET provides classes for adults in Edinburgh who speak English as a second language. Classes are free and are held in schools and community centres all over the city: Corstorphine, Newington, Leith, Dalry, Tollcross, Wester Hailes and Canonmills. A creche is available for most classes. Home tuition is also available on a one-to-one basis. Contact Elizabeth Currie, The Roundabout

Centre, 4b Gayfield Pl EH7 4AB, 556 1168. See also below the 'Roundabout Centre' under the subheading 'Women's Support Groups'.

FRESH START COURSES FOR THE UNEMPLOYED

These courses aim to ease the transition back to employment. They help you to build on past experiences, learn how to learn, find out where your talents and interests lie, and help you to take the next step either into further training or employment. The courses described here either provide childcare facilities or make you eligible for a training allowance from the Manpower Services Commission. A course without childcare is run by The Adult Learning Project, 184 Dalry Rd, Dalry, 337 5442.

Second Chance to Learn
Edinburgh University Settlement, Wilkie House, Guthrie St
226 3801 Prue Pullen

Free course for unemployed adults who left school with no educational qualifications. 2 days a week for 10 weeks. Creche available 9-5. Courses in creative writing and communicating better are also run as an extension of the basic course.

Extra-mural Department
University of Edinburgh, 11 Buccleuch Pl, Newington
667 1011

'Wider Opportunities for Women' is 6 week full-time course for women over 19 who have not worked outside the home for 2 yrs. Participants are eligible for a TOPS allowance. Contact Joanna Highton 667 1011 ext 6397 or 6523 (evenings and weekends 667 6097).

The Department also runs the 'New Horizons' course for men and women over 21. However no creche or allowance is available for this programme.

Stevenson College of Further Education
Bankhead Ave, Sighthill
453 6161

'Wider Opportunities for Women' course with creche for 1-5 yr olds.

PARENTING CLASSES AND DISCUSSION GROUPS

For groups for single parents, see 'Health Care Facilities, Problem Solving'

Craigmount High School Community Wing
Craigs Rd, Craigmount
339 8278 T McLean

Among its many informal activities the centre sometimes has a parents' discussion group. Creche is usually available Mon afternoons at a cost of 50p/child. See also below 'Women's Support Groups'.

Growing Up in Lothian
Contact Jennifer Brown 453 4042

A newly-formed offshoot of 'Growing up in Scotland' which aims to spread awareness of the needs of children, with particular emphasis on their home and community environments. The group's main activity at present is the promotion of the Open University packs on parenting and childcare, which they lend cheaply to groups and individuals. These packs start with

'Preparing for Pregnancy' and cover all stages of child development through to teenage. The group also has social meetings.

Life-saving Classes for Parents
See below 'Specific Sports Activities, Swimming, Summer Classes'

Montessori Diploma Course in Nursery Education
William Robertson Building, George Sq
441 2392 Jackie Ley

Evening course over 3 terms open to anyone interested in working with pre-school children, either in nursery schools and playgroups or as parents with their own children. Run by the London Montessori Centre.

The Parents' Centre
St Brides Community Centre, Orwell Ter, Dalry
337 5442 Gerri Kirkwood
Mon 9.30-11.30.

A centre which allows parents to come together and learn from each other's experience and support each other in practical ways. All activities are organised by the participants, and there are regular planning meetings where everyone can contribute to preparing the programme. Some activities are open, ie new people can join in at any stage. However the discussion group closes after the initial 2 weeks of a programme. Activities are free; membership of St Brides costs 50p; creche costs 20p a time.

PARENTS' DROP-IN CENTRES
The aim of these centres is to provide somewhere local to meet other parents, and somewhere to turn with problems.

Broomhouse Neighbourhood Centre

79-89 Broomhouse Cres, Broomhouse
443 7795 Pauline Marengin
Fri 1-3 during the school year.

Creche caters for under 5s only. Parents can either leave children and go off to shop etc or socialise in the centre. There are at least 3 staff to look after the children. Cost 50p for 2 hrs.

The Harbour

5b Hailesland Pl, Wester Hailes
442 2474
Mon-Fri 9-5.

Well-staffed creche. Children from birth to over 5s. Centre is open to all parents in Wester Hailes and the immediate vicinity. Parents (all Mums at present) run the centre themselves, arranging activities (swimming, daytrips, videos, etc.) and choosing topics for discussion.

The Middle House

Ainslie Park High Schoolhouse, 206 Crewe Rd Nth
Contact Pamela Murphy or Heather
552 2884
Wed 11-4.

Specifically for teenage parents aged 16-20 with children under 5. A chance to meet other young parents and join in activities. Also help with DHSS problems, and generally someone to listen. Help with children.

Muirhouse Under Twelves and Parent Centre

Silverknowes Primary School, Muirhouse Gdns
336 5527 Willie McPherson or Josie Auld

Informal social centre offering support, help and friendship to parents.

Activities include keep-fit, swimming and outings. Most are free. No creche as such, but staff help parents with children.

Sycamore Centre

St Catherine's Argyll Church Hall, Grange Rd, Grange
667 3994 Margaret Dunbar or Church Hall 667 7220
Thurs 10.30-4.

Drop-in centre for all ages, and not just for parents. Children welcome — toys available although no creche. Aerobics class on Thurs lunchtime, with children in same room.

Women's Flat

20/1 Muirhouse Park, Muirhouse
336 4804 Heather

Centre open to all local Mums offering a place to meet people and get support with parenting. Lots of activities organised by women themselves. Past topics have included depression, numeracy, nutrition and childcare.

SPORTS CENTRES

We outline below only the centres which offer cheaper membership and regular creches ie the public centres. It is worth becoming a member if you intend to become a regular user. Many of these centres offer special rates to the unemployed, disabled and OAPs. See also above 'Centres Offering a Variety of Activities, Wester Hailes Education Centre'.

Craiglockhart Sports Centre

177 Colinton Rd, Craiglockhart
443 0101/2

Mon-Fri 9 am-11 pm (last booking 10 pm); Sat, Sun 9 am-10.30 pm (last booking 9 pm).

This is the city's main public centre for racquet sports with indoor facilities for tennis, badminton and squash as well as archery, fencing, yoga, keep-fit. There are also several outdoor tennis courts and a boating pond. No cafeteria, but the space set aside for it can be hired for birthday parties. Facilities are all on the same level so there are no tricky stairs.

Membership for adults, £7.70/yr; family membership, £13.75 (Covers 2 adults and children.)

Creche available Tues, Wed, Thurs 10-12 for participants in the Ladies' Club, 60p/child. Qualified creche staff. At the Club aerobics/keep-fit, squash, badminton, and tennis are available for a try-out fee of £1.50. Thereafter it costs 90p plus membership of the centre. The Ladies' Club also operates without creche on Tues and Thurs 7.30-9.30 pm.

Dunfermline College of Physical Education
Cramond Rd Nth, Edinburgh EH4 6JD
336 6506

'Dunf' runs a variety of daytime and evening courses for adults throughout the year. Times and days vary slightly from term to term but the basic range of classes is the same. All courses must be booked and paid for in advance. The adult fitness course includes jogging, calisthenics and circuit-training and is suitable for beginners and advanced students. Sessions are held 3 or 4 times per week with creche available for the morning sessions.

Cost: on average £1.80/week, plus 65p/child for creche. The ladies' aerobics class is a 1 hour session of fun and fitness to music. Cost: £1/session, plus 40p/child for creche. There are also evening courses in ski fitness (autumn only) and 'jazzercise' with no creche. For information about swimming at DCPE see 'Activities for Children, Swimming'; 'Specific Sports Activities, Swimming' below.

Jack Kane Centre
208 Niddrie Mains Rd, Niddrie
669 0404
Mon-Sun 9 am-10.30 pm (last booking 9.30 pm)

Facilities available for badminton, judo, keep-fit, gymnastics, football, basketball, weight-training, lacrosse, hockey, tennis, volleyball etc. Membership: adults, £7.35/yr, families £13. Creche for under 5s is available free of charge to women participating in the Ladies' Fitness classes, Mon and Wed 10-11.30. (Dads can use the creche too.) The class costs 30p for members, 90p for non-members, 20p for unemployed, and is taught by a qualified instructor. You do not have to be superfit to take part. No cafetaria at present, but there are moves afoot to reopen it. See also 'Activities for Children, Play Centres'.

McLeod Street Centre
22 McLeod St, Dalry
337 3252

Independent sports centre where activities available include football, ladies' and men's keep-fit and basketball, mixed circuit-training, weight-training, ladies' badminton. No creche but parents can take turns to look after children. Classes cost £1; activities £7.50/hr, shared among participants.

Meadowbank Sports Centre

139 London Rd, Meadowbank
661 5351
Mon-Sun 9 am-11.45 pm (last booking 9.30 pm)

Excellent centre on 3 floors built for the 1970 Commonwealth Games. Facilities for 30 sports including racquet sports, yoga, fencing, judo, football etc. There are several sports halls, fitness rooms, squash courts as well as a 400m outdoor athletics track. Facilities are well sign-posted from the entrance hall. Access easy due to ramp outside, and doors are just wide enough for a double buggy. Lift for disabled is also available to parents. There are toilets on all floors.

Membership: adults £12.50/yr, families £20 (covers any number of children). Creche provided in Hall 4, Mon-Fri 9.30-12, 2-4. Good range of toys, plenty of space, carpeted floor. Never less than 2 staff. Qualified nursery nurse in charge. 60p/child/session.

Bookings. You can either book activities as an individual or join one of the many activity groups within Meadowbank which have sessions booked for set times each week. The Ladies' Club for example reserves squash courts, Hall 1 and a fitness studio on Tues 9-12, 2-4 and Thurs 9-12. Cost £1/session, plus centre membership. You choose your activity when you arrive. See also 'Activities for Children, Play Centres'.

Cafeteria
Mon-Sun 10 am-9.30 pm
£, Bottles heated.

Self-service cafe serving snacks, light meals and ices. Children are welcome and there is plenty of room for buggies. Staff request that parents stop their children running around in the temptingly large entrance. Toilets close by.

SPECIFIC SPORTS ACTIVITIES

This section is essentially a supplement to 'Sports Centres' above. See also above 'Centres Offering a Variety of Activities', and below, 'Classes and Courses for Women Only'.

BADMINTON

An informal activity widely and cheaply available in many church halls and community centres as well as at the following venues. In the main it is mums who participate.

Corstorphine Youth Centre

Kirk Loan, Corstorphine
334 8956 Brenda McLean
Mon-Thurs 9.30-11.30 am

Children in separate room supervised by mums not on court.

Rannoch Centre

6 Rannoch Ter, Clermiston
339 5351 Faye Stevens
Tues, Thurs 10-12.30

Creche available 10-11.30, 25p/child. Also mixed badminton Fri 7-10 pm — older children come too and amuse themselves in centre.

DANCE

Evening classes for adults are widely available — see 'Activities for Children' for a list of teachers. The following welcome accompanying children in some way:

105

Manor Ballet School
4 Manor Pl
225 6456

Ballet, modern, keep-fit and aerobics for all stages. Daytime and evening. Creche by arrangement.

Rebecca Walker Dance Studios
14 Orwell Ter, Dalry
337 0748

Tap, ballet and exercise classes to all levels. Free informal creche by arrangement.

Kicks
Classes in Goldenacre and Stockbridge
552 7613 Carole Robertson

Multi-dance/exercise classes for all ages. Young children may attend if in prams or buggies.

KEEP-FIT/AEROBICS

Bodytalk Fitness Centre
Semple St, Fountainbridge
228 2426
Mon, Wed 10.45-11.30

Aerobics is the only activity here for which creche is provided. Other activities include jazz, ballet, self-defence, yoga and karate. £1.75/class.

Heriot-Watt University Sports Centre
Riccarton Campus, nr Riccarton
449 5111
Mon 10.15-11.15

Cost: £1 (80p for members). Creche costs 50p and is only provided at this time. Other activities available at the centre include squash, tennis, table-tennis, football and multi-gym. 'City membership' is available to the public.

Jack Kane Centre
See 'Sports Centres' above.

Marco's Leisure Centre
Grove St, Haymarket
228 2141

Aerobics and Stretch and Tone, Mon-Fri mornings. Free creche in Little Marco's for under 4s — book 2 days in advance. For classes and activities at other times (eg lunch-time work-out, afternoon aerobics, jazz-exercise, squash, multi-gym, yoga etc) creche for under 4s costs £1/hour, while over 4s get ½-price entry to Little Marco's. Book two days in advance for under 4s.

Muirhouse Under Twelve and Parent Centre
Silverknowes Primary School, Muirhouse Gdns, Muirhouse
336 5527
Keep-fit Thurs 1.30-2.30. Women only, 40p. Childcare provided.

Ratho Community Centre
Off Main St, Ratho
333 1055
Ladies' keep-fit, Fri 9.30-10.30. 70p plus 20p/child for creche.

Sighthill Community Centre
Sighthill Wynd
453 6078 Sheila Brown
Aerobics Fri 10.30-11.30. Creche available if requested in advance.

SKATING

Murrayfield Ice Rink
Riversdale Cres, Murrayfield
337 6933

Beginners are advised to start with group tuition, available to adults and children together, Sun 10-11.30 am and Wed 5.15-7.15 pm. £1 admission plus 30p for skate hire.

(Sizes start at child's 8.) A 'Mum-skate' is run Tues and Thurs 10-12. (No creche.)

SWIMMING

Some parents find evenings the easiest time to swim, but for day-time swimmers both the Royal Commonwealth Pool and Portobello Pool provide creche facilities: at RCP Mon-Fri 9-3; and at Portobello Mon-Fri 9-1. Cost is 30p/hour/child. In addition Leith Baths have a 'Women only' session on Fri 2-3 with free creche for children aged 18 mths to 5 yrs.

Classes:

Adult classes are available in Edinburgh for beginners, 'improvers' and those interested in swimming for fitness, although the full range is not available at each pool. All the pools except Infirmary St offer classes of some sort. Most are run in the evening, however daytime classes are available on weekdays for adult beginners and improvers at the Commonwealth Pool and at Portobello, while Wester Hailes runs adult classes on Sat. All classes must be booked in advance, except at Glenogle where you can just turn up at the class time and ask for a lesson. Classes at the Commonwealth Pool, Dalry, Portobello and Wester Hailes must be paid in full in advance. At Glenogle and Leith you pay 95p as you go along. Cost: £8.80 for a course of eight 25 min lessons (£7.60 at Commonwealth and Portobello). £9 at Wester Hailes for ten 40 min lessons. This covers further swimming at your leisure after the lesson.

Dunfermline College of Physical Education in Cramond also runs swimming classes for adults of all abilities. The charge for a course of 6 lessons is £6. Write to DCPE, Cramond Rd Nth, Edinburgh EH4 6JD for details. Enclose a large SAE. During the summer the college also runs intensive learn-to-swim courses as well as individual lessons.

Swimming for fitness

Contact the Commonwealth Pool or Dalry Baths 667 7211.

Summer classes

Over the summer intensive courses are offered in swimming, diving etc. They usually involve daily lessons over a 2 week period. A course in lifesaving is also run during the summer catering mainly for parents who want to learn what to do in an emergency situation. It covers the potential dangers of water, basic rescue skills and resuscitation techniques. (Throughout the year bronze medallion classes are run, mostly at Dalry. Currently there is a waiting list.) Phone Commonwealth Pool for details 667 7211.

Swim and Trim

Commonwealth. Under this scheme women book in advance for a course of 10 hr-long sessions in the Health and Fitness Room under qualified supervision. They can then have a swim. Cost: 85p/session, plus 30p/child for creche.

Portobello. Ladies-only sessions in the Fitness Room, Mon-Fri 9-11. No booking required. £2.75/session (£2 is the deposit for the equipment key and is refunded.) After 11 am room is open to men also. Creche: Mon-Fri 9-1, 30p.

For further information on the Edinburgh pools see 'Activities for Children, Swimming' and 'Classes and courses for Women Only'.

WOMEN'S SUPPORT GROUPS

The first of these to appear in Edinburgh started after the Scottish Women's Health Fair in 1983. Women get together informally to share their experiences and ideas on health and on coping with life in general. Each group is open to women of all ages, and you don't have to be ill to go along. Most groups have prearranged programmes of discussion and activities with topics suggested by group members eg PMT, AIDS, make-up, welfare rights, parenting etc. All welcome new faces and some offer woman-to-woman support with problems. Creche facilities are available at most groups, often free of charge. See also above 'Parents' Drop-In Centres' and 'Health and Hospitals'.

Craigmount High Community Wing
Craigs Rd, Craigmount
339 8278

Women's group Wed 9.30-11.30. Creche when funds available.

Crosswinds Centre
Earl Grey St, Tollcross
229 0321

Women and Health group Wed 10-12. 1 hr keep-fit and 1 hr discussion on prearranged topic, with break for coffee in between.

Drummond Community High School
Cochran Ter, Canonmills
556 2651

Women Talk Tues 10-12. Creche 30p/child.

Edinburgh University
The Societies Centre, 60 The Pleasance
Contact the Societies Centre to find out group leader 667 1011 Ext 4514

Women's group Thurs 7.30-9.30. No creche. Open to non-students.

Gylemuir Primary School
Wester Broom Pl, Wester Broom
334 7138

Women's group, Tues 1.15-2.45. Creche. Group meets in one of the school huts.

Roundabout International Centre (YWCA)
4b Gayfield Pl
Contact Randi Eden 447 8749 or the centre 557 4695

The Roundabout is open Mon-Fri 9-5 and provides a centre where women from abroad can meet and make new friends. Excellent creche Mon-Fri 9-5. Many organised activities including the following: Wed and Fri 10-12 social meetings — chat, coffee, knitting, sewing, cookery; Mon, Tues, Thurs, Fri 10-12 English classes. (See also above under subheading 'English Classes').

Royston Wardieburn Community Centre
Pilton Drive Nth, Pilton
552 5700

Women's group, Wed 1.30-3. Programme includes discussion, activities, demonstrations and visits. Women and Health group, Tues 1.30-3 — health topics.

St Brides Community Centre
Orwell Ter, Dalry
337 5543

Well Woman Centre, Tues 9.30-12 with free creche. Also Wed 7.30-9.30 pm — no creche.

Tollcross Community Centre
Tollcross Primary School, Fountainbridge
229 8448

Women and Well-being Group, Tues 10-11.30. Creche 25p.

Young Women's Group
St Philip's Church Hall, Brunstane Rd Nth, Portobello
669 6315 Pam Donaldson

Group meets every 2nd Wed 9.45-11.15. Wide programme of topics. Creche. £1.50/year membership.

Many churches have **Young Wives Groups** which meet regularly, often in the evenings. You usually do not need to be a church member.

CLASSES AND COURSES FOR WOMEN ONLY

The following list comprises mostly classes with creche. For an up-to-date list of classes run by the Community Education service 229 9166 Ext 2124. For ladies' exercise classes etc, see above 'Specific Sports Activities' and 'Sports Centres'.

ANTE-NATAL EXERCISE CLASSES

Catero Hawkins
78 Polwarth Ter, Polwarth
337 8474
Mon 10.30-11.45

Mostly exercise and relaxation with some discussion. Exercises are mainly based on yoga positions. Suitable for mums-to-be who are more than 14 week's pregnant. £8 for 4 lessons. No creche.

DRAMA, DANCE ETC

Women Live
Tollcross Community Centre, Tollcross Primary School, Fountainbridge
228 1669 Michelle Gunn

Classes are run occasionally in drama, relaxation, art, dance etc. No experience necessary. All ages. Creche 25p. The group also organises events and performances eg during the 'Spring Fling', usually with creche.

POST-NATAL EXERCISE CLASSES

Marco's Leisure Centre
51 Grove St, Haymarket
228 2141 or contact Gill Waterman 336 3860/339 4844

Fri 10.30-11.30. Free creche in Little Marco's for under 4s — book 2 days in advance. £1.75 (£1.25 to members).

SELF-DEFENCE FOR WOMEN

Classes with creche or in the evening are held in the following centres.

Pentland Community Centre
Oxgangs Brae, Oxgangs
445 2871 Clive Page

Tollcross Community Centre
Tollcross Primary School, Fountainbridge
229 8448

Wester Hailes Education Centre
5 Murrayburn Dr, Wester Hailes
442 2201

SWIMMING

Broughton Primary School
Broughton Rd, Canonmills
Contact Drummond Community
High School 556 2651
Mon 7-8, Thurs 8-9

Victoria Baths
Junction Pl, Leith
667 7211 ask for Leith Baths
Fri 2-3, 35p. Creche for 1½-5 yr olds. All attendants are also women.

TRAINING COURSES

Edinburgh Women's Training Centre
57 Jeffrey St
557 1139
Centre provides one-year full-time courses in computing and electronics for unemployed women over 25. No academic qualifications necessary. Course is free and attenders are given a weekly training allowance, plus travelling and childcare expenses. Advice on benefits and childcare available. Women do not have to be registered unemployed: single parents, married women returning to the job market after a long gap, and women facing redundancy are also eligible.

Stevenson College of Further Education
Bankhead Ave, Sighthill
453 6161
The college runs an 'Access to Technology' course for which no formal qualifications or scientific background is required. It covers electronic/electrical engineering and is a 15-mth full-time course for women over 25, which aims to take students up to the standard of basic grade technician. The college also runs a 'Wider Opportunities for Women' course. See above under subheading 'Fresh Start Courses' for more information on such courses. The college creche is available to children aged 1-5 yrs.

Telford College of Further Education
Crewe Toll
332 2491
Courses specially geared to women include 'Women in Technology' and 'Women's Health Studies'. The college creche takes children aged 3-5 yrs. For fuller information on Telford College see above under subheading 'Centres Offering a Wide Variety of Courses'.

FURTHER SOURCES OF INFORMATION ON ADULT CLASSES

The first place to try is your local high school, many of which are now offering classes to adults eg Ainslie Park, Broughton, Castlebrae etc. Two other excellent sources of information are the 'Edinburgh Advertiser' and the 'Evening News'. The following offer classes:

Adult Learning Project
184 Dalry Rd, Dalry
337 5442

Edinburgh Walk-in Numeracy Centre (EWINC)
67 Bread St, Tollcross
229 0382

Lothian Region Dept of Education
Community Education Service, 40 Torphichen St, Haymarket
229 9166 Ext 2124

Napier College
Colinton Rd, Merchison
444 2266 Ext 2573
Learning-by-appointment Centre

University of Edinburgh,
Dept of Extra-Mural Studies, 11
Buccleuch Pl, Newington
667 1011 Ext 6246 (667 6097 evenings and weekends)

Workers' Educational Association (WEA)
Riddle's Court, 322 Lawnmarket
226 3456

YWCA
Randolph Centre, 7 Randolph Pl
225 4379

111

Places to Visit

Places to visit; including art galleries, museums, historic buildings, animals in the city and boats, trains and planes.

We are lucky in Edinburgh to have a wealth of historical buildings, museums and art galleries. However many of these, due to their content, physical structure (eg 17th century tenements), or both, are unsuitable for young children. Here we have concentrated on those places which most children enjoy, and that you will therefore also enjoy, because of the intrinsic interest and the relaxed atmosphere. We have also listed some of the other better known attractions in the city giving an indication of what you may expect to find.

Unless specified, entry to the museum/art gallery is free, although you usually have to pay for special exhibitions but this is indicated within the building. 'Sights of Edinburgh' discount vouchers are given away with ticket purchases at the

tourist office and at many of the places mentioned here.

The police have asked us to remind parents of the importance of supervising young children wherever they are, for their own safety, and emphasize the importance of teaching small children 'not to go with strangers'.

For city centre locations, refer to map.

For further details on where to go/ what's on, see 'Sources of Information'.

ART GALLERIES

Children can be fascinated by paintings and sculpture, although holding them up to see properly and constantly telling them not to touch can be tiring.

The City Art Centre
2 Market St
225 2424 Ext 6650
Oct-May: Mon-Sat 10-5; June-Sept: Mon-Sat 10-6; Suns during Festival 2-5

Stages temporary exhibitions, often with a very broad appeal, and Scottish art work. Accessible with buggy and there is a lift behind the shop at the entrance. Toilets on ground floor are very small, but there is a very spacious disabled toilet. Friendly, helpful staff.

Cafe: See 'Eating Out in Central Edinburgh (8)'.

Fruitmarket Gallery
Market St
225 2383
Tues-Sat 10-5.30

A small contemporary art gallery. The long flight of steel steps between the ground and the 1st floor (no lift) makes access with a buggy very difficult. The staff are friendly though. Toilet is very small, no room to change or feed a baby.

Cafe (1st): Sells good expresso and delicious homebakes, salads and soups, but no high chairs or feeding cups.

National Gallery of Scotland
The Mound
556 8921
Mon-Sat 10-5; Sun 2-5. Longer during Festival

An outstanding collection of paintings, drawings and prints by the most famous artists from the Renaissance to the post-Impressionists. Also holds the national collection of Scottish Art. Buggies have easy access to most of the building. There is an entrance ramp and a lift at the back of the building to the lower ground floor and the back of the 1st floor. The toilet isn't large and has nowhere to change a nappy, but there's quite enough space to take a chair in (if you wanted to!).

Netherbow Arts Centre
High St
556 9579
Mon-Sat 10-4. Closed 1st fortnight in Sept

Children's theatre events are held here, eg stages a puppet festival every Easter. Also there are exhibitions in the galleries, up a flight of stairs (watch for unsafe railings). Ask at the box office/reception to use the theatre's dressingroom for nappy changing or breastfeeding.

Cafe: see 'Eating Out in Central Edinburgh (32)' and 'Theatres and Cinemas'.

Scottish Craft Centre
140 Canongate, Royal Mile
556 8136
Mon-Sat 10-5.30

Displays of quality craft work by Scottish men and women, for sale. Totally unsuitable for toddlers — too much fragile stuff at floor level. Nowhere for buggies inside. There is a most attractive courtyard with a seat. No toilets, go to Huntly House next door.

Scottish National Gallery of Modern Art
Belford Rd
556 8921
Mon-Sat 10-4.30; Sun 2-4.30

The gallery is set in its own grounds with a large lawn in front and parking to the rear. Once a school, it has been beautifully converted to house a permanent collection in which most of the major 20th century artists in Europe and America are represented from Matisse to Hockney. There are pieces of sculpture in most rooms and outside on the lawn. The gallery also holds special exhibitions.

The whole gallery is easily accessible with buggy — ramp to entrance and lifts inside. The ladies' toilet is spacious and has a low chair in it. There are also low comfy chairs (suitable for feeding but not very private) in the passage next to the very pleasant cafe. The staff are very friendly and sympathetic to children.

Cafe: see 'Eating Out in North Edinburgh'.

Scottish National Portrait Gallery
Queen St
556 8921
Mon-Sat 10-5; Sun 2-5

No facilities for changing or feeding, no lift.

MUSEUMS

Museum of Childhood
42 High St
557 1625 Ext 211
June-Sept: Mon-Sat 10-6; Oct-May: Mon-Sat 10-5; Festival Suns 2-5

A museum devoted to the history of toys, it is of interest to both children and adults. Trains, boats, planes, dolls and many, many more playthings of the past. These are displayed in 5 galleries. Gallery 2 has a children's playtable and rocking horse. Gallery 5 has 'Scenes from the Past', a 1930s schoolroom, a nursery, a Victorian street. Gallery 1 has a few working models including a nickelodeon.

It is encouraging to see some of the displays at low level, suitable for viewing by small children, but even so, small children may get bored. The museum is not buggyable, there are many steps and it can become very congested. It is requested that buggies are left downstairs where they can be supervised. There is a lift up to the 3rd floor, the toilets are situated on the 4th (lift to 3rd and up ramp to 4th) and are badly signposted. There are no nappy changing or breastfeeding facilities, but there are a few chairs in the corridor near the 3rd floor lift which could be used at a pinch. There is a good shop at the entrance, see 'Shopping, Toy Shops etc'.

Edinburgh Wax Museum
142 High St
226 4445
Daily: Oct-Mar 10-5 (last entry 4.30); Apr-Sept 10-7 (last entry 6.30)
Adults £2.20, children 50p, OAPs 70p, discounts for groups.

Despite the inclusion of a fairy tale section in this wax portrayal of Scotland's past, this museum is not recommended for small children. Most will find the lifesize, lifeless wax figures very frightening and this is compounded by gloomy lighting and narrow, dark passages between the scenarios. See also 'Shopping, Toy Shops etc' for details of candle-making in the premises next door.

Huntly House, Canongate Tolbooth, Lady Stairs House
225 2424
Oct-May: Mon-Sat 10-5; June-Sept: Mon-Sat 10-6; Festival Suns 2-5

Like many buildings in the Royal Mile, these museums are on many levels with narrow steps, often turnpike staircases. Huntly House covers local history, Lady Stairs House commemorates Burns, Scott and Stevenson, and Canongate Tolbooth houses temporary exhibitions.

Royal Museum of Scotland
Chambers Street
225 7534
Mon-Sat 10-5; Sun 2-5
Museum cafe Mon-Sat 10-4; Closed Sun

Don't be put off by the rather imposing entrance, as it opens into a large, glass-roofed building, a wonderful example of Victorian Architecture at its best. Here fish ponds (just about toddler proof!), plants and artefacts give the foyer a distinctly Eastern feel. Of most interest to the under 5s is the large collection of stuffed animals, from Aardvark to Zebra, and the working model engines, operated by push buttons. Both of these are conveniently situated on the ground floor. The rest of the museum houses on its upper floors most forms of European decorative art and oriental culture as well as a large mineral display. It is the largest comprehensive museum in Britain under one roof.

The main entrance involves a long flight of steps, but these can be avoided if you enter from the 'disabled' entrance in Lothian St (rear). Ring the bell and wait, you will be ushered through to the main hall. For safety reasons buggies are allowed only on the ground floor, but can be left under guard at the main door.

The ladies' toilet is down a long flight of stairs, but has a table and a chair and plenty of space. The staff are helpful and friendly, and if asked are happy to let you use the First Aid Room for breastfeeding.

Museum Cafe
Mon-Sat 10-4
£, Feeder beakers

A cheap, self-service cafe which is being gradually upgraded. There are no facilities for children except baby feeding cups.

NB. The Royal Museum of Scotland also has a branch in Queen St (formerly the National Museum of Antiquities of Scotland). This museum is not of great interest to children under 5, and has no facilities for this age group.
225 7534 ext 360
Mon-Sat 10-5; Sun 2-5
No cafe.

Scottish Agricultural Museum
Ingliston
333 2674
1 May-30 Sept: Mon-Fri 10-5; Sun 12-5; Closed Sat

Presents a history of farming life in Scotland through relics, photographs and displays. No working models or live animals.

HISTORIC BUILDINGS

Camera Obscura and Outlook Tower
Castlehill, Royal Mile
226 3709
Mon-Fri 9.30-4; Sat, Sun 10-6 (Apr-Sept); 10-4 (Oct-Mar)
Adults £1.25, child 60p

Victorian optical device giving magnificent views over Edinburgh — best on a sunny day. It is a long climb up winding stairs to the outlook tower but there are seats at the top. Not recommended for toddlers. There is also a holographic display. Bookshop and toilets.

Craigmillar Castle
Craigmillar, off A68
661 4445
Apr-Sept: Mon-Sat 9.30-7; Sun 2-7; Oct-Mar: Mon-Sat 9.30-4; Sun 2-4
Adults 50p, child 25p. There is a 10% discount for large parties

Lovely little castle, dating from the 14th century. It was once the favourite residence of Mary, Queen of Scots. The grounds are attractive and there is a little garden to one side with a seat. Nice place for a picnic. One small toilet.

Dalmeny House and Estate
See 'Walks and Country Places'.

Edinburgh Castle
Top of the Royal Mile
225 5898
Oct-Mar: Mon-Sat 9.30-5.05; Sun 12.30-4.20; Apr-Sept: Mon-Sat 9.30-5.05; Sun 11-5.50
Adults £2, child £1, ask about family tickets

There are good views of the city from the esplanade and no charge for access. The castle itself houses St Margaret's Chapel (built in 1073) and the Scottish Crown Jewels, the National War Museum and military museums and regalia. Not recommended for toddlers or buggies as there are steep cobbled paths and lots of steps. Quite an expensive outing unless you are passionately interested in military history. There is a large toilet with a chair where you could sit to feed a baby but nowhere to change a nappy. Benches outside could be used. There is a small souvenier shop. The Military Tattoo is held on the esplanade during the Festival. 'See 'Annual Events, August'.

The Georgian House
7 Charlotte Sq
225 2160
Apr-Oct: Mon-Sat 10-5; Sun 2-5; Nov: Mon-Sat 10-4.30; Sun 2-4.30
Adult £1.10, child 55p

This is a National Trust property and is furnished and decorated in Georgian style (including gas lights). In the basement there is a slide and tape show about the New Town, and a video of life in Georgian Edinburgh is available. Most interesting for adults but not suitable for young children, as there are many things which must not be touched. Staff are welcoming. No toilets or place to feed. The National Trust Shop is housed here. See 'Shopping, Toy Shops etc'.

Gladstone's Land
Lawnmarket, Royal Mile
226 5856
Apr-Oct: Mon-Sat 10-5, Sun 2-5; Nov closes at 4.30
Adult 90p, child 45p

This 17th century merchant's house is another National Trust property. A clay pig lounges outside on the pavement. Inside it is not particularly safe for toddlers as there are steep winding staircases and open fires. Staff are friendly and cooperative. Small gift shop. No toilet or place to feed.

Greyfriars Tolbooth and Highland Kirk
Greyfriars Pl (Off Forrest Rd)
225 1900
Sun services 11, Gaelic 4
Kirkyard open 10-5
Kirk open May-Sept: Mon-Fri 10-12, 2-4

Edinburgh Burgh Church, Scotland's finest collection of monumental sculpture in kirkyard. Covenanters are buried here. A secluded and peaceful spot in the city centre much used for picnics at lunch time as there are sandwich bars in the vicinity.

Greyfriars Bobby
Situated outside the entrance to the Kirk. The story of the faithful dog is always popular. His master is buried in the churchyard.

Hopetoun House and Estate
See 'Walks and Country Places'.

John Knox's House
45 High St
556 6961
Mon-Sat 10-5
Adult 70p, child 50p

This picturesque house is of no interest to small children as it only displays information about John Knox's life. No toilets.

Lauriston Castle
See 'Walks and Country Places.'

Palace of Holyrood House
Queen's Park, foot of the Royal Mile
556 1847
Apr-Sept: Mon-Sat 9.30-5.15; Suns 10.30-4.30; Nov-Mar: Mon-Sat only 9.30-3.30
The Palace is closed to the public when the Queen is in residence
Adult £1.20, child 60p

The Palace is the Queen's official residence in Scotland and the part open to the public is fairly small. Guided tours not really suitable for toddlers. Pushchairs are not allowed but backpacks are OK. The ropes dividing the exhibits from the tour are rather too easy for small children to negotiate. The ruins of Holyrood Abbey dating back to the 11th century can also be visited and would provide children with an opportunity to run about. Toilets — no special facilities but staff very helpful. Public toilets at foot of the Royal Mile have baby changing room.

St Giles Cathedral
High St
226 2998
A landmark on the mile and probably Edinburgh's most imposing church. Many historical connections. The crypt and Thistle Chapel are visited from within the cathedral. Souvenir shop. Pleasant 'Lower Aisle Restaurant', see 'Eating Out in Central Edinburgh (29)'.

Scott Monument
See 'Walks and Country Places, Princes St Gardens'.

TELLING THE TIME

A cannon is fired from the castle at 1 o'clock everyday and can be heard from a considerable distance. The floral clock in the Princes St Gardens is very popular with children, who love waiting for the bird to pop out on the hour; Spring-late Autumn.
The House of Fraser, West End — a clock outside the building, with soldiers and a castle.

ANIMALS IN THE CITY

Butterfly Farm
Situated in Dobbie's Garden Centre, On the A7, just outside Dalkeith
663 4932
Mid-March-31st Oct: Weekdays 10-5; Weekends 10-4.30
Adults £1.50, children over 5, 90p; family ticket (2 adults, 4 kids) £4.50

The butterfly farm has many attractions and is popular with the very young (as well as older children and adults). It is a large heated greenhouse with free flying tropical butterflies and birds among scented flowers and lush foliage. There is a stream with terrapins and fish, also spiders, beetles and developing butterflies in cages. Some birds and fish are for sale. Entrance is through the shop. There is a car park. Toilets (no nappy changing facilities). Situated within the garden centre is a small cafe and children's play area.

Cat and Dog Home
26 Seafield Rd East
669 5331
Mon-Fri 9-4
Free

Used to showing visitors around — if asked in advance they will cater for group visits — eg from play-groups or nurseries. Very friendly staff.

⁋Edinburgh Zoo
Corstorphine Rd
334 9171
Mon-Sat 9-6; Sun 9.30-6
In winter, closes at dusk or 5 pm
Adults £2.50, children 3-14 yrs £1.25, 20% discount for groups booked in advance (min 10)
Car park: 50p at Post House Hotel, or on road (tickets and regulations)
Pushchairs may be hired at entrance.

A great day out for families. A large, leafy zoo situated on a hill which provides good views south but makes pushing difficult. Over 200 species of animals including the big cats, gorillas, giraffes, an elephant, reptiles etc and the famous penguin parade takes place at 2.30 daily throughout the summer months. Some of the animals are separated from the public by moats, walls and glass rather than traditional wire fences. There is also a children's farm and an exciting play area with slides etc. There are other activities to interest older children eg brass rubbing and animal handling sessions (min age 3) (stroke a snake, Easter and summer school hols and summer weekends — enquire at the bookshop).

There are numerous kiosks throughout the zoo but many of these only open in summer, also a gift shop and bookshop with a good range of toys and books on the animal theme.

If you are regular visitors it is worth considering membership (annual or life) which may save you admission money and which entitles you to use the Members' House and to park within the zoo.

A picnic area is provided near the 'Den', and the following catering facilities are available (for an explanation of symbols see 'Eating Out'):

The Den
Summer only 11-5.30

Currently being re-furbished; in the meantime may be used for picnics (you may leave packed lunches here to be collected later). No pushchairs inside but covered area to secure. Chair suitable for feeding in cloakroom.

The Penguins' Pantry
Daily in summer 11-5.30; winter — varies
£, High chairs (4), breastfeeding permitted, bottles heated, nappy changing surface.

Large self-service restaurant, fast food, children's menu, burgers etc. No pushchairs inside but covered area to secure outside. Chair suitable for feeding in cloakroom.

Members' House
Lunch Mon-Sat 12.30-2.15; Sun 12.30-1.45
££, High chairs (4), bottles heated, nappy changing surface, parties hosted.

Large table service restaurant for zoo members and their guests. No pushchairs inside but area to secure. Chair suitable for feeding in cloakroom. Tea/coffee and light snacks are served all day in the lounge, upstairs in the Members' House.

⁋Gorgie City Farm
51 Gorgie Rd (about 300 yds from junction with Dalry Rd)
337 4202

118

Mon-Fri 9.30-5; Sat 9.30-4.30, Sun 10.30-4.30
Free, donation box
Group visits should be arranged in advance, and a small charge is made. Membership can be taken out — £1.50 annual subs/individual, £2/groups.

This community farm affords real down-on-the-farm sights, sounds and smells in the centre of the city. Friendly sheep, goats, rabbits, ducks, hens, pigs etc. A herb garden has recently been added and a DIY workshop and craft room can be used by groups or individuals. A creche is available for people using the workshop, craft rooms and farm. Tea, coffee, homebaking and snacks are available from the farm kitchen. Produce from the vegetable garden and fresh eggs for sale. There is a staff toilet which visitors could use if necessary. Easy access for buggies. See also 'Activities for Parents'.

Lothian and Borders Police Stables and Dog-handlers
Apply to: Police Headquarters, Fettes Ave EH4 1RB
331 3131

Entry is at discretion of Police Headquarters and is restricted to groups with a genuine interest. Services include videos, talks, pictures for children to colour-in etc. Admission is usually on Tues 2-4, Nov-May.

Roseburn Open Farm
Kirkgate, Currie (about 6 miles from Edinburgh, A70)
449 4401
Easter-end Oct: Daily 11-7 or 8

Adults £1, children 50p
Parties over 10 reduced rates, preferably booked.
A real working farm (wear old shoes) owned and run by the Steven family, with the idea that visitors can touch, feed and enjoy the friendly animals which include sheep, hens, calves, goats, pheasants, chicks, donkey. Also pony rides and a children's play area. There is a car park and small shop selling teas, coffee, juice, souvenirs. Toilets available.

Royal Highland Show
See 'Annual Events, June'.

BOATS, PLANES AND TRAINS

More Ideas for Places to Visit

For more details of what you will find at these places, as well as tips for journeys, see 'Travel and Transport'.

Cramond
Pretty village at river mouth, many boats. See 'Walks and Country Places, Cramond'.

Edinburgh Airport
Off the A8
333 1000
Admission free but the car park is expensive

There is a viewing gallery and you can also see the planes from the cafeteria. The cafeteria provides high chairs. There is a changing room with a sink, changing surface, comfortable seats and a machine dispensing nappies. There are miles of corridors to explore, shops with toys, books etc. Plenty to entertain children here. Don't forget to show

young 'Mr Boom' fans the 'flying sock'. See 'Travel and Transport, Air Travel'.

Leith Docks
554 4343

Interesting to drive round — not safe for toddlers on the loose. Weekday evenings are the best time to go — not too busy but not too quiet. The 'Scotsman' newspaper gives daily information on ships using the port. Occasionally it is possible to tour a cruiser.

Newhaven Harbour

The harbour is peaceful and attractive and the village of Newhaven is worth a look too. There is a fishmarket here on Thurs am starting about 6.30.

Union Canal

Canal boat trips are available from the Bridge Inn at Ratho. See 'Eating Out in West Edinburgh' and 'Birthdays and Celebrations'.

Waverley Station
556 2477

Free tours are only for older children (8 and over) but young children will enjoy the atmosphere of bustle and expectancy. The central hall is a nice big area for letting off steam and the notice boards are an attraction too. There is plenty to see but now that there is open access to the platforms toddlers must be closely supervised. For details of facilities see 'Travel and Transport'. Two recommended short journeys are return trips to Haymarket, and across the Forth Bridge to Inverkeithing (or Aberdour and down the hill to the beach). Look out for Santa's steam train at Xmas, see 'Annual Events, December'.

THEATRES AND CINEMAS

A regular look at the 'What's On' columns reveals that there's a lot on offer for young children in Edinburgh's theatres and cinemas. 'See 'Sources of Information'.

In general, theatres are not well designed for a visit with toddlers — buggies are not allowed in the auditoria (although they can usually be left in cloakrooms) and toilet facilities are usually cramped, with no breastfeeding or nappy-changing areas. Some theatres have restrictions on admitting babies and toddlers under 3 so it's best to check beforehand what the situation is, and also to find out the duration of the show — some family pantomimes have a horrible habit of going on for far too long. Refreshments, when available, may not be suitable for children eg coffee or coke.

Cinemas tend to have spacious toilets, often with anterooms equipped with armchairs. Check press for details of the many film matinees suitable for under 5's (Certificate U). Of course, the list of venues and events expands enormously during the Edinburgh Festival. See "Annual Events, August'.

'Festival Venues: A Guide for Disabled People' is available from the Festival Office, and gives information on access, wheelchair spaces, parking, toilets, guide dogs and induction loops.

When buying tickets, it's worth remembering that discounts are sometimes available for block bookings, for matinees, and occasionally for dress rehearsals. Most theatres and larger cinemas accept bookings by phone if you have an Access or Visa card.

THEATRES

Churchill Theatre
Morningside Rd, Morningside
447 7597

Favourite venue for amateur dramatic companies. Steps up to theatre and to toilets. Sometimes self-service coffee bar on ground level.

George Square Theatre
George Sq
667 1011 ext 6530

University lecture hall which doubles as theatre. Popular with touring companies and hosts children's show during Festival. Auditorium up 2 long flights of steps, toilets down 1 flight (ie 3 flights away!)

Kings Theatre
2 Leven St, Tollcross
229 1201/229 4840

Christmas pantomime; children's plays, some with special all-one-low-price tickets, so book early for a front row seat in the Grand Circle and a good view of what's going on in the orchestra pit. NB Grand Circle has very low parapet and no guard rail. Boisterous toddlers could topple over!

Leith Theatre (Thomas Morton Hall)
Ferry Rd
554 1408

Level access. Toilets

Netherbow Arts Centre
43 High St
556 9579

Many events for young children, puppet shows at Easter, Christmas pantomime. Very small, intimate theatre, so every seat has a view.

Cafe. See 'Eating Out in Central Edinburgh (32)', and also 'Places to Visit, Art Galleries'.

Playhouse Theatre
Greenside Place
557 2590

Mainly a rock gig, but occasional children's shows.

Portobello Town Hall
High St, Portobello
669 5800

Toilets on ground level.

Queen's Hall
Clerk St
668 2019

Some orchestral concerts for children. Bar and cafe. Ground floor toilets.

Royal Lyceum Theatre
Grindlay St
229 9697.
Credit card ticket sales: 229 4353.

Christmas shows for young children; family tickets; babies not allowed in. Lifts to all levels. Disabled toilet on ground floor. Bar at stalls level; restaurant with separate entrance on ground level.

Theatre Workshop
34 Hamilton Pl, Stockbridge
225 7942

Many shows geared for school-children and occasionally under 5's. Also exhibitions and classes. Disabled toilet. 2 adults can bring 2 children for ½ price.

Cafe. See 'Eating Out in North Edinburgh'.

Traverse Theatre
112 West Bow, Grassmarket
226 2633

Occasional Christmas shows for children. Bar and cafe. (Closed Mon).

Usher Hall
Lothian Rd
228 1155

Orchestral concerts, very occasionally something for under 5s. Must be 3+ to get in. Disabled toilet in stalls foyer.

CINEMAS

ABC Film Centre
Lothian Rd
229 3030

Cameo
Home St, Tollcross
228 4141

Dominion Cinema
Newbattle Ter, Morningside
447 2660

As visited by Maisie the cat, and illustrated by Aileen Paterson in 'Maisie Comes to Morningside'!
Cafe: Mon-Fri 10-12 noon, coffee; 12 noon-2, Lunch. Tues-Sat 3-11 (Mon 6-11) cooked meals till 9.15 pm (bacon rolls, hamburgers, reasonable price).

Filmhouse
88 Lothian Rd
228 2688

Matinees Sat afternoons only, term time. Bar, restaurant: 12 noon-10.45. Half portions, quiches, salads. Must be 3+ to be admitted.

Odeon Film Centre
7 Clerk St
667 7331

Annual Events

Pantomimes at Kings; Royal Lyceum; Theatre Workshop. See press for details and 'Theatres and Cinemas' for addresses and facilities.

FEBRUARY

Snowdrops at Cammo Park and Dalmeny House, South Queensferry, where gardens open one Sun for charity. Lots of space to work off excess energy! See 'Walks and Country Places'.

EASTER

Puppet Festival, Netherbow Arts Centre, 43 High St, 556 9579. See 'Theatres and Cinemas'.

Animal handling sessions at Edinburgh Zoo. See 'Places to Visit, Animals in the City'.

Playscheme at Dunfermline College of Physical Education. Mime, music, art and craft, quizzes, games, films. Morning or afternoon sessions for 3-5 yr olds. Approx £8/child for the week. Application forms from DCPE, Cramond Rd Nth EH4 6JD, 336 6506

Easter Egg Rolling in West Princes St Gardens on Easter Sun. Also puppet shows and horse and cart rides. Also egg rolling at Dunsapie Loch in Holyrood Park.

APRIL

Student Charities Week

Procession of floats along Princes St on last Sat of the week at the end of April. For details: 225 4061.

Funfair in Meadows at end of week. Stalls, sideshows, music, face painting.

Ideal Home Exhibition, Ingliston. The many advertised attractions for children (eg Three Bears House, Giant's Castle etc) are very disappointing and it is not worth making a special trip. Creche.

MAY

Spring Fling Community Arts Festival organised by District Council. Music, dance, theatre, children's events and exhibitions. Many shows FREE, otherwise low priced. Creche at many events. Programme from libraries or contact Arts Outreach Team, 1 Cockburn St, 225 2424 Ext 6623/6625. See also 'Activities for Parents, Women Live'.

May Day at South Morningside Primary School.

JUNE

Meadows Festival, Sat and Sun beginning June. Lots of stalls, jumble to home baking. Many organised by charities. Sideshows, funfair, puppets, face painting, live music, fancy dress, mime. A lively place for a picnic if weather fine. See press for details or call Crosswinds Community Centre, Tollcross 229 0321.

Royal Highland Show, Sun-Wed, 3rd week June. Ingliston Showground, Newbridge. Lots of animals to look at, tractors to climb on. Creche. Daily arena events — gymkhanas' to marching bands. Under 5s — FREE admission. Reduced prices for adults after 4 pm and Sun. See press for details or contact Royal Highland and Agricultural Society of Scotland, 333 2444.

Gorgie/Dalry Festival. Puppets, pet shows, theatre events for children. See press for details or contact Gorgie/Dalry Community Workshop, 204 Dalry Rd, 346 0772. Most shows free or cheap.

Craigmillar Festival. Concerts, puppets, music. Details from Craigmillar Festival Society, 661 2202 or see press.

Leith Links Festival. Stalls, sideshows, etc (smaller version of Meadows Festival).

Blackhall Sports Day. Races, puppets, fancy dress.

JULY

Most Edinburgh schools break up for the summer around the 1st week.

Animal handling sessions at the Zoo. See 'Places to Visit, Animals in the City'.

Summer Playscheme. Dunfermline College. Details as in Easter entry. 6 weeks during July/Aug. Playscheme for 3-5's, also dance lessons for over 4's.

Punch and Judy and magic shows, Braidburn Park, Comiston Rd. Twice weekly in July/Aug.

Mini Rail Exhibition of model railways and meccano held at weekends in the new Refectory building of George Heriot's School, Lauriston Place during the final weeks of July, or at the end of July and beginning of Aug. Snack bar and souvenirs. Admission 60p (adult) 30p (child). Contact Mr Crawford, 442 1969 for details.

AUGUST

The city centre bursts into activity this month. (A bad time to try and shop on Princes St — just enjoy yourself!). Apart from official and fringe events, street entertainers are a great attraction too. Best places to find them are outside the Fringe Office in the High St and in 'Festival Place' (at the bottom of the Mound beside the Galleries), although the crowds here can be so thick that movement with buggy is impossible and toddlers are in real danger of getting lost and/or being trampled underfoot.

Book Festival. Charlotte Sq Bi-annual event in 'odd' years, ie '87, '89, '91. Children's Book Tent, storytelling by authors, visits from characters from books etc. Creche (organised by NCT). Details from Festival Society, 226 4001.

Edinburgh International Festival. Details from Festival Office, 21 Market St EH1 1BW, 226 4001. Programme available end May. Some performances for children eg foreign circuses and puppets. Bargain ticket booth at foot of Mound selling ½ price tickets for shows that day.

Festival Cavalcade. Procession of floats, pipe bands etc along Princes St on first Sun of Festival. A must! See 'Evening News' for route map and get your buggy parked beside the kerb early to beat the crush and ensure good view.

Festival Fireworks. A spectacular weekday evening display to musical accompaniment. Large crowds on streets in city centre — apply early for free tickets for standing room in Princes St Gardens or pay for seats. Small children may find all the noise, crush and strange sights overwhelming and frightening.

Festival Fringe. The many children's Fringe shows are an ideal introduction to the Arts for little ones — performances are short and less formal, with smaller audiences in smaller venues. Programme available mid-June from Fringe Office, 170 High St, 226 5257. Included in children's section are circuses, puppets, drama, music.

Fringe Sunday. Lots of free performances in Holyrood Park.

Grassmarket Fair. Sats during Festival. Lots of market stalls, junk, home-baking, plants, live music (pipe bands to buskers) bustle and excitement.

Jazz Parade. Procession along Princes St and through the centre of town on a Sunday afternoon.

Military Tattoo. Pipes, drums and marching bands on the Castle Esplanade, after dark, but a few early evening shows on Sats. You will be confined on high, hard and cold seats on terraces. So if you think your child can cope, take blankets, and refreshments. Cushions can be hired.

Schools and playgroups generally re-open mid-month for a new academic year.

OCTOBER

Children's Book Week. Competitions and readings organised in several bookshops.

Half-Term Holiday Highlights organised by District Council. Puppet shows, special events at sports centres and swimming pools. Exhibitions at museums and art galleries. Programme from libraries or Recreation Marketing Unit, 225 2424 Ext 6632/6639.

NOVEMBER

Fireworks at Meadowbank Stadium. Large, well organised display. Entry around £1.
There are also several smaller local firework events around town, eg: Portobello Beach (bottom of Brunstane Rd) FREE; Balerno Round Table Fireworks display on Currie playing fields; Fairmilehead Scout Fireworks; Donaldson's School; Gracemount School.

Charities Hypermarket. Assembly Rooms, George St. Craft stalls, gifts, Christmas cards, second hand toys, clothing, home baking.

YWCA Toy Fair, Randolph Pl. Bring and Buy toys for Christmas; 50% of sale price to seller, rest to YWCA.

DECEMBER

Pantomimes and Christmas Shows
(see Jan).

Steam Train Trips around Edinburgh's suburban Circle with Santa on board. Details from Scottish Railway Preservation Society Railtours, 7 Craigmount Ave Nth EH12 8LD, 339 5646.

Santa in residence at various stores — Jenners, Goldbergs and Debenhams are especially nicely decorated. Also at Foam Centre, 163 Causewayside, along with vast numbers of Christmas trees for sale, and free balloons, chocolates and apples.

Sources of Information

MAGAZINES

What's On
Published monthly
Cinemas, theatres, shops, restaurant guide. Art galleries and exhibitions.
Distributed free, available at Tourist Office and many other public places.

'The List'
Published fortnightly
Includes a section 'Kid's List' providing information about events in and around Edinburgh and Glasgow.
Available at newsagents.

NEWSPAPERS

The Scotsman and the **Evening News**
20 North Bridge EH1 1YT
225 2468

The Scotsman
Daily morning paper, birth announcements; details of exhibitions, theatre, art galleries etc, especially on Mon Church service information on Sat.

Evening News
Daily afternoon and evening paper full of local news. Full details of cinema programmes daily. Theatres, sales, fetes etc, especially on Fri.

Edinburgh Advertiser
7-9 Newhaven Rd
554 9333; to advertise
553 3255; to arrange delivery

Published every Thurs and delivered free to most homes in Edinburgh. Details of sales, fetes etc. Large 'for sale' columns.

RADIO AND TELEVISION

Radio Forth
Forth House, Forth St
556 9255

BBC Scotland
5 Queen St
225 3131

TELEPHONE INFORMATION LINES

Leisureline
246 8041
What's on in Edinburgh (1st May-30th Sept).

Scottish Tourist Board Information Centre

23 Ravelston Ter EH4 3EU

332 2433

Tourist information for the whole of Scotland.

Tourist Information Service

3 Waverley Market

also at 5 Waverley Bridge

557 2727

Tourist information for Edinburgh.

BOOKS

Tips for Trips

Published by The Environment Centre, Drummond Community High School EH7 4QP

For suggestions of places to visit in Edinburgh and Lothian Region

Cafuf (The Committee on Facilities for Under Fives)

'What is there for the Under Fives in Tollcross/Pentland?' April 1986.
'What is there for the Under Fives in Leith?' Jan 1986.
Available from the Regional Community Work Team, 14 Alva St EH2 4QG (225 3226)

The Red Book: Lothian Directory of Local Services

Available from libraries and contains details of voluntary and statutory organizations in the fields of health, social work, community and allied services.

The Edinburgh Information Pack is a blue file held in local libraries which lists local and regional councillors; members of the children's panel; local churches; consulates in Edinburgh; information on private nurseries and playgroups and nursery education in Lothian; information on drama groups etc and contains statistics from the census.

The Community and Amenity Associations' file is held in local libraries and lists resident associations, community councils, and local projects oriented largely towards social, environmental and self-help groups. Published by EDC Planning Department from whom it is also available.

See also individual chapters for other useful books.

Playgrounds & Parks

Playgrounds for young children in Edinburgh are, on the whole, extremely poor. The District Council have made some recent improvements, but it is obvious that they are working with a limited budget to tackle an inheritance of badly designed and poorly-sited equipment. A member of the Council staff said that she felt that most of the city's playgrounds are unsuitable for children under 6 or 7. Nevertheless, there are 'bucket' (or 'cradle') swings in many playgrounds, and recently, small climbing frames and the very popular 'buckabouts' (wobbly animals and vehicles) have been installed. In all playgrounds close adult supervision is required, particularly if your toddler chooses to use some of the non-toddler equipment (particularly the still prevalent old-fashioned high slides) or to dash in front of unprotected swings, or even out on to nearby roads. Visits can be dangerous, particularly if there is more than one child per adult. Other very common hazards to watch out for are broken glass (we found it on all but one of Edinburgh's playgrounds), litter, and dog excrement (almost as common). Dogs are not allowed in children's play areas, but there are seldom fences to keep them out, or posts at which to tether them.

Nevertheless, although our survey of all of Edinburgh's playgrounds mostly took place in bitterly cold winter weather most were in use, and there is clearly a demand for good outdoor play areas for children. Most of the children we saw in the playgrounds were under 10, and many were under 5. Playgrounds can be a good place for both parents and children to make new friends, as well as to burn up some energy. If you would like to express an opinion on playground matters, write to: Mr Horsfall, Assistant Director (Parks), Department of Recreation, Edinburgh District Council, 17 Waterloo Pl, 557 1265.

Here are some of our findings, with an emphasis on the better and busier playgrounds (not necessarily the same thing!).

Bruntsfield Links and The Meadows

An extensive area of flat grassland and paved walks through avenues to the south of the city centre, incorporating a putting green, and also suitable for ball games, picnics, learning to cycle etc. Surrounded by busy roads. There are 2 play areas:

Although really for older children, there are a few bucket swings (as well as other swings, 2 climbing frames and a high slide) at the **Bruntsfield Links Playground** to the north of Melville Dr, but they are unfenced and close to a very busy road. Nevertheless, this playground is usually busy, and the **Toddlers' Play Area** at the east end of the Meadows is enclosed and dog-free and there is a paddling pool in the summer. Also 2 slides (one of which is wider than average), 4 buckabouts, bucket swings, a rocking horse etc. All on grass. (Parking nearby at Buccleuch St.)

Colinton Mains Park
Oxgangs Rd Nth, Firrhill

Most of the equipment is on hard surfaces, although some rubber matting has been provided. It includes 4 bucket swings, a helterskelter and 4 buckabouts. It is planned to install further equipment. The playground is adjacent to a large area of playing fields, and road safety is good.

Dalmeny Park
Iona St, Lorne (nr Leith Walk and Albert St)

A playground with potential for toddlers, which suffers badly from wind-blown litter. One of the few playgrounds in the city where a slide has been built into a bank, which makes it far safer than usual, as long as the bank itself is not slippery. There are bucket swings, ordinary swings, climbing frames and a rocking boat, and a hard area which could be useful for tricycles, wheeled toys, etc. There are trees and seats, and the 2 acre park is fenced, so road safety is good provided the gates are shut.

Falcon Gardens
nr St Peter's Primary School, Churchhill

A small park, safe from roads, with an adjacent grassy area. Relatively clean. Equipment includes 3 bucket swings and a high slide on rubber matting. There are also ordinary swings, 2 climbing frames and 2 seats.

Haugh Park
Brae Park Rd, Barnton

This playground is attractively situated down in a dell close to the River Almond Walkway. There is a paddock close by in which a horse can sometimes be seen. With an attractive wooden fort and bridge, and a set of swings, it is more suitable for older children than toddlers.

Inverleith Park
Arboretum Rd, opp Royal Botanical Gardens

61 acres of playing fields and allotments, as well as a rose garden and a pond on which there is curling when it is frozen, and radio-controlled model boats when it is not (particularly on Sat and Sun afternoons). Also some small fish (which do not live for long in a jam-jar) and occasionally, ducks. The playground is in the SW corner (off Arboretum Rd) and is unusual in that it incorporates a large wooden 'ship' the 'HMS' Edinburgh'. Although there are 2 low slides, they are built over hard surfaces, and as children climb up vertical ladders inside the ship and slide into 'the sea' adults desperately try to be both sides at once. Inside 'the ship' there is a climbing frame now very unsafe for small children as its

very popular orange tubular slide was vandalised and replaced by a 'fireman's pole'. There are also 6 animal swings, very popular, but dangerously heavy. Also a variety of buckabouts, 2 bucket swings, and a further climbing frame. Hard surfaces throughout.

Leith Links

50 acres of attractive parkland, dominated by hillocks which are 16th century gun emplacements and great for toddler mountaineering. The paths are suitable for pushchairs, prams and tricycles. There are 2 playgrounds, one of which contains little to recommend it to small children. However, the other, in the centre of the park is fenced and set aside as a **Toddlers' Play Area**. It is relatively clean and dog-free, although we did find some broken glass. Surfaces are rubber and grass, except under one of the 2 climbing frames where it is tar. There are 2 bucket swings, a low slide, a moon-buggy, a balancing rail, and a bench too.

Liberton Recreation Ground
Liberton Gdns

Safely tucked away from traffic, the equipment is set in grass and mud and is surrounded by playing fields, which seem very popular with the local dog-owners. There are 3 bucket swings, a medium-sized slide with a drop at the bottom, as well as climbing frames, a rotating sphere and a roundabout. What may make this park useful however, is that there are toilets near the entrance in the old tram terminus, which have benches which would be suitable for changing and feeding a baby in warm weather (no heating).

Lochend Park
To the SW of Lochend Rd

Ordinary swings, a high slide, a roundabout and 3 buckabouts and benches away from the road in a large grassy area (23 acres) with a path on one side of the loch. You may be able to feed ducks through gaps in the wire-mesh fence!

Morningside Park
Between Balcarres St and Morningside Dr

8 ordinary swings, 3 bucket swings, a high slide on a hard surface, a roundabout, and seats. Also an area of grass on which to play. The park is safely away from roads and there are plans to improve it.

Pilrig Park
Pilrig St

The 21 acres of Pilrig Park contain football pitches and 2 playgrounds. The one to the east of the park, off Pilrig St, has recently been renovated and this is a sign that local playgrounds are gradually improving. The equipment is all on a bark chip base for softer falls, and not as likely to break glass bottles. There is a commando bridge (not suitable for young children), 2 tyre swings and bucket swings, 4 buckabouts, a climbing frame, log planks and chains to walk along, and a playhouse and slide as well as 2 tables and benches. It is a pity that there is still no gate in the wall separating the play area from Pilrig St, and that the whole area is not fenced to keep dogs out. There is another fairly new playground on the other side of the park (also accessible from Stead's Pl). Here, hard surfaces are used throughout. Despite being built next to a sloping former railway embankment, the slide is free standing. The wooden bridge climbing frame looks attractive and 'designed', but could be dangerous to all children without outstanding agility and good sense. There are also 5 bucket swings, a see-saw, and a bench.

Princes St Gardens
See 'Walks and Country Places'.

St Margaret's Park
Corstorphine High St

An attractive and clean wooded and grassy park, but with only 1 bucket swing. Apart from some rubber at the base of the high slide, the equipment (3 further swings and 2 climbing frames) is on a hard surface. 1 bench.

Saughton Park
Entrances on Gorgie Rd, Balgreen Rd, and Stevenson Dr

The 47 acres of the park are mostly given over to football pitches and a putting green. However there are 2 features worth mentioning here, both of which are accessed from Balgreen Rd. Saughton Gardens have been developed especially for the blind, with an emphasis on scented plants. They are attractive and well paved. And there is also Fort Saughton, Edinburgh's most exciting children's playground, which is well set back from the road and very popular. The equipment, all of which is on a bark-chip base, is divided so that older and younger children are at different ends of the well fenced playground. There are 'bucket' and animal swings, buckabouts, a helter-skelter, a roundabout like a flying saucer, a huge climbing frame and a 'commando' slide (rope on a runner). No dogs.

Towerbank

Corner Promenade and Beach Lane, Portobello

This playground is very safe from traffic and is adjacent to the Promenade and close to the beach. A limited amount of rubber matting has been installed, but there is a high slide without effective rubber surrounds. Also 4 swings, 2 bucket swings, 1 large and 1 small climbing frame, 4 buckabouts and a see-saw.

Victoria Park

Between Newhaven Rd and Craighall Rd, Trinity

One of the better playgrounds for younger children — it is fenced and gated in the middle of an attractive grassy park (18 acres), and although surfacing is predominantly hard, effective rubber matting has been installed. The centre-piece is a climbing frame-house with a low double width slide which gives more scope for sociable play than most playgrounds. There are also 3 bucket swings, 2 buckabouts, a roundabout and benches.

White Park

Gorgie Rd

A busy playground conveniently close to Gorgie shops and the City Farm, but gated and fenced with some rubber surfacing. There is a small area of grass (usually littered) and 2 seats. For toddlers there are 4 bucket swings (over rubber) as well as 2 small climbing frames shaped like 'YES' and 'NO' and 5 buckabouts on hard surfaces. There is also another climbing frame, 4 swings, and a high slide, all of which are surrounded by rubber matting.

ADVENTURE PLAYGROUNDS

Adventure playgrounds are less formal than the playgrounds described above, and offer greater opportunities for creative play and boisterous behaviour, so they are hard work for parents! There is usually provision for barbequeing as well.

Pilton Youth Retreat

70 Baird Rd, Ratho (on B7030 just north of old village of Ratho)
333 1659 (Warden)

The approx ½ acre site is fenced off from adjacent fields and roads. Car parking is provided. There are 3 parts to the site:

On the grass to the left of the entrance is an enormous wooden play structure with many levels, ramps, ramparts, ladders, hidey-holes, cat walks, rope swings and nets for climbing. When visited, this structure was in need of repair, and there were some rusty nails and a few fallen planks to watch out for. Agile parents were certainly required to safeguard excited and adventurous small children. This structure is in a grassy field which is also suitable for ball games etc.

To the right is a barbeque and playground area, with a high slide set in a cobbled bank, 3 tyre swings over sand, a concrete tunnel and a sandpit, and grassy mounds. There is also a paddling pool (you will need to make your own arrangements to fill it). Take your own sausages, charcoal, barbeque forks, grills, etc, as well as toys for the sand, footballs etc.

There is also on the site a cottage with a large open fire, kitchen, piano, and snooker and table-tennis tables, as well as 8 bunk beds.

The Retreat may be hired by groups (eg playgroups) for a nominal sum, but is not generaly open to the public.

Scotland St Yards
Prospect Bank, Canonmills

The MSC and EDC are jointly developing a play area which will eventually include an area for toddlers, as well as facilities for handicapped and older children. There will be toilets, no dogs will be allowed and there will be free access. May be partly available summer 1987.

Vogrie Estate and Country Park

B6372 between Dewarton and Newlandrig. 12 miles south of Edinburgh, signposted from A7 at Gorebridge and A68 just before Pathhead. Ranger: Gorebridge 21990; Midlothain District Council 440 0352. Open all year. Free, except for £1 for barbeque which should be booked and paid for in advance. A

room in Vogrie House may be hired for £3.

Adventure playground may be used from toddling upwards, as long as parents are prepared to clamber about too. As well as the official barbeque site, there are paved areas where you may use your own portable barbeque. For both you should provide your own utensils, charcoal and food. The playground is part of a very attractive large park, with gardens, nature trails and country walks.

Wester Hailes

5 'venchies' are built on waste land. There are full-time playworkers and sometimes special events eg barbeques, children's circuses, and festivals. The clubs which meet in the evening are for school age children. However Clovenstone (443 3140) and The Wester Hailes Adventure Playground (443 1030) both aim to include provision for younger children. They will re-open in summer 1987 after rehabilitation.

Walks & Country Places

There are a variety of green and open places where adults and children can relax without having to travel for miles, ranging from carefully tended parks to wild hillsides and streams. We have endeavoured to give an indication of the surfaces you will find, so as to indicate the feasibility of walks with wheels, but some paths will be muddy after rain and overgrown in summer. (Of course, children can also walk or be carried in a sling or backpack!)

For keen walkers, the following may be of interest:

Edinburgh National History Society (1982) 'A Guide to Edinburgh's Countryside — Habitats and Walks Within the City Boundaries', Macdonald Publishers, Edinburgh, ISBN 0 904265 83 8 £4.95.

This book will enable adults to identify geological features, as well as the flora and fauna in many of the areas we have described. It also contains some excellent sketch maps.

Colinton Amenity Association 'Colinton: Seven Walks'

Edinburgh New Town Conservation Committee '4 Walks in Edinburgh New Town'.

Lothian Regional Transport 'Walks from City Buses'. Available from the Tours information desk and the Transport Office, see 'Travel and Transport'.

THE BRAIDS

A golf-course and grassy slopes and hills, good for kites, walking and sledges. Best on Sun when there is no golf. There are horses nearby at Liberton Tower Farm.

THE HERMITAGE OF BRAID AND BLACKFORD HILL
Ranger: 447 7145

3 car parks at the Royal Observatory, Braid Rd and Cluny Gdns (for the pond). Ice-cream vans often park here in summer. Maps of walks at the entrances.

An extensive and attractive area of countryside within the city, comprising the **Blackford Hill** (540') and an area of woodland along Braidburn. Walks at lower levels are negotiable with wheels and at higher levels, with determination. Beware of the cliffs of the old quarry. Also several picnic sites. Autumn blackberries. Good bridges for 'Pooh Sticks'. Sledging in winter.

The beautifully situated **Blackford Pond,** to your right as you enter from Cluny Gdns, contains some of Edinburgh's best fed ducks, moorhens and geese. Sometimes there are squirrels to be seen too.

In **The Hermitage** there is a Visitor Centre where maps and trail leaflets are available. Also public toilets, although not ideal for nappy changing or feeding.

ROYAL OBSERVATORY
667 3321
Mon-Fri 10-4; Public holidays, Sat, Sun 12-5. Adult 65p, child 35p.

Excellent views of the city, but the exhibition of the history of modern astronomy (including many telescopes) contains little to interest most young children. Many steps, so not suitable for buggies or toddlers. However, there is a clean spacious cloakroom. Floodlit over the Festival and at Christmas. Souvenir shop.

BRAIDBURN VALLEY PARK
Pentland Ter

There is a stream, hilly slopes and walks, but no play equipment. The stream is suitable for fishing, but is a bit deep for small paddlers. Also an open-air amphitheatre in which puppet and magic shows are held twice-weekly during July and Aug.

CALTON HILL

Main entrance at Regent Rd. Parking in centre of park at top of hill.

A grassy hill (355') with many famous monuments, and offering wonderful panoramic views over the city, most interesting to children when city landmarks are floodlit over the Christmas season and during the Festival. A popular kite-flying spot. The **Nelson Monument** may be climbed, but this is not safe for children who are unsteady on their feet. Mon-Sat, 1 Apr-30 Sept 10-7; 1 Oct-31 Mar 10-3. Closed Sun.

Adult 40p, child 20p.

The Time Ball drops at 1 pm daily.

CAMMO AND THE RIVER ALMOND
Cammo Rd, Barnton

The paths along the River Almond can be joined from Cammo. If you are determined, the routes described here are passable with a pushchair in dry weather.

Start the walk along Cammo Rd. Just past the last house is a gate on the right, and a rough wide path down to the river. Very steep banks down to the water many feet below. The path can be continued and follows the river upstream towards the airport. It can be very overgrown. There are stepping-stones over the river about halfway along. OR Turn up the path to the left near the bridge. This eventually joins up with Cammo Rd again. Along this path you pass Craigiehall Temple — a locked tower. Good for holly picking. OR Turn right over Grotto Bridge. The river is very narrow under the bridge and after rain it looks quite spectacular as it thunders underneath. Just over the bridge there is a cattle grid, which has been known to capture clambering youngsters! The path follows the river downstream; it is fairly rough and there are some very steep drops to the river. It ends near the Cramond Brig Hotel, see 'Eating Out in West Edinburgh'. For a walk further downstream, see below 'Cramond, South: The River Almond Walkway'.

CAMMO PARK
Main gate at Cammo Rd, Barnton

Cammo House has disappeared, but its 104 acres of lawns, woodlands, avenues, gardens and pond have developed into a 'wilderness park', and the intention is to keep it this way. There are many paths to wander along and explore.

CEMETERIES
There are several overgrown cemeteries in the city which are now almost nature reserves. Do be careful if you explore them. The headstones may not be secure and there have been tragedies.

COLINTON DELL
See below, 'Water of Leith Walkway'.

CORSTORPHINE HILL
Panoramic views of the city and beyond are offered by the 530' summit of Corstorphine Hill. The terrain is varied; with a rocky and steep section — which includes a flooded quarry — between the Cairnmuir Rd and Clermiston Rd entrances, and large areas of woodland. Flora and fauna include conkers, acorns and pine-cones, raspberries and blackberries, squirrels, badgers and foxes too. There is also **Clermiston Tower**, built in 1851 to commemorate the centenary of Scott's birth, which is sometimes floodlit, but can no longer be climbed.

There are several routes to the summit of the Hill: **Clermiston Rd** (3 paths: the path near Fox Covert is rough and steep); **Queensferry Rd** (steep and rugged); **Craigcrook Rd** (a long push, between new houses, up a fairly steep gradient. Reasonably smooth path); **Ravelston Dykes Rd** (nr Mary Erskine School and about 200 yds north of Murrayfield Golf Clubhouse); a one-way revolving gate (out!) of the Zoo in Corstorphine; and from Cairnmuir Rd, at the junction with Kaimes Rd. This latter route is the easiest way for a pushchair and there is a car park too. There is a grassy slope on the left near the entrance where there are some picnic tables. (This is also a good place for sledging.) The toilets always seem to be locked. The path to the summit follows the edge of the Zoo (some animals can be seen) and it then joins the paths from the Ravelston Dykes and Craig-crook entrances.

CRAIGMILLAR CASTLE AND GROUNDS

See 'Places to Visit, Historic Buildings'.

CRAMOND

Walks radiate in all directions from the yachting centre at Cramond. Toilets. There is a large car park on Cramond Glebe Rd just below Cramond Kirk and above Cramond Inn. Sloped exit on to the Prom.

South: The River Almond Walkway

Length ±1⅓ miles. The walkway starts on the esplanade, and passes the boats and swans at the river mouth before entering a wooded glen. The path is rough, but wide and on the level. There is a more open grassy area around Cockle Mill cottages at the foot of School Brae. (Also a small car park at this point.) The path continues to Fair-a-Far Mill where there is a spectacular waterfall and fish ladder (although we have never seen any fish). The mill is now a ruin and children will enjoy running about through the arches and up a few steps. The river is railed at this point, but toddlers can easily run underneath. People throw pennies into the water at the top of the fall. (Boys collect them later!) The path continues to Cramond Brig Hotel (see 'Eating Out in West Edinburgh'), but there are several flights of steps and a pushchair would have to be carried. See also 'Cammo

and the River Almond' above, for a description of the route further upstream.

North: To Cramond Island

There is a rough causeway across the tidal mudflats out to Cramond Island, which is negotiable, on foot only, at low tide. Tide charts are displayed at the start of the walk. Take a picnic to your own small uninhabited island! Good views of the Forth Bridges.

East: The Esplanade

A broad paved footpath runs for 2 miles from Cramond through Silverknowes until it reaches Granton Point (West Shore Rd). An attractive area for promenading with a pram or on a tricycle and learning to ride a bike, particularly when there are clear views across to Fife. Suitable for picnics. At Silverknowes there are toilets and a booth which sells snacks in the summer. Also icecream vans, pipe bands and entertainments over some summer weekends. The beach itself is sandy at Cramond and stony elsewhere. It is gently sloped, but beware of the tide which comes in fast and could cut you off on a sandbank. The beach can be oily too.

West: Across the River Almond

There is no bridge across the Almond at Cramond, but it may be crossed by foot passenger ferry. This small boat operates Apr-Sept 9-7; Oct-Mar 10-4. Closed 1-2 and Fri. Adults 20p, children under 6 free. Folding pushchairs allowed, but no dogs, picnic cases or large baskets. The land to the west of the river belongs to the Dalmeny Estate (see below). There is a path (approx 2 miles) to Dalmeny House, but it is not negotiable with a pushchair. There is also a 4½ mile shore walk to South Queensferry along a woodland path.

DALMENY HOUSE AND ESTATE
A90 and then B924, 331 1888 Administrator

House and estate are open all yr, Sun-Thurs 2-5.30 (last admission 5). Guided tours of the house are not of great interest to children.

The estate is pleasant to walk around — fields, shore and woodland, with cows, sheep, pheasants and a statue of a horse. There is a sheltered woodland walk through the rhododendrons and azaleas of the garden valley. No fires or dogs. Picnics only by pre-arrangement. (Permits for parking at the beach can be obtained from the administrator.)

As well as the walks above (West: across the River Almond), the house may be reached on a walk from Long Craig Gate, South Queensferry (2½ miles). This walk is negotiable with a pushchair.

FIGGATE BURN PARK
28 acres of parkland along the Figgate Burn in Duddingston. Easily negotiated paths meander down gentle wooded slopes and across the burn. On the Figgate Burn loch there are ducks and swans. There is a disappointing children's playground (but with a slide set in a bank and 2 wobbly buckabouts, no swings) in the land which rises to the north-east above the burn. Next to the playground are the Craigentinny Carriage Sidings, off the main railway line, and which are of interest to young rail enthusiasts, particularly when shunting is in progress.

HILLEND
Biggar Rd

There is a chairlift at the artificial ski-slope at Hillend and this may be used by non-skiers. It will carry you into the open walking country of the Pentland Hills. Not suitable for pushchairs. (For details of the ski-slope itself, see 'Activities for Children, Ski-ing'). The walk to Swanston Village from Hillend is pretty, but is really only suitable with babies in a sling or backpack as the going is far too strenuous for most young children. There are lambs at Swanston Farm in the spring and it is a pleasant area for picnics.

HOLYROOD PARK
Car parks at Dunsapie Loch and near the entrances at Duddingston Loch, Holyrood Palace and Meadowbank Ter.

A large area including Arthur's Seat (823') and several other grass and gorse covered hills, the Salisbury Crags, the Radical Road and 3 small lochs. There is a Visitor Centre near Holyrood Gate, where maps of the park are displayed. With the exception of the Queen's Drive (a road), there are no surfaced walks in the park, and the climb to the top of Arthur's Seat is a steep one for a young child. Dunsapie Hill (523') might be a better choice, although the views are not quite as panoramic. (Both climbs start from the car park at Dunsapie Loch.) Circular walks may also be made in the park.

Duddingston Loch is a bird sanctuary with ducks but beware, the geese and swans can be aggressive. Rowing boats are available on **St Margaret's Loch** in the summer.

137

The northern area of the park is the venue for 'Fringe Sunday' during the Festival. There is a children's playground at **Dumbiedykes,** near Holyrood Gate, but the provision is very poor. (7 (!) climbing frames, 1 high slide, 1 sphere, 1 rocking horse. No swings. Hard surfaces throughout. Improvements are planned, and much needed). Pushchairs will be a liability off the road in the park, particularly when the ground is soft under-foot, but the **Innocent Railway** footpath and cycle track departs from the Queen's Drive to the south-east of Pollock Halls and below the Salisbury Crags and continues for 6½ miles to Craigmillar and Bingham. A tarred surface makes for easy walking along a pleasantly wooded path. Stinging nettles in summer.

The Scottish Wildlife Trust, 25 Johnston Ter, have produced a booklet describing a nature trail in the park.

HOPETOUN HOUSE AND ESTATE
on A904 from S Queensferry
331 2451
Apr-Sept: daily 11-5.30
House and grounds adult £1.90, child 90p. Grounds only adult 50p, child 30p. Garden centre open all year

Scotland's greatest Adam mansion and the ancestral home of the Marquis of Linlithgow. The house has superb rooms and state apartments, a magnificent art collection and is about a mile's walk along the coast from S Queensferry. For an outing with young children there is plenty to do without visiting the house itself. In the grounds there is a deer park, a nature park, a stable museum and a walled garden centre. Also a picnic area, a self service cafe and gift shop. There is a

surface for nappy changing in the toilets and a seat in the powder room where a baby could be fed.

INCH PARK
Old Dalkeith Rd

A large area of grassland with playing fields, deciduous trees, slopes for sliding down, paved paths for prams and learning to ride a bike. No play equipment. Edinburgh District Council's Nurseries are situated here, and during school holidays activities are sometimes organised (eg planting flowers, taking cuttings etc).

LAURISTON CASTLE AND GROUNDS
2 Cramond Rd South (just beyond Safeway, Davidson's Mains)
336 2060
Castle Apr-Oct: daily except Fri 11-1, 2-5 (last admission 4.20); Nov-Mar: Sat, Sun only 2-4 adults 80p, children over 6 40p. Grounds free. Car park free.

The house has remained unchanged since 1926 and has a secret room and a notable collection of Blue John china. Guided tours only, lasting about 40 mins, and not really suitable for young children as once inside the castle you cannot leave until the tour is finished. There are pleasant walks, suitable with a pushchair, in the peaceful and extensive grounds with fine views ovr the Forth estuary to Fife. They are particularly lovely in spring when the daffodils are out. There are usually ponies in the fields and there is a box hedge maze and a croquet lawn. Ball games may only be played in The Glade. No dogs or cycling. There is a picnic area with tables and arrangements can be made for large parties (apply to the Recreation Dept, 27 York Pl). Toilets have a convenient bench seat where one could sit and feed a baby or change a nappy. There is also a toilet for the disabled. For the nearby Lauriston Farm Restaurant, see 'Eating Out in West Edinburgh'.

PORTOBELLO BEACH AND PROMENADE

The paved promenade runs for 1¾ miles from Seafield Rd, past the Seafield Industrial Estate, south past King's Rd in Portobello to Morton St in Joppa. This latter stretch through Portobello is the most popular. There is a permanent funfair, amusement arcades and 10p rides on space ships etc, as well as the usual take away snacks. The beach is sandy but used by dogs. There is a summer beach programme of entertainments and events for all ages, and donkeys on the beach. See also Towerbank playground in 'Playgrounds and Parks'.

PRINCES STREET GARDENS
(see Map)

The city's most famous park runs to the south of Princes St and beneath the dramatic skyscape of the Old Town. There are access points from King's Stables Rd, Lothian Rd, the Mound, and Princes St itself. It's worth pausing here during shopping trips, there are lots of benches to rest on. The more formal paths and gardens are on the northern side of the park; there are more rugged steep and trickier paths beneath the castle. Access to the grassy slopes involve steps, unless you use the extremely steep and cambered path from opposite the junction of Castle and Princes St. Children enjoy the **railway** which runs through the

park. Trains are best viewed from the bank beneath the National Gallery in the East Gardens or from the lattice bridge near the Ross Bandstand in the West Gardens. Another very popular attraction is the **floral clock** (see 'Places to Visit; Historic Buildings') in the corner closest to The Mound and Princes St. Entertainments at the **Ross Bandstand** (eg Highland dancing, bands) are displayed on the hoardings along the railings of the Gardens. **The Scott Monument,** a Victorian Gothic spire and landmark may be climbed and a certificate will be earned. However, it is not recommended for small children, particularly when crowded, as there are very tight spiral staircases. Mon-Sat: Oct-Mar 9-3; Apr-Sept 9-6 45p. There is a **playground** with bucket swings, a rocking horse, roundabout and multigym all on rubber mats set in tar. The Gardens are a good place for **picnic lunch,** sandwiches, yoghurt, apples etc can be bought from Marks & Spencer, BHS, and Littlewoods. There is also an open air cafe selling fast foods. Toilets are marked on the map

RIVER ALMOND

See entries for Cammo and Cramond above.

ROYAL BOTANICAL GARDENS

Gates on Inverleith Rd and Arboretum Rd. Car parking at the latter
552 7171
Daily, except 25 Dec and 1 Jan; Mon-Sat 9-sunset in winter, 1 hr before sunset BST; Sun opens at 11. Times displayed at gates.

Plant Houses Mon-Sat 10-5 (or ¼ hr before gates shut); Sun open 11.

A beautifully landscaped and well-signposted garden, wonderfully clean and pleasant, perhaps because no dogs or picnics are allowed. (Nor are ball games, wheeled toys or sledges.) Tarred paths, grassy slopes and a pond with ducks. Plant houses at several temperatures, also indoor fish pond with viewing windows in the aquarium underneath, and an exhibition hall. No buggies or prams allowed in the hothouses or the rockery. There are toilets at the hothouses, West Gate and Inverleith House (no changing surface at any of these). There are 2 cafes:

Rachael's Tearoom, East Gate: Wed-Sun 11-5, Lunch 12-2, closed Mon, Tues.

You must leave your buggy unattended on the path outside the entrance to this cafe.

Tearoom, Inverleith House: 1 Apr-30 Sept: Mon-Sat 10-5; Sun 11-5. Open weekends in winter.
£, Breastfeeding permitted, bottles heated, feeder beakers.
Very basic self service cafe. Seats outside and in.

RAILWAY PATHS AND CYCLE TRACKS

Railways were developed throughout Edinburgh by rival companies; all that remains now are flat routes which are gradually being developed into a network of footpaths and cycle tracks. 'Spokes' (the cyclists' organisation) is hoping to bring out a map but in the meantime you may find it useful to join them in order to receive up-to-date information, or to campaign for the development of more paths. Send 15p plus SAE for a fact sheet to 'Spokes', 53 George IV Bridge EH1 1EJ; 225 6906. A 'Spokes' member,

Alison Ruddock (229 9916), will organize cycle rides for parents and young children if sufficient people phone her to express an interest. There are developed routes between Corstorphine, Balgreen and Dalry; from Dalry to Davidson's Mains; from Craigleith to Leith; from the New Town to Trinity; and from Easter Rd via Seafield to Leith Links. The paths although flat have often been re-developed and are no longer straight (and boring), but meander between birch trees, rowans and brambles.

RED MOSS WILDLIFE RESERVE BALERNO

Follow the signs to Marchbank hotel, Balerno, pass the hotel and take the next road to the left, then continue on until reaching the sign prohibiting further access by cars. Car parking available here. Rough and muddy track leads on left of road to Threipmuir and Harlaw Reservoirs. Not suitable for pushchairs although if you walk back along the road there is a turning on the right which also takes you past the worst track to the reservoir. Very exposed walk and inclined to be cold. Metalled road continues on from car park up a hill, a tree lined avenue (acorns in season) to track passing Bavelaw Castle (private). Signpost at top gives walking options. Left turn continues to be suitable for pushchairs and prams until reaching field gate and stile opening on to Pentland Hills, the nearest being Hare Hill, 1472'. Sheep and lambs in fields, waterfowl on reservoirs, good hills for sledging, wildflowers and lovely fresh air.

SAUGHTON GARDENS

See Saughton Park, in 'Playgrounds and Parks'.

SWANSTON VILLAGE AND FARM

A small picturesque village at the foot of the Pentland Hills (nr Fairmilehead). At first it is grassy slopes with sheep grazing but higher up becomes rough ground. Can walk over the top to Hillend. Not suitable for buggies. Nice for picnics.

THE UNION CANAL

The Union Canal runs, with obstructions, from the Lochrin Basin in Edinburgh's West End (access from Gilmore Park and Leamington Rd) to Falkirk. The towpath is on the north bank and is in parts a combined cycle and footpath. Obviously children need close supervision. From the centre of the city and industrial buildings (but where swans sometimes nest) the canal goes past suburban gardens and parks and eventually into woods and open countryside. The canal is carried by aqueducts over the Water of Leith at Slateford (you can join up with the Water of Leith walk here, see below), and over the River Almond beyond Ratho. It disappears for a mile into culverts beneath Wester Hailes and is cut through again by the M8 between Broxburn and Ratho. The canal boat **The Pride of the Union** operates from the Bridge Inn at Ratho (see 'Places to Visit' and 'Eating Out'). A leaflet is available which describes the route and history of the canal from the Union Canal Ranger: Helen Rowbotham, Canal Office, Station Rd, Drumshoreland, Broxburn EH52 5PG (0506) 856624. She is keen to encourage children to use the canal and its footpaths, and can arrange talks, guided walks and help with other activities related to the canal.

THE WATER OF LEITH WALKWAY

The Water of Leith rises in the Pentland Hills and runs from Currie in the East through the city until it reaches the Firth of Forth at Leith Docks in the West. In its 23 miles it flows through wooded dells and past abandoned mills, beneath the high terraces of the New Town, under a spectacular road bridge, meanders around cemeteries and past new housing developments until opening out into a broad river surrounded by the dignified commercial buildings and docks of Leith. The walkway runs along most of the river and most parts are negotiable with a buggy. Prams are more difficult as access to some perfectly flat and well paved stretches is down steps. Tricycle riding could be dangerous on stretches where the banks are steep, watch your step too as sections are badly fouled by dogs. The brown water is due to peat and although it is generally safe for paddling there is always the possibility that it does contain sewage from overflows due to heavy rain or failures within the sewage system. Don't drink it. Giant Hogweed, a giant umbellifer with large white flowers has established itself on several stretches. Touching this plant or blowing through sections of its hollow stem may cause allergic reaction and photosensitivity of the skin. These plants are routinely treated with weedkiller and hacked down. Along stretches of the river there are raspberry canes and blackberries which should be safe to eat but remember dogs may have been there before you. Leaflets giving maps and details of some parts of the 'walkway' are available free from the City of Edinburgh District Council, Planning Department, 18 Market St and

141

in some libraries and bookshops. Nature trails have been devised for primary school children along some stretches and leaflets describing them are available from St Bernard's Education Resource Centre, Dean St, and in some bookshops. See also:

Juniper Green Village Association: 'A Water of Leith Walk' (J Tweedie). This includes the industrial history of the Slateford to Balerno section.

The Water of Leith Project Group: 'The Water of Leith' (ed S Jamieson).

Juniper Green to Currie (1½ miles)
Leaflet available for Balerno to Juniper Green

There are no picnic spots on this stretch and not much safe access to the river as it runs in a deep wooded valley. There are 4 access points: **Access at Baberton Loan,** next to Juniper Green Post Office. Public toilets. Park cars in Baberton Ave opposite. Wide, surfaced, safe road downhill to walkway. Excellent for pushchairs or prams. Turn right to Currie, left to Colinton. Good wide and level track (old railway line). Prams may find wooden bridge beyond back of Veitch's Garden Centre difficult but not impassable. All track is muddy when wet with the added hazards of horse manure and dog droppings. **Access at Blinkbonny Rd** (leading to the Glenburn Hotel from Lanark Rd West) at the bridge over the river. Steep muddy wooden steps on right. Not recommended for wheeled transport. No parking. **Access from Blinkbonny Rd** through the Kinleith Industrial Estate. Follow main road through estate and it opens directly on to the walkway. Parking possible. Wooden bench seat 50 yds or so

from here. **Access from Kirkgate, Currie:** Wooden steps, quite steep and muddy nr bridge on left. Wider, level track on left further along.

Juniper Green to Slateford
(inc Craiglockhart Dell), leaflet available

Along this particularily attractive section of the river, the walkway follows the bed of an old railway line, and passes through a railway tunnel at Colinton. A good access point is near here as the former Colinton Station, off Gillespie Rd, is now a car park. The walkway crosses Lanark Rd at Slateford and it is possible to join up with the Union Canal here. There are several other access points too. Craiglockhart Dell, near Slateford, provides old grottoes and beautiful walks in the wooded estate of Craiglockhart House. At Spylaw Rd, in the central Colinton Dell section of the walk, there are 8 swings (4 bucket type) and a high slide on a hard surface.

Slateford to Belford Rd

There is no 'walkway' or river path along much of this section, although you will be able to follow the river with the aid of a street map, as it passes through Saughton and Roseburn Parks, and around the ice-rink and rugby ground at Murrayfield. Those inspired by Dr Livingstone will be able to follow the rest, but should anticipate a lot of scrambling up banks, pushing through undergrowth, and crossing of the river. So wear Wellingtons; the route via the old iron bedstead ferry and the bread-crate stepping stones, which we were shown by a group of 10 yr olds, may no longer be available! Definitely not for pushchairs or anyone who wants to be carried when the going gets tough.

Dean Bank Footpath
Leaflet available

This section follows the north side of the slow moving loop of river which runs in a deep hidden and wooded glen from the Dragonara Hotel to Dean Path. The path is muddy and uneven and not recommended for prams. It is accessed down many steep steps opposite the Dragonara Hotel at Belford Bridge; and also from Dean Path a little way up the hill in the village of Dean. There is also a footbridge about half way along the path to Sunbury Mews, in the new housing development. The track runs on the river bank, a precarious few feet above the water. Some sections have handrail at about 3 ft — useful for adults, but small children can slip straight underneath!

Dean Path to Stockbridge

This established railed and paved section runs along the south bank from Miller Row in Dean, to Saunders St in Stockbridge. As the river gushes beneath the dramatic Dean Bridge, it is hard to imagine the urban bustle only 10 mins walk away at the West End of Princes St. The depth of the steep wooded valley is emphasised by the views of the backs of Moray and Ainslie Pl. St Bernard's Well (a Georgian statue and temple) is halfway along the path; and there are several flights of steps down to paddling and fishing spots. There are upper and lower routes between St Bernard's Well and the bridge at Saunders St. You'll find fewer steps on the higher path.

Deanhaugh Footpath, Stockbridge
Leaflet available

A very short stretch (less then ¼ mile) in Stockbridge. There are steps down near the TSB on Raeburn Pl or ramps at Falshaw Bridge and Haugh St. Although it is a useful secluded spot to remember about if you're feeling hassled at the nearby shops, unfortunately it is always very fouled by dogs. Sometimes ducks to feed.

Rocheid Path

An attractive established section running between Stockbridge and Canonmills. Trees and slopes provide seclusion from the nearby houses. Sledging in winter. Access from Arboretum Rd in Stockbridge, over a wooden bridge that is the continuation of the road between Glenogle Pl and Bell Pl in the Stockbridge colonies, and from Inverleith Ter Lane, off Howard Pl in Canonmills.

Warriston — Coburg St
Leaflet available

This section of the route commences at Warriston Cres and runs for 2 km until it reaches Leith. From there the Water of Leith is followed on its journey to the sea by public roads. It is the most diversified section of the Walkway, following the line of the former North British Railway. It is at times hidden in woodland, at others is high above the surrounding land, giving open views of the city. There is a boat launching area at Coalie Park, and a muddy children's playground at St Marks Park at Warriston Rd, where there is a climbing frame, a slide and a roundabout.

Travel & Transport

BUSES

Daytime buses in and around Edinburgh are operated by two companies: Lothian Region Transport (maroon buses) and Eastern Scottish (green). LRT run most of the city services.

Night-buses are run by Eastern Scottish. Five circular services leave Waverley Bridge 4 times per night serving many parts of the city. A flat fare of 75p is charged for any distance.

Rules for under 5s

Both companies have the same policy. As regards fares, the under 5s travel free on the understanding that they give up their seats for fare paying passengers. An adult can be accompanied by up to 2 free children. The standard children's fare must be paid for any more children under 5. With regard to pushchairs, parents are expected to fold them before taking children on board a bus. LRT say that sometimes (in wet weather or if a bus is less busy)

144

parents may be allowed to board a bus with a child still in a pushchair. This is up to the driver. Only folding pushchairs are permitted on buses — not prams or non-folding push-chairs.

Coach Tours

Both LRT and Eastern Scottish run coach tours round Edinburgh and to places further afield, the former all year round and the latter between April and October. The tours are reasonably priced but are suited to parents with babies (or older chil-dren who can sit still) as even the shortest takes 2 hours. Brochures available.

Longer Distance Buses

Eastern Scottish operate services to many parts of Scotland, where they link with other members of the Scot-tish Omnibus Group. They also run services to London and other parts of England. Fares compare well with train fares, eg £23 return to London compared with £45 off-peak by train. (Can be less with railcard.)

LOTHIAN REGION TRANSPORT

Waverley Bridge Ticket Centre
226 5087
Mon-Sat 7 am-8 pm; Sun 8-8

Head Office
14 Queen St
554 4494
Mon-Fri 9-5

Both offices deal with general phone enquiries and sell travel cards, bus maps, tokens and publications. In addition Waverley Bridge handles tours, while Queen St deals with OAP tickets and all postal enquiries. Tickets and information can also be obtained from specific shops in

Balerno, Currie, Wester Hailes and Cameron Toll.

Lost Property Office, 14 Queen St; Mon-Fri 9-1, 2.15-5.

Fares and Frequency

Adult fares range from 20p-90p. You must offer the exact fare — drivers cannot give change. (Remember to take your ticket from the automatic dispenser.) Dogs travel free. Buses run every 12, 15 or 20 mins on weekdays 8 am-6 pm depending on the route. After 6 pm and at week-ends frequency lessens to every 30 mins or 'irregularly' (quote from timetable).

Cheap Tickets

'Ridacards' can be bought giving unlimited travel on LRT services in and around Edinburgh (including Balerno, Riccarton, Dalkeith etc). A weekly ticket costs £5, 4-weekly £17, and a yearly ticket £193.60. The 'Edinburgh Freedom Ticket' gives one day's unlimited travel for £1.25. The 'Touristcard' gives visitors unlimited travel, reductions on coach tours, a map of Edinburgh, plus concessions at various shops, restaurants, theatres and museums. One day costs £1.25, 4 days £10.80 etc.

You will need a passport-sized photo for your ridacard, but both offices have booths — photos cost 60p.

EASTERN SCOTTISH OMNIBUSES LTD

Bus Station
St Andrew Sq
Enquiry Office (Platform E) 556 8464
Mon-Sat 8-6; Sun 9-5
(Calls are answered in rotation, so

145

don't be surprised if you continue to hear the ringing tone for a while.)

Lost Property Office (Platform A)
Mon-Fri 8.30-12.30, 1.30-5.30

Left Luggage Office (Platform A)
Mon-Sun 7 am-10 pm

(46) **Snack Bar** (Platform A)
Mon-Sat 7 am-8 pm; Sun 9-7
£, breastfeeding permitted, bottles heated.

Self-service cafe, clean but smoky. Main meals and snacks. Steak pie, fish, pizza, hamburger, king-ribs always on menu. Vegetarian dish always available. Children's menu. Buggies must be folded as space is limited. Toilets: ladies next door, gents downstairs. (More toilets on Platform E.)

The bus stops for city buses are not in the Bus Station itself, but on St Andrew Sq.

Fares and Frequency

Adult fares on city routes range from 20p-90p. At present some drivers of green buses can give change, but gradually all buses are being altered to operate an exact-fare-only system. For dogs you pay one quarter the adult fare. During the daytime, frequency ranges from every 5 mins on the C5 Wester Hailes to Restalrig service, to every 30 mins on the C6 route. The usual wait between buses on city routes is 15-20 mins. During the evening and on Sun, services run from ½ hourly to hourly.

Cheap Tickets

'City-go-Round' tickets give unlimited travel on green buses. 1 week's travel within the city (including Currie and Balerno) costs £4.50, 4 week's travel £15, 1 year's travel £169. In addition 'Travel Club'

tickets are available offering unlimited weekly travel between Edinburgh and the Lothians. The cost to Dalkeith or Musselburgh is £5 weekly, to Livingston £9. This pass entitles the holder to ½ price travel on green buses in the city. An initial fee of £1 is charged for entry to the 'City-go-Round' and 'Travel Club' schemes. You also need two photos for your pass. (Booth on Platform A.) The 'Edinburgh Explorer' gives 1 day's unlimited travel on city green buses and costs £1.75.

Where to buy tickets

Weekly tickets can be bought from the driver, your local Post Office, or from the Bus Station. 4-weekly and yearly tickets can be obtained from the Post Office or Bus Station.

TAXIS

There are 4 radio-cab companies in Edinburgh: Central 229 5221, City 228 1211, Radio-Cab 225 9000 and Castle 228 2555. All black taxis charge the same rates: a basic charge of 70p, plus 10p for every additional 345 yds. This covers 2 adults and 1 child under 12. Extra charges are as follows: 40p call-out charge, 5p/item for luggage held in the section next to the driver, 5p for each additional adult (2 children under 12 count as 1 adult.)

SAFE TRAVEL BY CAR

Statistics show that hundreds of children are killed each year because they are not properly secured while travelling in cars. Since 1983 the law has required passengers travelling in the front seats to be properly restrained, but so far no law compels us to restrain passengers in the back seat, although they can be equally at risk. You may have seen on television accident reconstructions which show how children especially can be tossed around.

How to protect your child

Various types of child restraint are available and all safe ones carry the British 'Kitemark' or European 'E' to show they meet recommended standards.

For babies up to 10 kg or 9 mths old, the 'Love-seat', and equivalents made by Mothercare and Britax, are available. These sit on the front or back seat facing rearwards and are held in place by the normal diagonal seat-belt. Fife Health Board has set up a scheme for lending these seats to new parents. Groups interested in setting up a similar scheme can get guidance from The Child Accident Prevention Trust, 75 Portland Pl, London W1N 3AL. Tel: 01-636 2545.

An alternative is to use a carrycot strapped to the back seat of the car. Special car straps are available. Remember also to clip the baby into the carrycot with a harness for added safety.

For children aged from 6 mths to 4 yrs car seats are the best idea. Upright and reclining seats are available. These seats may fix on to existing rear seat-belts. If not, you will need an anchorage kit and possibly also a special bar for fixing, depending on the car. When comparing prices in shops remember to check if the anchorage kit is included — Mothercare, for example, sells it separately. If buying second-hand, remember to ask for the fitments and instructions.

For children aged 4 yrs and upwards a special harness is probably the answer. Alternatively if your car has adult rear seat-belts, a stable cushion or booster seat will raise your child high enough to fit them.

Local shops which sell all the equipment outlined above include Mothercare, John Lewis, Halford's in Hanover St and large branches of Boots. Prices vary so it's worth shopping around. The National Childbirth Trust also sells the 'Love-seat' by mail order.

Prices also vary in garages which fit the seats. The following have been recommended for service and/or price:

T C Juner and Son

13 Montague Ter, Canonmills
552 4173

Supply and fit the Kangol Dreamseat cheaply.

Heriothill Garage

18 Manderston St
553 1012

They successfully fitted a child seat to the back seat of a VW caravanette without removing the engine, which was advised by other garages.

For further information see the leaflet 'Protect Your Child in the Car' available from the Dept of Transport, Room C16/12, 2 Marsham St, London SW1P 3EB. For free advice call the Dept of Transport, Freephone 234 888.

Car Hire and Child Seats

Most local rental firms seem to offer car seats for the 9 mth to 4 yr age group. Avis and Europ Car charge

147

£10/rental while Budget charges £5. Forth Car Hire usually supply seats free of charge and also harnesses for 4-11 yr olds. However best by far are Mitchell's who supply seats, straps for carrycots, a 'Love-seat' equivalent seat for babies and harnesses — all free of charge.

Tel. Mitchell's Self Drive 229 5384; Forth Car Hire 343 1001.

Road Safety

The Tufty Club teaches children the following basic rules of road safety:

— Never go out without an adult
— Always hold an adult's hand
— Stop, look, listen before you cross the road

Individual children can join the Tufty Club, as can playgroups, nurseries etc. It costs nothing. Members receive leaflets and advice, a news-letter 3 times a year, and books, games and visual aids to help teach children road safety.

Write to: The Tufty Club Office, RoSPA, Cannon House, The Priory, Queensway, Birmingham B4 6BS. (RoSPA also publish easy-to-read leaflets on all aspects of safety — in the home, in the water, camping and caravanning etc.)

TRAVEL BY TRAIN

Enquiries

Waverley Station Enquiry Office
Mon-Sat 8 am-11 pm; Sun 9 am-11 pm
Passengers train enquiries 556 2451 (Calls are answered in rotation, so be prepared for a wait at peak hours.) 24 hr telephone service.
Sleepers 556 5633
All other enquiries 556 2477

(See Phone Book under British Rail for numbers of other information services.) Edinburgh is a major station in the BR network. Trains travel from here all over Scotland and south of the border.

Stations

Edinburgh is currently served by 5: Waverley and Haymarket in the city centre, and South Gyle, Kingsknowe and Meadowbank. By October 1987 2 further stations will be open — at the Wester Hailes Shopping Centre and at Curriehill both on the Edinburgh to Glasgow Central line.

Waverley is the principal station serving all destinations. It provides many amenities all on one level: a large airy Victorian waiting hall — great for restless children to charge around in, but beware the automatic doors which allow easy exit.

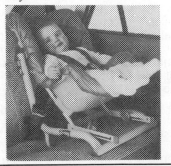

This is surrounded by the ticket and reservation counters, 'superloos', self service food units and a bar. Elsewhere in the Station there are snack kiosks, a bookshop/newsagents, florists, shoe repair shop and various fast food counters selling baked potatoes etc. The 'superloos' cost 10p to enter, are clean and have many facilities. The ladies have toilets, showers and a comfy waiting area, a long well-lit mirror, and a small separate mothers' room with chair, sink, nappy changing surface and bin — perfect for feeding baby in private. Ask the attendant if you wish to use this room as it is kept locked.

The Food Court

Mon-Sun 6.30-12 m'night
£, High chairs (2), breastfeeding permitted, bottles heated.

Self-service cafeteria selling meals and snacks. There are 3 counters. 'Casey Jones' serves burgers, bacon rolls, French fries etc. 'Hot Favourites' is licensed and serves breakfasts, fish and chips, chicken nuggets etc. 'Upper Crust' serves cakes, filled French bread etc. All 3 serve drinks. Cold drinks come in lidded cups with straws. No toilets in Food Court but station 'superloos' not far away.

Haymarket serves all points west and north. Lots of steps to platforms. The short trip between Waverley and Haymarket is popular with playgroups as an outing.

South Gyle is a suburban halt serving all Fife trains. A return trip to Waverley Station (9 mins away) costs 80p, single 50p. Tickets are obtained on the north platform from a ticket machine which takes all silver and £1 coins. Large car park

on south side. No steps. Trains run ½-hourly to Waverley.

Kingsknowe lies west of Waverley on the Edinburgh to Glasgow Central line. Trains run hourly in each direction and more frequently at peak hours. It takes 11 mins to get to Waverley and the fare is 50p single, £1 return, payable on the train.

Meadowbank is on a branch line east of Waverley. It is currently only used for special trains, eg football specials when Hibs are playing at Easter Road, or for large sporting events at Meadowbank Stadium.

Future Plans

Scotrail are currently seeking funding for a circular suburban route using the existing freight line which takes in Gorgie, Morningside, Blackford, Newington, Niddrie, Portobello, and Meadowbank. If funds are made available construction will take about 5 years.

Fares and Rules

As a general rule children under 5 travel free, on the understanding that they give up their seats to fare-paying passengers. An adult can be accompanied by up to 4 free under 5s.

Folding pushchairs and prams are permitted on trains but not their non-folding counterparts. Guards vans are very small nowadays (where they exist).

Return fares are usually twice the single fare.

Cheaper Tickets

'Off-peak Day Returns' are available but only on less busy routes and to destinations within 50 miles of Edinburgh, eg to Stirling, Glasgow and all points west, but not to Fife. On a weekday you must travel after 9.15 am. On Sat and Sun you can travel at any time. Over long-distance routes 'saver tickets' are widely available. A leaflet explaining 'savers' is available from Waverley Station.

Railcards

BR offers railcards to many users including families and senior citizens. Cards for these 2 groups cost £15 and £12 respectively and are valid for 1 year from the day you buy it. These are excellent value and if used carefully can save you lots of money when you travel with children. The railcard entitles you to a reduction of 34% on the normal adult fare. The amount you save on one long-distance journey will probably cover the cost of the railcard, so it's worth getting the card for only one long journey per year. The Family Railcard is issued to adults both of whom are pictured on the card. If both holders travel they can take with them up to 2 other adults at the reduced rate, plus up to 4 children. If only 1 card holder is travelling he can take up to 2 other adults and 4 children. A useful feature of this card is that the 2 holders need not be in 1 family, so you and your sister or friend can jointly buy 1 card which is then valid for both families. For children over 5 you pay a flat-rate of £1 each. If all the children travelling are under 5, you pay a token £1 to qualify for the scheme. An adult holding a Senior Citizen Railcard can also take up to 4 children.

Foreign Travel by Train

For an extra payment of £5, holders of a Family Railcard can buy a Rail Europ Family Railcard which entitles the holder to reduced railfares in Europe.

See BR leaflets for full details of all railcards. Available from Waverley Station.

Tips

1) Seat reservations. £1 reserves one 2nd class seat but it costs no more to reserve up to 4 seats.
2) Avoid travelling Fri or Sat if you want cheaper tickets.
3) Best and most private place to change a baby's nappy on a train is sitting on the toilet seat lid with the baby balanced on your knee!

AIR TRAVEL

👫 Edinburgh Airport

A8, 4 miles west of Edinburgh (near Ingliston showground)
333 1000

Reservations British Airways 225 2525; Air UK 225 3978; British Caledonian 041-887 0101; British Midland 447 1000. (For full details of all airline numbers, see Phone Book under 'Airports' or individual airlines.)

The airport terminal is modern, spacious and clean. The lay-out is simple: a 3-storey building with a long tail, with all the principal facilities housed in the former: snack bar, restaurant, shop, bank, bar, spectators' gallery and most of the information desks. The external doors are automatic and lots of luggage trolleys are available. Lifts at Gates 3 and 5. There are toilets everywhere, and doors are wider than average — a boon for buggy-pushing parents!

Spectators' Gallery

Reached by the lift at Gate 5, the gallery is open during daylight hours. The best time for viewing if you want to see lots of planes is during the summer, on Sat and Sun and Mon-Fri 12-2.30. In winter the airport is much quieter.

Mother and Baby Room

Located at Gate 6 the room is excellent if a bit cramped. It has comfortable chairs, a deep sofa, play-pen, sinks, nappy-changing surface, large bin, nappy-and-wipe machine (50p for 1) and an en-suite toilet. The latter has larger than normal floorspace and a door that opens outwards, so that (for once!) you don't trap your toddler in the door as you enter. There is also a pull-cord for medical assistance which summons one of the enquiry desk staff, all of whom are trained nurses. Fathers may use the room also. Unfortunately the room is only signposted once you get to it, so it is easy to miss.

The Sky Shop

The shop sells an amazing selection of goods, ranging from small travel packs of baby-wipes and baby lotion to sewing kits, luggage labels, straps and souvenirs. In addition it carries magazines and books (including a reasonable range for the under 5s), as well as story tapes, colouring books and toys.

EATING PLACES

Pie In The Sky
Mon-Sun 6.30 am-9 pm
£, High chairs (3), bottles heated.

A self-service snack-bar in an open area off the main ground-floor concourse. Offers sandwiches, rolls, salads, fruit, yoghurt, pastries etc. Bright, clean and spacious and welcomes children. There is a no-smoking area and lots of room for buggies and prams. Beware — there is no door, so kids can wander off. (Nappy-changing in nearby Mother and Baby Room.) Tables not suitable for clip-on seats.

Algy's International Diner
Mon-Sun 7 am-10 am, 12-8.30 pm
£££, High chairs (2), bottles heated, children's menu.

Small, waitress-service restaurant on the 1st floor. Standard grill menu featuring steaks, hamburgers etc with salad bar. Plenty of room for buggies and prams.

Which Airline is Best?

All airlines like to know **in advance** that you are travelling with babies and children.

On short flights you may not require much by way of help. Most airlines seem to offer similar services: families are boarded before the other passengers; cabin staff stock supplies of nappies and juice, and will heat or cool bottles and baby food as required. In addition, British Caledonian (B Cal) and Air UK both say they give parents an extra seat to spread out into, if there is room. Air UK mentioned that on certain aircraft families are seated in a section of the plane which has extra emergency oxygen masks, to allow for children sitting on parents' knees.

On longer flights many airlines offer extra services to parents, in addition to the above. British Airways (BA) and B Cal provide 'skycots' (similar to carrycots) for babies up to 9 mths old. (It is worth asking for one even for a toddler, as sleeping in a cot curled up or with feet over the edge may be better than sleeping on the floor.) Both BA and B Cal try to seat families in the bulkhead to give them more room. They say they supply baby milk and special meals for babies (but experienced travellers warn not to rely on this). A member of staff is allocated to look after the families on board. Both airlines allow you to bring your buggy into the cabin if they are not too full, so that you can wheel your child from the departure lounge on to the plane. If there is no room, they will at least stow the buggy in the hold last, so that it is first off. You can request that your buggy be fetched as soon as you leave the plane. Some airlines have special amusement packs for children with hat, sweets and colouring book. Although geared to school-children they can be useful to distract younger children.

Pregnancy and Air Travel

Flying is unlikely to be harmful in a normal pregnancy, but airlines will not as a rule carry women after the 35th week. Some airlines require a note from your GP as to your fitness. Anyone who has had a previous miscarriage or premature baby is advised not to embark on long jet flights during pregnancy.

Nappy-changing on Board the Plane

Facilities vary with each aircraft. In the toilet of the larger trans-atlantic planes there is a changing surface which folds down. The similar planes used on European routes may not have this facility.

152

'Airlink' Bus

Operated by Lothian Region Transport this service runs every ½-hour Mon-Fri from 8.30 am-8.30 pm, and hourly outwith these times. The single fare is a flat-rate £1.75 for adults, £1.20 for children aged 5 and over. The return fare is £3 and £2 respectively for adults and children. A special Family Day Return costs £3.50 for 2 adults and up to 3 children. You catch the bus at specially marked stops on Waverley Bridge, Princes St, Haymarket and points west. Look out for stops with blue plates embellished with a white aeroplane. The buses themselves have a black and white livery. The journey between Waverley Bridge and Edinburgh Airport takes 25 mins.

'Citylink' to Glasgow Airport

Eastern Scottish operate a ½-hourly service to Glasgow Airport. Journey time is 1 hr 44 mins. The single fare is £2.80, return fare is £4.25 (children over 5 ½ price).

Welfare

If you have any problems with Maternity or Child Benefit, Social Security, marriage or divorce and are seeking counselling or legal advice the following organisations may be of some help:

Benefits Advice Shop

Sighthill Community Centre, Sighthill Wynd
Volunteers contact David Gardner 442 1009 (office hours)

Joint venture between Sighthill Community Centre and Wester Hailes

Citizens Advice Bureau. Provides free and confidential advice on all aspects of welfare benefits and social security.

One morning a week, Tues 10.30-12.30

Citizens Advice Bureau
Central Office, 58 Dundas St
557 1500
Mon-Fri 9.30-4. Closed Wed 12.30-2.30. Answer-phone when closed.

Apart from giving more general advice and information most branches have an evening clinic once a week where a qualified lawyer can be seen by sppointment to give free advice. Local branches at Gorgie/Dalry, Leith, Pilton, Portobello and Wester Hailes. See phone book for details.

Citizens Rights Office
43 Broughton St
557 3366

Mon-Fri 10-4; Tues, Wed, Thurs 1-4

DHSS
Central Office for Scotland, Argyle House, 3 Lady Lawson St
229 9191

Gingerbread
5 Casselbank St, Leith
553 3970/553 4169

Legal clinics and counselling provided every 2nd Tues and Wed (respectively). By appointment. Clinics start at 5.30.

Granton Unemployed Information Centre
134 West Granton Rd
551 2459 Cassie Stewart
Mon-Fri 10-1.30

For information about social security, housing, job vacancies, welfare rights, assistance with filling out forms, interviews etc.

Legal Aid Dispensary
Old College, Edinburgh University, South Bridge
667 1011 Ext 4214 Miss Lorimer
Wed 6.30-7.45

Free legal advice organised by the Law Faculty. In the Old College Common Room.

Lothian Marriage Counselling Service
556 1527

Simpson House (Counselling Service)
225 6028/225 1054

Under the auspices of the Church of Scotland the service offers counselling to anyone with personal problems.

Welfare Advice Clinics
Leith Community Centre, New Kirkgate
553 3970/553 4169
Tues 10-12

Clinics offering advice for people with questions and problems regarding Social Services.

The Lothian Directory of Local Services
The 'Red Book' is a useful reference book giving the names and addresses of all local government departments, churches, schools, libraries, police stations etc. This should be available in libraries. See 'Sources of Information'.

See also the following chapter **'Health Care Facilities, Problem Solving**.

Health Care Facilities

This chapter describes resources available in Edinburgh for family health care; maternity and paediatric hospital facilities; and lists contacts for advice and assistance with specific problems. We have checked that all the organisations mentioned, many of which are charities with volunteer staff, are active and, wherever possible, we have given a local address and phone number.

The Scottish Health Education Group have published several guides to certain aspects of health care which provide more detailed information. We acknowledge the assistance given by the SHEG booklets, listed below.

'Well Woman — A Guide to Women's Health'; 'Getting the Best for Your Child'; 'The Book of the Child Pregnancy to 4 Years Old'; all published by: The Scottish Health Education Group, Woodburn House, Canaan Lane EH10 4SG, 447 8044

Useful addresses:

Lothian Health Board
14 Drumsheugh Gdns EH3 7QG
225 1341

Edinburgh Local Health Council
21 Torphichen St EH3 8HX
229 6605

GENERAL PRACTITIONER (GP) SERVICES

Everyone is entitled to receive services from a GP, but an individual GP is not obliged to accept a particular patient on his or her list. Lists of GPs are available in post offices, and from the Lothian Health Board or Local Health Council (addresses above). These show the doctor's name, practice address, phone number, consulting hours and the range of services offered. Both you and your GP should sign part A of your medical card. If you have lost it, you can still sign on a doctor's list by using a form which you can get from the surgery, or apply to the Health Board for a new card.

If you want to change your doctor (but have not changed your address), you may do so at once if your present doctor has given consent by signing your medical card. If you do not want to let your doctor know that you intend to change, you can do this by writing to Lothian Health Board but there will be a 14 day gap until the changeover takes place. If you have difficulty in finding a doctor to accept you as a patient, contact the Health Board which has an obligation to find you a GP.

ALTERNATIVE MEDICINE

This covers a number of fields such as oesteopathy, chiropractice, homoeopathy, medical herbalism, hypnotherapy, acupuncture and many other forms of medical treatment. Most of these services are offered privately by individual practitioners who charge a fee for consultations and treatment. Your GP may be able to refer you to an alternative medicine specialist or you can approach one yourself.

Libraries and good bookshops may have books which describe specific types of therapy or books which refer to individual problems such as back pain or allergy and these may describe the appropriate therapy which could be tried.

Homoeopathic treatment is available on the NHS at the **Glasgow Homoeopathic Hospital,** 1000 Great Western Rd, Glasgow (041-339 0382). Outpatient referrals to 5 Lynedoch Cres, Glasgow (041-332 4490). You must be referred to the hospital by a letter from your own GP and you will then be sent an appointment.

British Homoeopathic Association
27 Devonshire St, London W1

Supply a list of Medical Doctors practising homoeopathy.

CANA (Centre of Advice on Natural Alternatives)
Catherine Barrett, 26 Lighthorne Rd, Solihull B91 2BD
021-705 9961 (before 9 pm)

Information referral service. SAE required.

The Institute for Complementary Medicine
Miss Helen Campbell, Armadale, West Lothian
0501 30935

Directory of registered therapists in various branches of alternative medicine.

Napier D & Sons
17 Bristo Pl EH1 1EZ
225 5542

Herbal remedies, health food supplies, vitamins etc in shop. Also consultation facilities for specific problems.

The Templegarth Trust
82 Tinkle St, Grimoldby, Louth, Lincolnshire
050782 655

'Encourages health cultivation in individuals, families and neighbourhoods. Its work complements contemporary efforts to establish alternative methods of healing'. Literature on pregnancy and nutrition.

FAMILY PLANNING

GPs give family planning advice and some prescribe contraceptives but do not supply free condoms. They can be obtained free, or at very low cost, from the family planning clinics listed below.

Family Planning Centre
18 Dean Ter EH4 1NL
332 7941

Free and confidential advice on birth control and free supply of contraceptives. Sexual problems clinic, vasectomy service and pregnancy counselling. Waiting room with toys, staff accommodating to young children.

The Brook Advisory Centre
2 Lower Gilmore Pl EH3 9NY
229 5320

Free and confidential advice on birth control and free supply of contraceptives. Counselling service, particularly for young people.

Catholic Marriage Advisory Centre
205 Ferry Rd EH6 4NN
440 2650 (Tel: Mon-Fri 10-5)
Mon, Tues, Wed 7-9 pm by appointment only.

Natural Family Planning
28 Lauriston St EH3 9DJ
665 2759

No appointment necessary.
1st and 3rd Weds of each month 7-9 pm.
Teaches the Billings (or Ovulation) Method of natural family planning to avoid or achieve pregnancy. Service is free. Literature and teaching aids.

PRE-CONCEPTUAL CARE

Foresight — The Association for the Promotion of Pre-Conceptual Care
The Secretary (Mrs J Barnes), The Old Vicarage, Church Lane, Witley, Surrey GU8 5PN
04279 4500

Leaflets and publications; help and advice on pre-conceptual care to help prevent congenital deformity and mental damage. Information may be helpful to those with infertility or recurrent miscarriage problems. Send large SAE.

Genetic Counselling
Your GP may refer you to the Western General Hospital for this service if medical history indicates this would be useful.

PREGNANCY TESTING

Free pregnancy testing is available from GPs (2-3 days for results). Home testing kits (from good chemists) give reasonably reliable results in an hour or two.

Lifeline UK Pregnancy Advice & Care Service
9 Albany St EH1 3PY
557 2060
Mon-Fri 9.30-3.30

Free, confidential service to anyone who is or thinks she may be pregnant. Pregnancy testing, material help, professional counselling, information. Post abortion counselling.

Newington Laboratories
26 Clerk St EH8 9HX
667 7534

Private pregnancy testing for a fee.

PREGNANCY, MATERNITY CARE, AND CHILDBIRTH

This section is intended to be a general guide to facilities available in Edinburgh; for more detailed information, contact the Edinburgh Local Health Council (address at beginning of Chapter) who will be happy to discuss any aspect of hospital facilities.

There are four maternity units in Edinburgh:

Eastern General Hospital
Seafield St EH6 7LN
554 4444

Elsie Inglis Memorial Maternity Hospital
Spring Gardens, Abbeyhill EH8 8HT
661 3234

Simpson Memorial Maternity Pavilion
Lauriston Pl EH3 9EF
229 2477

Western General Hospital
Crewe Rd EH4 2XU
332 2525

The Lothian Health Board is currently planning to reorganise the maternity services in Edinburgh. The plan is to close the small units at Elsie Inglis and the Eastern General and to build a new larger unit of 100 beds at the Western General Hospital. This should be in operation by the early 1990s. Both the choice and availability of facilities, particularly for mothers on the eastern side of the city, will be profoundly affected. Elsie's has been the popular choice of maternity unit for many women because it pioneered a more relaxed approach to delivery, initially with considerable opposition from some health professionals. More recently, however, all the local hospitals have made concessions to the requests of some women for 'natural birth' opportunities, including ambulant labour and alternative birth positions.

The Elsie Inglis Action Group has been formed to campaign to keep Elsie's and the Eastern open. Details from Moyra Burns (669 5277).

HOME CONFINEMENT

You may of course choose to have your baby at home instead of in a hospital (if your medical history indicates this would be safe). However, very few GPs offer home deliveries. If you want a home delivery and your GP is unable to be involved, try to find another GP or contact the Nursing Officer in charge of Community Nursing Services through the Lothian Health Board (225 1341).

The organisations mentioned below will give you advice and support for your request.

Birth Rights
Yvonne Baginsky, 2 Forth St EH1 3LD
557 0960

Society to Support Home Confinement
Margaret Whyte (Organiser), 17 Laburnum Ave, Durham
0385 61325

ANTE-NATAL CARE

As soon as you think you are pregnant you should visit your GP. Usually you will be asked to choose where you would like to have your baby. Basic facts to bear in mind are your preference and comfort, closeness to home, your medical history, the consultants' policies, hospital facilities and the size of the maternity unit. The Eastern General and Elsie Inglis are smaller units than the Western or the Simpson. A mother's specific requests will be met (circumstances permitting) in all of the units.

Options for ante-natal care if you are having your baby in hospital are usually:

Shared Care: You attend a Booking Clinic and one other hospital clinic before 32 weeks, seeing your own GP regularly in between. After 32 weeks you may attend the hospital clinic more often;

GP Care: You attend only the GP's local ante-natal clinic and he or she will deliver your baby in hospital and visit you there afterwards. A few GPs in Edinburgh offer this type of care but your choice of where you have your baby will be restricted;

Hospital-only Care: You attend only the hospital ante-natal clinic throughout your pregnancy.

Unless you are having full GP care you should be given a choice of Consultant Obstetrician (the most senior hospital doctor concerned with pregnancy and birth); your GP, friends, or ante-natal class teacher may be able to guide your choice. Although you may not meet your Obstetrician at the hospital clinic he or she will supervise your maternity care and you may request a personal consultation.

ANTE-NATAL TESTS

Routine testing of blood and urine, as well as regular blood pressure and weight checks, will occur throughout your pregnancy.

A Scan (Ultrasound scan) may be performed at your hospital ante-natal appointment (or more rarely at your GP's surgery). A 'picture' of the baby is build up on a small television screen using sound waves and can provide an accurate 'due date' as well as checking the progress of the baby.

All pregnant women in Edinburgh are offered AFP (Alpha Fetoprotein) screening. This is a simple blood test usually taken by your GP between 16 and 18 weeks of pregnancy to detect possible spina bifida in the baby.

Amniocentesis (testing the amniotic fluid to check for abnormalities such as Down's Syndrome in the baby) may be offered to women over 35 or others whose babies may be at risk. It is usually performed at a maternity unit as an outpatient.

ANTE-NATAL APPOINTMENTS

Unfortunately there are sometimes long delays at hospital antenatal clinics. During your appointment a creche may be available for young children but check with the hospital as times may vary.

Eastern General
Supervised creche.

Elsie Inglis
Toys in waiting areas.

Simpson
Supervised playroom and creche (ask at reception).

Western General
No creche.

ANTE-NATAL CLASSES

You will be offered the opportunity to attend ante-natal classes provided free by all the hospitals. Classes to prepare you for labour (not held at the Eastern) are usually held in the later weeks of pregnancy but early pregnancy classes may be available (check at your first ante-natal appointment). Classes at Elsie's may include preparation for using the birthing room. 'Mothercraft' classes are provided at all hospitals.

Local clinics and health centres sometimes offer classes organised by Health Visitors (sometimes with a creche).

Non-NHS classes are also available in Edinburgh from:

Birth Rights
Yvonne Baginsky
2 Forth St EH1 3LD
557 0960

For classes contact: Beatrice Carline
0875 340239

A sister group of the Birth Centre (London). Ante-natal classes run for 10 weeks and aim 'to give parents the information, skills and confidence needed to reclaim the responsibility for their very own childbearing experience'. Labour and post-natal support available. Classes cost £25 (concessions available). Venues vary.

Nadine Edwards
229 6259

A birth teacher, affiliated to the London Birth Centre, runs classes including stretching for active birth, information and discussion. She is particularly interested in working with single young pregnant women.

The National Childbirth Trust
Stockbridge Health Centre, 1 India Pl EH3 6EH
225 9191
Mon-Fri 9.30-11.30

A registered charity devoted to 'education for parenthood'. Classes (£25 for a course of 9 classes) give mothers-to-be and their partners (if they wish) an opportunity to learn about pregnancy and childbirth from a practical and emotional point of view. Breathing and exercise are an important part of these classes. Breastfeeding counsellors help with feeding queries. Post-natal support groups operate locally where pregnant women, new and not-so-new mothers can meet for a chat to give and gain support and friendship. Refresher classes are available (reduced fee) for second- and subsequent-time-mums. Help with fees may be available. Venues vary.

Antenatal Exercise Class
See 'Activities for Parents, Classes and Courses for Women Only'.

ANTE-NATAL INFORMATION

Active Birth Movement
32 Willow Rd, London NW3
01-794 5227
11 am-2 pm

Preparation for birth which emphasises self-responsibility, self-help and natural healing.

Association for Improvements in the Maternity Services (AIMS)
67 Leonard Rd, London SE20

Campaigning group which provides information, excellent booklists and advice to parents about all aspects of maternity care. Quarterly journal.

Maternity Alliance
309 Kentish Town Rd, London NW5 2TJ
01-267 3255

Campaigns for the rights of mothers, fathers and babies. Literature available.

MISCARRIAGE

Any bleeding once your pregnancy has been confirmed should be reported to your GP as it may mean you are threatening to miscarry. You may hear your doctor call this a threatened abortion because the medical term for miscarriage is abortion. Many women find this word upsetting because of the way it is used in other contexts but it does not have these connotations for your GP. You may be admitted to the ante-natal ward of the hospital where you are booked for delivery and find yourself in distressingly close proximity to mothers with babies. However it is difficult to avoid this in the current design of Edinburgh's maternity units.

Your Health Visitor may be able to give you support and advice after a miscarriage.

The Miscarriage Association

18 Stoneybrook Close, West Bretton, Wakefield WF4 4TP
092 485 515

Aims to provide support, help and information, and to set up local groups. SAE required.

LABOUR

All the hospital staff we spoke to emphasised that they wished childbirth to be a safe and happy experience for everyone. It is as well to keep an open mind about labour — it is not an exam to pass or fail. Discuss what you would like to happen during labour with the staff and listen to the replies. All the hospitals said they were willing to comply with mothers' wishes 'within the bounds of commonsense and reason'. All women having a hospital delivery are entitled to make a 'birth plan' — ie a written statement of wishes and preferences during labour and at delivery, which will be included in the hospital case notes. It is very important to discuss **'birth plans'** prior to admission in labour so that any problems can be resolved. It should also be reviewed on admission to the labour ward because you may not necessarily meet the same people when you are admitted in labour as you did at your hospital ante-natal appointments. At the **Western** a 'birth plan' is offered to mothers at the booking clinic.

Policies on induction, acceleration of labour, foetal heart monitoring, use of drugs, episiotomy etc vary from consultant to consultant, as well as, of course, being determined by individual circumstances. This may be something you may wish to find out about before you choose your consultant; ask your GP, hospital clinic or friends for advice.

The hospitals all encourage women to be mobile during a straightforward labour, and all now have portable fetal heart monitors.

Women are encouraged to have a labour 'companion', who may be her husband or partner, a relative or a friend, to be with her throughout labour and delivery.

Conflict occasionally arises between doctors and mothers and may involve midwives. Midwives are bound by codes of practice and professional conduct, and also, as NHS employees, by the approved policies of the Lothian Health Board, and thus must follow the instructions of the consultant obstetrician. In all circumstances the welfare of the mother and baby is of primary importance.

DELIVERY

The 4 hospitals all have the traditional delivery beds, 'high-tech' equipment, facilities for drugs etc. Although an anaesthetist may not be resident, epidurals and Caesarean Sections are always available in emergency and usually .in most other circumstances too. Husbands may be present at some forceps deliveries, and also Caesareans (especially if performed under epidural anaesthetic) but this should be arranged with your consultant.

The traditional 'birth-on-the-bed' is

no longer compulsory at any of Edinburgh's hospitals, and all have made provision for other positions to be adopted:

Eastern General

Birthing chair, bed and a bean bag. Mattresses may be put on the floor for supported squats etc.

Elsie Inglis

The 'birthing room' is a small room minimally equipped with armchair, stool, a mattress and casette recorder. You may bring with you items you think will be useful (but discuss intentions in advance). If you hope to use the birthing room this should be mentioned to the clinic staff early in pregnancy. If it is in use when you need it beds can be removed from the other delivery rooms and mattresses provided for birth on the floor.

Simpson

Birthing chair. Mattresses can be provided for alternative positions. Bean bags.

Western General

Birthing chair and bed. You may not deliver on a mattress on the floor, but may adopt alternative positions on the bed (this makes many positions impractical).

POST-NATAL CARE

You may choose to have your post-natal care in hospital or at home. The normal length of stay after a first baby is 5 or 6 days. You may arrange to go home after 6 or 48 hrs if you wish. Options for early discharge have to be arranged

between your GP, the hospital, and the community midwives and this must be done before your baby is delivered.

POST-NATAL WARDS

You may prefer company or privacy and quiet; you may also want your baby to stay next to your bed or to be cared for in a separate nursery. However, larger wards where babies are 'roomed in' (beside the mother's bed) can make nonsense of the idea of staying in hospital 'for a rest'. Mothers recovering from Caesareans or difficult deliveries are usually assigned to the smaller wards. All hospitals except the Western allow fathers open visiting 'within reason' and will also make arrangements for visitors who cannot come during the set times. See the Ward Sister. Children can also visit, but only at the discretion of the Ward Sister. Your own will nearly always be allowed. Remind friends and relations that they should not visit you at all if they have colds or other infections.

Eastern General

Single to 4-bedded wards. Two single beds can be pushed together for use by couples during prolonged labour or following a difficult delivery or stillbirth.

Rooming in: During the day; at night on request.

Visiting: 3-4, 7.30-8.30.

Elsie Inglis

Single to 7-bedded wards.

Rooming in: At all times, although babies can be taken out by request at night.

Visiting: 3-4, 7.30-8.30.

Simpson

Single to 10-bedded wards.

Rooming in: During the day; at night on request.

Visiting: 2.30-4.30, 7-8.30.

Western General

One 3-bedded ward; others of 10 beds.

Rooming in: Day only.

Visiting: 3-4, 7.15-8.15. Fathers may be allowed to visit outside these hrs.

SPECIAL CARE BABY UNITS

All the maternity units have these in case of anything going wrong. Ill babies are transferred from Elsie Inglis to the Simpson and all the units transfer any baby requiring surgery (eg for cardiac problems) to the Royal Hospital for Sick Children (see Paediatric Hospitals for address).

The units encourage early handling of babies and breast milk can be expressed for individual babies if normal feeding is not possible. Breast pumps are available for the use of mothers of sick or premature infants from the hospital or Community Midwives. (The NCT also have breast pumps available. See Ante-Natal Classes for Address.) Accommodation may be available for mothers (and sometimes fathers) if it is required.

All Special Care Units allow babies to be christened in the unit either by the Hospital Chaplain (of the appropriate denomination) or by the parents' minister.

Support for parents of babies in Special Care is available from:

Friends of Simpsons Neonatal Intensive Care Unit

Peter and Sue Heatly
449 6719

Raises funds to 'maintain and improve facilities in the unit and to support parents who had and have babies in the unit'.

NAWCH National Association for the Welfare of Children in Hospital

(See below Paediatric Hospitals and Wards.)

Scottish Premature Baby Support Group

Maggie Pringle, 12 Corstorphine Hill Cres EH12 6LL
334 1934

Help and friendship for families whose baby requires admission to a neonatal special or intensive care unit. Branches all over Scotland. Affiliated to NIPPERS (National Information for Parents of Prematures: Education, Resources and Support).

REGISTRATION OF BIRTH

The hospital or doctor notifies the Lothian Health Board of the birth of your baby within 36 hours. In addition, you or your husband must register your baby's birth with a Registrar of Births, Marriages and Deaths within 21 days. Your hospital, midwife or health visitor will know which office you should contact. You will be given a Birth Certificate for your baby which you may need to produce for various purposes (such as claiming Child Benefit).

STILLBIRTH AND NEONATAL DEATH

All the hospitals will advise parents about what to do if their baby dies. Lothian Health Board will make arrangements and pay for the funeral of a stillborn baby.

The Stillbirth and Neonatal Death Society (Local Group)
Zania McKenzie, 55 Buckstone Cres
EH10 6PP
445 3856

Offers support to parents who have suffered a stillbirth or neonatal death. Local self-help group. Literature. SAE required.

POST-NATAL SUPPORT AND NEW BABIES

Community Midwives visit you at home after the birth of your baby (and will attend the delivery if you have a home confinement). If you go home early they will visit twice a day until the baby is 3 days old, thereafter they will visit once a day until the baby is 10 days old (or for longer if there are any problems).

Health Visitors are nurses with special training and are often midwives as well. They work in close contact with your GP from the surgery or a Well-baby Clinic. You should be visited at least once by a Health Visitor after you have your baby and she may be contacted by telephone for advice and reassurance. She will want to keep a check on your baby's weight, make sure that the baby is developing properly, will give hearing tests and she will guide you about the immunisation programme. Your

Health Visitor should be a valuable source of information and tips and no problem should be too trivial for her. She will give advice on feeding, nappy rash, teething, weaning etc. If you are not happy with the relationship you have with your Health Visitor, discuss the possibility of seeing another one with your GP.

New Friends can provide valuable support once life eventually starts getting organised. Meeting other mothers who are experiencing similar joys and trials can be very reassuring. Some mother and toddler groups have 'baby groups' attached (see Pre-School Play and Education). Birth Rights and the NCT both arrange meetings for mums to get together (see Ante-natal Classes for addresses).

The National Childbirth Trust (address see Ante-Natal Classes) offers extensive post-natal support in the form of local groups which meet on a regular basis. If you go to NCT Ante-Natal Classes your name will be given to your local group representative who should contact you around the time your baby is due, if not before. She will give you details of local meetings and may be able to advise you of who to contact if you have any specific problems. The NCT Office will tell you who your local group representative is if you are not an NCT member. You are welcome to join a Post-Natal Support Group, even if you have not been to NCT Ante-Natal Classes. Activities include coffee mornings or afternoons, evening talks, fund-raising events, picnics, local newsletter etc. Annual membership costs £5 locally, £10 nationally. National members receive the quarterly magazine 'New Generation'.

Birth Rights
See above 'Ante-Natal Classes'
557 0960

MAMA (Meet-a-Mum Association)
Kate Goodyer, 3 Woodside Ave, London SE25 5DW

Self-help groups throughout the UK for mothers with new babies and/or young children. SAE required.

Twins Club
Hedda Gregg, 48 Corstorphine Hill Ave EH12 6LE
334 4698

Post-Natal Exercise Class
See 'Activities for Parents, Classes and Courses for Women Only'.

POST-NATAL DEPRESSION

Local support groups are occasionally set up for mothers with post-natal depression and your Health Visitor may be able to advise you.

The Church of Scotland Family Counselling Centre
52 Queen St EH2 3NS
225 6028/1054

Offers individual counselling to mothers and fathers, and also a weekly group meeting, with creche and child care provided, every Mon morning. Phone the centre (Mrs Rosemary Dempster) or speak to your GP or Health Visitor.

Post-natal Depression Support Group
Leith Community Centre
New Kirkgate, Leith
669 3355 Laura Bryden-Reid or
554 4433 ext 244 Anne Simpson

Group meets Wed 10-12 for coffee, chat and support from former sufferers. For individual help contact the above people, your Health Visitor or doctor. Health Visitors also run groups in different parts of the city.

Association for Post-Natal Illness
7 Gowan Ave, Fulham, London SW6

Counselling, literature and local support. Send large SAE.

BREASTFEEDING

The National Childbirth Trust
(Address see Ante-Natal Classes)

Provides advice and individual support through contact with Breastfeeding Counsellors. The NCT actively encourages breastfeeding because it can be such a rewarding experience for mother and baby. However the best method of feeding a baby is the one that makes both of you happy and healthy so Breastfeeding Counsellors will also advise on bottle feeding. They can also arrange for you to borrow electric breast pumps if you need to express milk.

Association of Breastfeeding Mothers
71 Hall Dr, London SE26
01-461 0022

Counselling service through support groups offering advice from personal experience.

La Leche League
BM 3424, London WC1V 6XX
01-404 5011; (24 hrs) 01-242 1278

Self-help group providing information and support to women who wish to breastfeed their babies.

Comprehensive literature and discussion groups. Send large SAE for information.

LEAD POLLUTION

Apart from the dangers posed by lead in exhaust fumes (which are at pushchair passenger height), and the possibility of children chewing lead-painted surfaces, Edinburgh has problems with lead plumbing in older parts of the city, which contaminates drinking water. Grants towards the removal of old lead plumbing are available from Edinburgh District Council (225 2424).

In the meantime, if you live in an older, lead-plumbed house, and particularly if you are bottle feeding, use only water drawn off the kitchen cold tap (fed from the rising main) and run off about a bowlful every morning. Also empty the kettle completely now and again, and don't fill it from the hot tap. This is good advice to follow if you are trying to conceive and also antenatally.

PARENT AND BABY PROBLEMS

Sometimes a loving relationship between parents and the new baby takes time to develop. Support for parents who find their new role distressing is available from:

Cry-Sis
Pauline Peat
333 1968

Telephone help for parents with persistently crying babies.

Parents Anonymous
41a Polwarth Ter EH11 1NL
(RSSPCC)
337 9743

ADOPTION

Scottish Adoption Association
69 Dublin St EH3 6NS
556 2070

Counselling for those who may wish to place a child for adoption as well as for prospective parents. Adoption placements and post adoption support.

Adoption Advice Centre (East of Scotland)
21 Castle St EH2 3DN
225 3666
Mon-Thurs 9-5; Fri 9-4.30

Counselling and advice on any aspect of adoption.

PAEDIATRIC (CHILDRENS) HOSPITALS AND WARDS

EMERGENCIES

If your child is in need of urgent medical attention you should contact your local GP's Surgery

GP Phone Number ....

If you can't contact your doctor go straight to the
Royal Hospital for Sick Children, Sciennes Rd EH9 1LF

Hospital Phone Number 667 1991

DON'T WAIT if your child

is unconscious
has a 'fit' or convulsion
goes 'blue' for more than a few moments
bleeds for more than a few minutes from any cause
has a bulging or sunken soft spot on top of the head
has difficulty breathing
has vomiting and/or diarrhoea for more than an hour

Royal Hospital for Sick Children
Sciennes Rd EH9 1LF
667 1991

Excellent atmosphere and obviously orientated to the needs of children in all areas of the hospital. Clinics, waiting areas, and accident and emergency department are all well stocked with toys and books etc. Extremely understanding staff and excellent reputation.

A resident area is provided for parents wishing to stay with children in hospital. It consists of 8 bedrooms, each with 2 beds, sitting room, kitchen and bathroom. This area is obviously apart from the wards themselves but parents can be contacted at anytime during the day or night to be with a distressed child or for feeding etc. 'Z' beds and reclining chairs can be provided if the parents would prefer to stay beside a child overnight.

No specific visiting hours, parents are welcome at any time. In surgical areas, depending on procedure or operation, the Ward Sister will discuss with the parents what is best for them and the child post-operatively. Siblings are welcome to visit but obviously adequate control and discipline must be exercised. Friends of the child in hospital may

also visit, at the discretion of the Ward Sister. Always phone and check.

'Play ladies' are present in most wards except the baby ward and ENT (Ear, Nose and Throat) ward where stay is only for 24 hours. Each play lady has a team of volunteers who come on different days to help her.

Playcentre at 11 Millerfield Pl EH9 1LW for children of parents visiting the hospital is open 9-4.30, Mon-Fri.

Arrangements for teaching provided by the Lothian Region Council Education Department are being changed in the hospital (phone 667 6811 for details).

There is a school in the grounds of the Astley Ainslie (Convalescent Hospital) where children are sent to recuperate. Policies there are the same as at the Sick Children's Hospital above.

City Hospital (Ear, Nose and Throat and Communicable Diseases Children's Wards)
Greenbank Dr EH10 5SD
447 1001

Friendly staff. Procedures in Isolation Units are necessarily strict. It is possible for parents to stay within the above wards. No special room is provided but a 'Z' bed can be put at child's bed or cot side. Visiting hours for parents not staying are 10.30-6.30 daily. There are no facilities for children of parents visiting a sick child and parents are therefore asked not to bring other children into the wards. Supply of volunteers from the National Association of Welfare of Children in Hospital has stopped but the Paediatric wards of the Communicable Diseases Unit have Nursery

Nurses employed as part of the ward team who initiate and participate in play for the children. No provision for education.

Western General Hospital Paediatric Wards G11-14, G7-10
Crewe Rd EH4 2XU
332 2525

Small friendly wards, one medical and one surgical. There are limited facilities available within the paediatric unit for parents who wish to stay overnight. Unrestricted visiting for parents. Other children may visit by arrangement with the Ward Sister. Play room and 2 part-time play ladies encourage children to participate in various activities.

There are also paediatric wards or beds at:

Astley Ainslie (Convalescent) Hospital
133 Grange Loan EH9 1HB
447 6271

Leith Hospital
Mill Lane EH6 6TJ
554 3548

Princess Alexandra Eye Pavilion
Chalmers St EH3 9ES
229 2477

Princess Margaret Rose Orthopaedic Hospital
41 Frogston Rd West EH10 7AH
445 4123

National Association for the Welfare of Children in Hospital
(Scotland) (NAWCH)
94 Murrayfield Gdns EH12 6DJ
337 6412

A charity for all children in hospital and for all adults caring for them. Information for parents with babies in Special Care Units'.

Play for Children in Scottish Hospitals
15 Smith's Pl EH6 8HT
553 2189
Mon-Fri 8.30-12.30

'Provides books and leaflets, for sale or to borrow. The Group can help you to prepare a child for planned admission. They can advise about appropriate toys and books; provide information about the hospitals' policies on visiting and staying in and give details about the provision of play'. Promotes play for children of all ages in hospitals, clinics and health centres.

DENTAL CARE

All dentists providing NHS care can be found on the list held by the Lothian Health Board (see address at beginning of Chapter), or at your post office or library. Listen to recommendations by friends and neighbours when choosing a dentist, although what may suit them may not suit you. Community dentists are paid a salary rather than for individual items of work; many deal almost exclusively with children and are also involved in dental health education, which means some appear at playgroups, accompanied by naughty mice and monkey puppets!

Mothers are entitled to free dental treatment throughout pregnancy and until the baby's first birthday.

Children under 18 are also entitled to free dental care. It is recommended that the first 'check up' is at about 2½ years, but of course you may consult a dentist earlier.

Average **fluoride** concentration in drinking water in the Lothians is

0·02 parts per million and dentists recommend that children take fluoride drops or tablets. These are available free at many dentists and baby clinics. Take very careful note of how to give them.

British Dental Health Foundation
88 Gurnards Ave, Fishermead, Milton Keynes MK6 2BL
0908 667063

Provides excellent pack of free information leaflets for SAE.

EYE CARE

All emergency eye treatment is given at the Princess Alexandra Eye Pavilion (see Paediatric Hospitals for address). Your GP may refer your child here for non-emergency eye treatments or surgery.

An annual eye examination is free from any optometrist and children do not need to be able to read before attending. A first eye test at 3 followed by annual check ups, unless there are obvious problems such as squint or difficulties with vision, is a good way to monitor your child's eyesight.

PROBLEM SOLVING

Most of us need advice, information or support at some time in the young lives of our children. This list is not exhaustive but may provide a starting point to help solve your problem. Your Health Visitor may know of local contacts and the Play Resource Unit of Moray House College of Education, Holyrood Rd EH8 8AQ (556 8455) maintain a

comprehensive list of useful addresses for people with special needs. We have checked that all the groups listed here are operational. See also 'Welfare' and 'Activities for Parents, Women's Support Groups'.

BEREAVEMENT

The Compassionate Friends
Vee Snodgrass
7 North Gyle Ave EH12 8JS
339 2981

Support and help for parents who have recently suffered the loss of a child. Lending library and link scheme.

Cruse
3 Rutland Sq EH1 2AS
229 6275

Weekdays 10-12.30; Wed 1.30-3.30

Although mostly concerned with the widowed, Cruse will usually help any bereaved person, with counselling, practical information and advice

Edinburgh and Lothian Cot Death Support Group
Mrs Linda McDonald
44 Clerwood Park EH12 8PP
334 7512

Gives personal support to bereaved families by letter, telephone and leaflets and puts parents in touch with formerly bereaved parents.

CRUELTY, ABUSE AND VIOLENCE

See also **CRISIS LINES** at the end of this book.

Edinburgh & Lothian Women's Aid
97 & 101 Morrison St EH3 8BX
229 1419 (24 hrs)

Confidential advice and refuge for women and their children abused by their male partners.

Lothian Victims Support Scheme
53 George St EH2 2HT
Mon-Fri 9.30-1.30
226 3563

Support and practical help for individuals and families who have experienced loss, distress or inconvenience caused by crime.

Royal Scottish Society for Prevention of Cruelty to Children
41 Polwarth Ter EH11 1NU
337 8539/0 (Day and Night 337 4891)

Help and guidance to families in crisis. Prevention of child abuse.

Scottish Women's Aid Federation
11 St Colme St EH3 6AA
225 8011

Temporary accommodation for physically, mentally or sexually abused women and their children.

INCEST

Church of Scotland Pastoral Foundation
Holy Corner Church Centre
552 4275

Support for incest victims.

Incest Survivors' Campaign
Wed 6-8
556 9437

MARRIAGE COUNSELLING

Catholic Marriage Advisory Centre
205 Ferry Rd EH6 4NN
553 5150

See above 'Family Planning'.

Lothian Marriage Guidance Counselling Service
9a Dundas St EH3 6QG
556 1527
Daily 10-4; Mon-Thurs from 6.30; Sat 10-12

Confidential counselling service for those who are experiencing disharmony and tension in their personal relationships. Appointment only.

Scottish Family Conciliation Service (Lothian)
127 Rose St Sth Lane EH2 4BB
226 4507
Daily 9-5

Appointments offered to divorcing couples and their families; advice and information on conciliation and divorce. Literature.

PHYSICAL AND DEVELOPMENTAL PROBLEMS

Asthma Society and Friends of the Asthma Research Council
300 Upper St, London N1 2XX
01-226 2260
Local Branch: Mrs Elizabeth Tait, 27 Combfoot Cottages, Mid Calder EH53 0AG

Scottish Society for **Autistic** Children
Gen Admin Sec Miss V Gillean Parker, Room 2, 2nd Floor, 12 Picardy Pl EH1 3JT
557 0474

Scottish National Federation for the Welfare of the **Blind**
8 St Leonards Bank, Perth PH2 8EB
0738 26969

Co-ordinates organisations concerned with blind people in Scotland.

Brittle Bone Society
Mrs M Grant, 112 City Rd, Dundee
0382 67063

Help and advice for those suffering from osteogenesis imperfecta.

International **Cerebral Palsy** Society
5a Netherhall Gdns, London NW3 5RN
01-794 9761

Cystic Fibrosis Research Trust
Mr D J Forbes, 33 Coates Gdns EH12 5LG
346 0844

Scottish Association for the **Deaf**
Moray House, Holyrood Rd EH8 8AQ
556 8137
Mon-Fri 8.30-5

Promotes the interest and welfare of the deaf in Scotland and is responsible for the co-ordination of welfare.

British **Diabetic** Association
Mrs D Baker, 157 Colinton Rd EH14 1BG
443 1492

Scottish Council on **Disability**
Princes House, Shandwick Pl EH2 4RG
229 8632

Scottish **Downs Syndrome** Association
Mrs Elise Selman, 74 Macdowal Rd EH9 3EG
667 3066

'Aims to make contact with parents of Down's children as soon as possible after birth, to offer help and encouragement, particularly through the early years'. Organises a mother and toddler group and provides information on research, facilities, meetings etc.

Epilepsy Association of Scotland
13 Guthrie St EH1 1JL
226 5458

National Association for **Gifted** Children
Mrs Sylvia Boal, 8 Hillview Ter EH12 8RA
334 5478

Association for Children with **Heart Disorders**
Mrs Lorraine Simpson, 37 Fountainhall Rd EH9 2LN
667 0589

Hyperactive Children's Support Group
Mrs Valerie McKitterick, 7 Craigleith Cres EH4 3JJ (SAE required)
332 7115

Infantile Hypercalcaemia Foundation
37 Mulberry Green, Old Harlow, Essex

Helps parents of children with the disease through the exchange of information on past experience and useful services regarding schooling, assessment and further education.

Invalid Children's Aid Association
126 Buckingham Palace Rd, London SW1W 9SB
01-730 9891

British **Kidney** Patient Association
Bordon, Hants
04203 2022

Leukaemia Society
Mrs Barbara Adamson, 'Rose Eden', Elliot, Arbroath DD11 2PE
0241 76214

Malcolm Sargent **Cancer** Fund for Children
Contact 'Malcolm Sargent' Social Worker at Royal Hospital for Sick Children
229 5837

Financial help for children suffering from cancer in all forms.

Directory of Services for People with a **Mental Handicap** in Lothian (2nd Edition) April 1986
Available from health centres and Shrubhill House, Shrub Pl EH7 4PA

18 pages of information for parents of mentally handicapped children and lists of many useful organisations.

Nucleus
Alison Patterson, 18 London Rd EH7 5AT
652 1480

Counselling and support services for **Mentally Handicapped** Children and their families from birth or diagnosis. Support groups and practical courses organised.

British **Nutrition** Foundation
15 Belgrave Sq, London SW1X 8PS
01-235 4904

Publications about healthy eating and special dietary needs.

National Society for **Phenylketonuria and Allied Disorders**
26 Towngate Grove, Mirfield, West Yorkshire
0924 492873

Advice, information, leaflets, dietary information and quarterly newsletter for parents of children suffering from phenylketonuria.

Lady Hoare Trust for **Physically Handicapped Children** (Allied with Arthritis Care)

Mrs Ann Lennox, 9a Forres St EH3 6BJ
225 4895

Welfare services for physically handicapped children.

British **Retinitis Pigmentosa** Society
Dr C Beevers, 82 Belmont Rd EH14 5ED

Family Fund
Joseph Rowntree Memorial Trust, PO Box 50, York YD1 1UY
0904 21115

Fund to help families with a **Severely Handicapped** child under 16. Help can be goods, services or cash for some definite purpose related to the problems posed by the handicapped child in the home and not covered by existing sources.

Association for All **Speech Impaired** Children (AFASIC)
347 Central Markets, Smithfield, London EC1A 9NH
01-236 3632/6487

Scottish **Spina Bifida** Association
Mrs A D Smith, Executive Officer, 190 Queensferry Rd EH4 2BW
332 0743

SINGLE PARENTS

Gingerbread, 5 Casselbank St, Leith EH6 5HA
553 3970
Mon-Fri 10-4.30; Mon 6-7.30

Self-help association for single-parent families (with creche at each group meeting). Holiday play-schemes for lone working parents. Legal advice and counselling.

Scottish Council for Single Parents
13 Gayfield Sq EH1 3NX
556 3899

Tollcross Community Centre
Tollcross   Primary   School,
Fountainbridge
229 8448

Single parents' group, Tues 7-9.30 every 2nd week. For parents aged 16+. Group leader is Charlotte Morton. No creche.

WOMEN'S PROBLEMS

See also **CRISIS LINES** at the end of this book.

National Association for Pre-Menstrual Syndrome
25 Market St, Guildford, Surrey GU1 5LB
0483 572806

Rape Crisis Centre
PO Box 120, Head Post Office, Edinburgh 1
556 9437

Information and support for women who have been raped or sexually assaulted. Run by women for women.

Tranquilliser Group
Ainslie Park High Schoolhouse, 20b Crewe Rd Nth
332 0871 Jane Jones
Mon 1.30-3.30

For women who wish to lose their dependency on tranquillisers. No creche.

Women's Support Group
Leith Community Centre, New Kirk-gate, Leith
554 4750
Thurs 1.30-3.30

Group for women with drug-related problems eg addiction, partner on drugs etc. Creche.

Well Woman Centre
St Brides Community Centre, Orwell Ter
346 1405

Information, mutual support, help, tea and a chat. Free child care. Tues 9.30-12 noon; Wed 7.30 pm-10 pm.

Women Talking To Women
St Brides Community Centre
Orwell Ter, Dalry
337 5543
Wed 4.30-7 pm

A chance for women to talk over problems with another woman in complete confidence. Please telephone first.